Ninette de `

Adventurous Trá

CW00922780

Ninette de Valois
Adventurous Traditionalist

Edited by Richard Allen Cave
and Libby Worth

To Jasmine ———

good to hear you have
graduated to the Company
from the School.
Good luck with your career

Richard Allen Cave

Libby Worth.

2 — vii — 2012

DANCE BOOKS

First published in 2012 by Dance Books Ltd.,
Charwell House,
Wilsom Road,
Alton,
Hampshire,
GU34 2PP

ISBN: 978-1-85273-157-1

A CIP catalogue record for this book is available from the British Library

Printed and bound in Great Britain by Latimer Trend & Co, Ltd., Plymouth

Contents

List of Illustrations
(between pages 142/143)

DVD Contents

DVD Track 1 David Bintley in interview, 31 January 2011 (11:26)

DVD Track 2 De Valois' Training Syllabus taught by Valerie Adams FRAD, 2 April 2011 (52:47)

DVD Track 3 The significance of the English Folk Dance Tradition in The Royal Ballet's history: Libby Worth with Ron Smedley and Simon Rice, 2 April 2011 (32:28)

DVD Track 4 Dance illustration of the Betrayed Girl's first solo for 'Benesh Movement Notation, Labanotation: an overview' by Victoria Watts (01:01)

DVD Track 5 *Dancing Across the Bosphoros* (2012), a film by Levent Kurumlu (45:28)

DVD Track 6 Madam and the Betrayed Girls: the Dancers' Perspective. Nicola Katrak with Julia Farron and Margaret Barbieri, 2 April 2011 (34:07)

DVD Track 7 Eurydice's solo from Ninette de Valois' *Orpheus and Eurydice* (1941), Pamela May coaching students of The Royal Ballet School, July 2003 (7:04)

DVD Track 8 "Promenade" girl's dance from Ninette de Valois' *Promenade* (1943), Pauline Clayden coaching students of The Royal Ballet School, June 2005 (6:59)

DVD Track 9 Re-creation of W. B. Yeats's *The King of the Great Clock Tower*, directed by Richard Allen Cave and filmed by Peter Hulton, 3 April 2011 (35:31)

DVD Track 10 Ninette de Valois: a filmed interview by David Drew, 1989 (14:26)

Foreword

This book about Ninette de Valois leaves me marvelling at her achievements and prompts me to pinch myself and think, is it really true that I have this amazing, privileged position of being the Director of The Royal Ballet, which she created. It was a job that I never applied for, I sort of landed in it by default. To date I've had the most wonderful time trying to honour her, and all the seeds that she sowed, all those years ago.

When I was appointed, one of the first things I wanted to do was to have a portrait of her in my new office. I spoke with Francesca Franchi [Head of Collections, Royal Opera House] and she came along with two or three photographs of Madam, and I chose one which I'd never seen before, or since. It was taken probably sometime during the forties or early fifties. It's very much a working picture of her; this is not dressed up and bejewelled and posed at all. It almost looks as if she turned round in her office and just looked into the camera. The thing about it, is that she is looking directly at the camera, and so wherever I am in the office she's looking at me. She wears really quite a quizzical expression, and one that I felt, from the beginning, would find me out. So I had to be particularly careful, and yet at the same time I felt challenged to be as brave as I possibly could.

Everyone involved in the preparation of this volume has demonstrated what this woman means to this art form. The way she crossed borders, and the way she involved herself with so many wonderful people – people that she must have listened to and learned from, and helped her to create this extraordinary thing, which is the Royal Ballet with its schools, its repertoire, its history and its remarkable legacy.

When I was first in the company – I joined when I was 16 – she was my Director for my first five years. During those five years I trembled at the sight of her. I always hoped I wouldn't see her very often, because she just scared me so much. I had witnessed her demolishing people, asking a question and when their answer wasn't what it should be she made them feel absolutely terrible and the whole thing ended in tears. So I tried to avoid her, but, of course, one often couldn't. On the other hand she gave wonderful opportunities, and took rehearsals, and was extraordinary; inspiring is an understatement. Later on in my life, after she'd retired, I got to know her. I used to drive her home to Barnes – I lived in Kew – I used to drive her in my mini. If I'd only had a tape recorder running imagine the treasures I would have. How I didn't crash my car, I'll never know, because very often she asked the most difficult questions, which required full concentration at the same time as going round Hyde Park Corner.

When the penny really dropped for me about her brilliance was when we went to Russia for the first time in 1961. I was twenty years old and we'd had a particularly tough year. We'd been in America for five months (we'd travelled the length and breadth, up and down, and we were completely exhausted) and we returned only to be told that we were going to spend six weeks in Russia later in June and July. Off we went, and we had performances every night. We knew that the pressure was really on us; The Royal Ballet was appearing for the first time in Russia. It was definitely the most nervous I've ever seen Margot, having to dance *The Sleeping Beauty* in St. Petersburg. In spite of the fact that she had done it so many times and over so many years, she was terrified. The audiences were amazing. Madam insisted on making sure that every single member of the company went to every single art gallery, every single museum, and on top of all of that, witnessed every possible demonstration of national dancing that it was possible to witness. It was a huge education, the whole thing was the most amazing experience. But what made the penny drop was the fact that she was able, on every single occasion, to speak. She never had a note, and yet I became aware that she somehow managed to say the most appropriate thing for every single occasion. It didn't matter where she was, she would get up and speak. It was then that I thought, my goodness, this woman is really quite something.

This extraordinary woman changed the lives of hundreds and hundreds of people. How many people have been touched and affected by her? There have been people who have worked closely with her, and known her over many, many years. This collection of essays, reminiscences, reflections, and performances reveals to us sometimes familiar things, sometimes unfamiliar, and we're forced to examine, look again and think again about the multitude of aspects that made up Dame Ninette's personality.

I feel that she didn't just create a school and two companies; it's as if she created a world, a universe for this art form. This universe is populated, and has been populated by the most passionate, loyal, brilliant people. Even with all the most brilliant people that inhabited this universe, somehow everybody knew that she was the brightest star of them all. She was, and remains endlessly fascinating. It's no wonder that she achieved what she did, and she inspired so many people over her long life. This volume offers us another opportunity to salute this great, great lady, and to say, from the bottom of our hearts "Madam, thank you."

Monica Mason
Director of the Royal Ballet

Acknowledgements

An editing project as large as this inevitably required us to call on help from a wide range of people. First we must express our gratitude to Dame Monica Mason for graciously contributing the Foreword; to Gailene Stock, Director of The Royal Ballet School, for kindly agreeing to the inclusion on DVD of filmed material showing many of her students; and particularly to Jay Jolley, Assistant Director of The Royal Ballet School, for being a massive support with his wisdom, patience and invaluable advice at all stages of the creation of this volume. Special thanks must be given to Anna Meadmore, Curator of White Lodge Museum and Ballet Resource Centre, for her tenacity, continuing assistance, insights and exacting input throughout the whole process of collecting and properly presenting the items in this book, which ensure its future as a resource for ballet lovers and dance scholars; to Marius Arnold-Clarke, IT and Theatre Manager for The Royal Ballet School, who gave unsparingly of his time to completing to the highest standards all the technical aspects of this venture and especially the making of the DVD. We owe our profound thanks to Jane Pritchard and her committee for organising the magnificent three-day conference in April 2011, *Ninette de Valois, Adventurous Traditionalist*, to which this volume is indebted for so much more than its title and to Jane too for her continuing guidance. Jonathan Gray, Editor of *Dancing Times*, generously gave us permission to reproduce the seven essays by Dame Ninette to be found here and the photograph of her by Mesdames Morter of 1932 used on the cover; and Simon Oliver, his Production Editor, meticulously prepared the essays for our transcription. We are grateful to Elizabeth Schafer and the Vic-Wells Association for locating and allowing us to re-publish the articles de Valois contributed to *The Old Vic* and *The Old Vic and Sadler's Wells Magazines*. Patrick Baldwin, Leslie E Spatt, Ben Blackall and Richard Farley kindly let us have permission to use their photographs for free. Francesca Franchi and Cristina Franchi of Royal Opera House Collections gave the whole project enormous practical support: their inspirational 2011 Royal Opera House Exhibition, *Invitation to the Ballet; Ninette de Valois and the story of The Royal Ballet*, provided crucial impetus for a timely re-examination of de Valois' legacy. Anna Fineman and Sabine Naghdi, Assistant Curators of The Royal Ballet School Collections, White Lodge Museum, assisted us over a long period with transcriptions, copyright, and project administration, while Edward Small, Cataloguer of The Royal Ballet School Collections, helped assiduously with the selection and preparation of many of the photographs included here. We are profoundly indebted to the Department of Drama and Theatre at Royal Holloway, University of London, for funding the costs of mass-producing the DVD. Liz Morrell, our editor, and David Leonard, our publisher, were tireless in their enthusiasm and support for the venture, patient, tactful and meticulous in preparing the volume for printing. Finally, we thank our many contributors – writers and practitioners, dancers and film-makers, teachers and students, administrators and archivists – who have made the task of editing such a pleasurable and rewarding undertaking by sharing their expertise and their enthusiasm for defining the many facets of de Valois' genius.

Libby Worth
Richard Allen Cave

Editors' Introduction

This collection of essays, photographs and DVD materials relating to Ninette de Valois is unusual in a number of ways that could be said to neatly reflect the diversity of de Valois' interactions within both the artistic and critical worlds of her day. Firstly it is notable that the contributors to the written chapters include professional dancers, experienced dance and theatre critics, museum archivists, dance notators, choreographers, dance teachers and academics. A brief survey of their bibliographies reveals that many of these writers themselves span more than one area of work. This cross-disciplinarity is integral to a collection that hopes to do justice to de Valois' extraordinary contribution to the creation and maintenance of a thriving ballet culture in the UK. She was at pains to insist on the essential connections between all the arts and the necessity of this for the vitality of ballet, having experienced for herself, both the inspiration and reality of close collaborative working across art forms. There are discussions in this volume, for example, of her involvements with popular theatre and revue, Diaghilev (the notable shaper of her ideas and philosophy of dance), the Cecchettis, Massine, Lilian Baylis, the Bloomsbury Group, with Turkish culture, with W.B. Yeats, Ashton, MacMillan and David Bintley. To offset this examination of her public persona, there is an exploration of the private self revealed in Dame Ninette's poetry and the inspired self voiced in her theoretical writings.

The major stimulus for the creation of this volume was the April 2011 Conference, *Ninette de Valois: Adventurous Traditionalist*, hosted by The Royal Ballet School in London and Richmond. Held close to the tenth anniversary of de Valois' death, it provided a forum for debate, appreciation and re-assessment of her career. This timing, given the sufficient distance from de Valois' active participation in UK ballet developments, allowed for a robust approach to the evaluation of her work, rather than memorialisation, and for the emergence of distinct areas of her career that records have previously skimmed over or ignored or that were in danger of being lost. Now was precisely the time for seizing an opportunity to dialogue with dancers who had worked extensively with de Valois as students, as members of her Companies and as interpreters of her choreographies and to hear testimony from a range of performers, highly regarded in their fields, who could recall and critique detailed experiences of their times with Madam (that favoured term of address for de Valois within the Companies and School). Considerable insights are gained from dancers, some in their eighties, looking back at their early careers and their contact with de Valois. These are juxtaposed with the experience of young dancers at The Royal Ballet School studying aspects of de Valois' curriculum (her highly individual ballet syllabus; her passion for folk dance) or learning roles in de Valois' ballets under the guidance of older generations of performers. The wide span of ages and their interaction is reflected in this book whether in the chapters or the DVD recordings of classes, rehearsals, re-creations and dance/theatre performances. The emphasis, therefore, is on the articulation between past records and current practices and responses. To further readers' appreciation of this context, two groups of de Valois' own early published writings about building up a company and training choreographers for the future, which have long-since been out of print, are again made available to readers. De Valois' body of work therefore stands in vibrant relationship with current thinking and practice in dance.

This is the first time that such an extensive range of materials on de Valois' thinking, practice and achievement has been collected in one volume with the aim of providing the practitioner or keen ballet enthusiast or academic researcher with an array of essential resources. To this end, no single argument is pursued throughout the volume, but a series of voices and practical examples is offered that can be mined for contrasting, sometimes combative viewpoints in response to de Valois' career. Writing alone, however brilliant the description or the analysis, cannot hope fully to capture the vitality of theatrical performance or the rigours of the training and rehearsal schedules that underpin its virtuosity. To help remedy this lack, the text of the book is accompanied not only by photographs but also DVD recordings, offering some four hours of filmed material of archival value and importance to complement the written word. For readers not familiar with the details of Dame Ninette's biography, an appendix gives a time-line of the major phases of her life and career up to the time of her retirement from the Directorship of The Royal Ballet. Further appendices give short accounts of the two main archival collections of materials relating to de Valois and details of how to access them.

It is apparent from the many contributions that this collection is not simply a record of de Valois' working life but a recognition and evaluation of the active legacy she leaves the dance world, even when her vision has resulted in developments somewhat different from ones she may have envisaged. That is as she would have wished. In her Foreword to Alexander's Bland's *The Royal Ballet, the first 50 years* (1981), de Valois expressed her hope that the coming generations would "guide our national ballet into the future as a group of adventurous traditionalists". It is without question that Dame Ninette's own unparalleled success derived from her unshaken faith that ballet in its training methods and its repertoire must be fearlessly adventurous, confidently traditionalist and always theatre-centred.

Libby Worth
Richard Allen Cave

Part One: Biography

David Bintley: filmed interview

Anna Meadmore

Many influential dance practitioners around the world can be seen as the inheritors of de Valois' artistic legacy; in the case of David Bintley (b. 1957), this inheritance seems to be particularly direct and personal. As becomes evident in this filmed interview with Bintley, recorded in his office at Birmingham Royal Ballet in February 2011, his response to de Valois' interest in him was profound and formative. From the time he was a student at The Royal Ballet Upper School, de Valois delighted in his unusual talent for choreography and mime; he won the School's prestigious Ursula Moreton Choreographic Award in 1975, and performed the role of Dr Coppélius in the School Matinée at the Royal Opera House in 1976. Bintley then joined the Sadler's Wells Royal Ballet, and within two years had begun to choreograph for the Company. In 1985 he became the Resident Choreographer of The Royal Ballet in Covent Garden, but later returned to his former Company (now Birmingham Royal Ballet) as its Artistic Director, following the retirement of Sir Peter Wright in 1995.

 track 1

From Bad Fairy to Gramophone Girl: Ninette de Valois' early career in English popular theatre[1]

Jane Pritchard

Ninette de Valois' stage career appears to have begun in 1911 when she had just turned thirteen and it may be said that the first phase of her career continued until her employment with Serge Diaghilev's Ballets Russes twelve years later in 1923. This chapter looks at her career, from her first stage appearances in productions created to show the strength of the dancing schools at which she trained, through to being invited to work with Russian ballet stars, Lydia Lopokova and Léonide Massine in their independent productions in Britain in the early 1920s. Her early career took in performances in music hall and variety, pantomime, opera and musicals. With a few exceptions de Valois did not dance on the stage of internationally recognised opera houses and most of her performances at this time were within areas defined as the popular stage. How could it have been otherwise? De Valois' early career coincided with the decline of the big ballet presentations at the Alhambra and Empire theatres in Leicester Square and their shift to the presentation of revues. The beginning of her career also coincided with the arrival of Diaghilev's Ballets Russes to perform at the Royal Opera House, Covent Garden (alternating with and sharing the programme with the local opera). This was the first real suggestion in Britain that ballet might be restored to being recognised as an opera house art in its own right.[2]

Comparing the career of de Valois with those of her young contemporaries reveals that she was always forward-thinking and planning for the future. Unlike many of her young peers who performed as much as possible, de Valois balanced her performances with periods of intensive training with the teachers she recognised would strengthen her technique (and who would also, ultimately, provide a secure foundation for her career as a pedagogue). Contact with a variety of teachers during her performance opportunities (many choreographers/dance arrangers were also teachers) enabled her to progress as an artist and reports of her development and growing strength of technique repeatedly appeared in the *Dancing Times*.

From appearing as one of twenty Bad Fairies for Mrs Wordsworth at the Royal Court Theatre, through to dancing the solo as the Gramophone Girl in the "jazzaganza", *You'd Be Surprised* when it transferred from

Covent Garden to the Alhambra, suggests a trajectory from traditional to modern. Many dancers began their careers as a fairy but appearing as a Gramophone Girl evokes the more modern world of the "jazz age". When de Valois embarked on her career the dance scene in London was changing. With the Alhambra folding its own ballet company in 1912 and the Empire's company following a few years later, the apprenticeship schemes at these theatres, through which young dancers received some training in exchange for appearing in the *corps de ballet*, ended. Although there was some possibility for training as a spin-off from the long seasons Anna Pavlova gave at the Palace Theatre 1910 -1913, Russian teachers had not settled in London when de Valois began to train. Seraphina Astafieva, the first Russian teacher based in London, established her school first at Chandos Hall near the Coliseum in 1915 and at the Pheasantry, Chelsea, the following year. The Italian ballet master, Enrico Cecchetti would open a London studio in 1918 and Nicolas Legat in 1923.

It was interesting that concurrently with The Royal Ballet School hosted conference, *Ninette de Valois: Adventurous Traditionalist*, in the spring of 2011, the National Portrait Gallery presented *Ballet in Focus*, a display of photographs by Bassano Ltd. and Emile Otto Hoppé of dancers appearing on the London stage between 1912 and 1925. This provides a useful context for discussing de Valois' career. Many of the dancers represented were of a senior generation: Maud Allan, Adolph Bolm, Adeline Genée, Tamara Karsavina, Lydia Kyasht, Unity More, Vaslav Nijinsky, Anna Pavlova and the exotic dancer Roshanara (Olive Craddock). Others, including Phyllis Bedells, Anton Dolin and Lydia Lopokova, were closer contemporaries. Although the exhibition's captions referred to the ballet companies at the Leicester Square theatres, what the images really emphasised was the importance of the London Coliseum, the NPG's close geographical neighbour, as the home of dance in London during the 1910s and 1920s. The Coliseum was dependent on visiting artists and companies (unlike the Alhambra and Empire it did not establish its own ballet) but it filled the vacuum left by the decline of "music hall ballet". De Valois danced at the Coliseum before joining Diaghilev and would indeed return there with Diaghilev's company in 1924-25 and with Anton Dolin's troupe in August 1926. The image of de Valois selected for *Ballet in Focus* showed her in *Oh! Julie!*, a musical revue in which she featured at the Shaftesbury and later the Princes Theatre in 1920.[3]

De Valois cannily seems to have controlled "the story" of her career, making it tidier than it was in truth. Her first theatre appearance seems to have been with Mrs Wordsworth's pupils, although de Valois always emphasised that Mrs Wordsworth was opposed to stage work. This implied that she did not perform in public until she joined Lila Field. Nevertheless, however much she disapproved of the theatre, Mrs Wordsworth must have recognised the advantages of a public showcase and at matinées at the Royal Court on 29 and 30 June 1911, Edris Stannus was cast as one of the Bad Fairies "in mauve" in *The Enchanted Rose*. (Molly Lake was another of the Bad Fairies but "in green".)[4] Mrs Wordsworth did not train performers for a stage career, disliked ballet and pointe work, probably associating these with the music hall, and *The Enchanted Rose* was a children's operetta by J.H. Dockery, with music by C. J. Bush, which included dances.

De Valois and her mother recognised the limitations of Wordsworth's "fancy dancing" if she was to make a career on stage. They also recognised the challenge of her name, Edris Stannus. She soon became Ninette de Valois of Lila Field's Wonder Children. It should be observed that her name-change occurred just before the trend for dancers to adopt Russian names as a passport to success. In addition, children's matinées, that is, afternoon productions performed by children, were popular in the later nineteenth and early twentieth centuries. Steadman's Academy, the training school that rivalled Lila Field's, and produced such dancers as Hilda Munnings (Sokolova), Hilda Boot (Butsova), and Vera Clark (Savina), regularly presented its own shows including frequent stagings of *Alice in Wonderland*.

De Valois liked to state that her performing career began with the Lila Field Wonder Children from 1913. Field put together a series of fairy plays including the much repeated *The Goldfish* (first performed in 1911), *The Lily Queen* and *The Children's Dream* but also had her young dancers perform divertissements and revues. In the latter her pupils would appear as the leading lights of music hall, including the cross-dressing Vesta Tilley, the Scottish entertainer, Harry Lauder, and others. Thus when de Valois danced *The Swan*, she was being Anna Pavlova in *The Swan*, rather than simply presenting her own version of Fokine's choreography.[5] This explains why de Valois went to the Wednesday ballet matinées at the Palace to study Pavlova's performance carefully and left a valuable record of how Pavlova danced this solo pre-War. The revues produced by Lila Field covered a wide range of song and dance. Among the productions sent up at the Ambassadors' Theatre, London, on 30 July 1913 was "Nijinsky's Spring Ballet", although details of the Wonder Children's response to the original *Le Sacre du printemps* (first performed in London nineteen days earlier) have yet to emerge.

Field clearly recognised de Valois' natural talent as a dancer and soon after joining de Valois took over roles from Marjorie Stevens, her previous ballerina and "Pavlova". Stevens had been one of the *corps de ballet* of forty children,"Pupils of Miss Lila Field and Steadman, Ltd." who danced in Pavlova's *Snowflakes* "A Ballet in Miniature" (loosely based on the Snow scene from *The Nutcracker*) in August and September 1911. *Snowflakes* was quickly mounted after the departure of Michael Mordkin, the year before Pavlova acquired Ivy House and began training her own "girls". Stevens would occasionally return to dance solos in Field's programmes but was busy performing Pavlova's dances (with the apparent approval of the ballerina) in music halls, including the London Palladium in 1912 and touring with Alex Goudin. From 1918 she danced in musicals and revues.

The Wonder Children toured extensively in Britain and were booked commercially for the London Palladium. De Valois recalled that they performed "only about two months, then we were brought back to London again, back to our school books and everything". She also remembered that "We played to very good houses always, and we returned to the same places year after year".[6] De Valois writes movingly in *Step by Step* of the collapse of the Wonder Children at Southsea in August 1914, with the outbreak of the First World War.[7] What she fails to acknowledge is that she was still dancing with them until she went into her first pantomime at the Lyceum Theatre, London. On 7 December 1914 she performed on the West Pier, Brighton, in *The Swan* "by popular request" and appeared as England in the patriotic "Grand Ballet" called *The Allies*. The circuits danced by the Wonder Children are interesting. De Valois often repeated her account of dancing *The Swan* on every pier in England. What needs to be recognised is that in the 1910s and 1920s there was a distinct, if not very clearly publicised circuit that took dancers round seaside towns and spas (Harrogate for example), places associated with leisure, where they gave between one and five performances, often presenting "split weeks". Seaside towns such as Eastbourne, Brighton and Bournemouth play a not inconsiderable role in the history of British ballet. To cite one 1920s example, it is exactly this same group of theatres to which Bronislava Nijinska took her tour of experimental divertissements in 1925. For de Valois, as for so many others, the War was a real watershed in her life and career so it is understandable that many years later she should remember its outbreak as the end of the era of the Wonder Children.

Appearing in large-scale pantomimes at the Lyceum was also not so much a break from her work with the Lila Field Wonder Children as it might appear. De Valois auditioned for the ballerina role in *Jack and the Beanstalk* in 1914 but Lila Field was supplying groups of dancers for the same production. Indeed the programme credit reads "Speciality Dances by Miss Ninette de Valois and Miss Edna Maude of the Lila Field Company". This suggests that she was still perceived as part of that organisation. The Lyceum and Drury Lane were widely considered the best pantomimes in London so an engagement here was significant. Between 1914 and 1919 de Valois featured as ballerina in *Jack and the Beanstalk*, *Robinson Crusoe*, *Mother Goose* and *Cinderella* (there was no pantomime at the Lyceum 1917-18). De Valois was allocated a male partner in her first and last pantomime (*danseurs* were in great demand during the War) and there was always an "infant phenomenon" to present competition. In *Jack* this was "Little Edna Maude" as she was designated in the programme, which also included a photograph by Hana showing just how tiny she was next to de Valois. In *Robinson Crusoe* and *Mother Goose* it was "Little Miss Joan King", described in the programme for the *Crusoe* as "the smallest dancer in the world", and in *Cinderella* "Little Miss Cecile Maude-Cole". The reviews suggest that these dancers made much of their impact by being cute rather than through their technical ability.

With her choreographers or ballet mistress it is also possible to locate de Valois as an artist in a changing world. For the first three pantomimes de Valois worked with Mme. Rosa, an ex-leading dancer at the Alhambra, and she seized the opportunity to learn what she could from the music hall traditions, while in *Cinderella* the dances were arranged by Euphan McLaren. However, for her penultimate pantomime, *Mother Goose*, in which she appeared as the Fairy of the Golden Valley (a title given to her in the picture captions rather than the production's cast list[8]), she introduced a variation specially created for her by Edouard Espinosa. This was probably more sophisticated, challenging and up-to-date than the other dances and was described by Philip Richardson (already a great supporter of her work) in the *Dancing Times*, which included a photograph of the young dancer on their cover. "It included an *enchaînement of petite batterie*, some *adage* and the very showy finish consisted of a series of *coupés*, *posés*, *attitudes en tournant*, about a dozen *fouettés rond de jambe en tournant*, ending with the familiar *déboulés*."[9]

Through the 1910s de Valois' career was essentially conventional for the period[10] and, like many of the successful child-dancer-pupils of the

Field and Steadman academies, she followed appearances in pantomime by dancing in opera-ballet and in the developing area of musical comedy. The more successful dancers established their own music hall act. In looking at the pattern of these acts, it is clear that the young women performed as soloists or with one or two others (including a partner, if Alex Goudin or the Belgian *danseur* Robert Roberty, was available) and they needed a repertoire of no more than five dances. Edna Maude, with whom de Valois danced on tour with Field's Wonder Children, in *Jack and the Beanstalk* at the Lyceum and on a 1915 music hall tour led by Roberty,[11] had a typically short but very successful career as the "Spirit of Dance", performing in music halls week after week, certainly through to 1926 and culminating with seasons at the London Coliseum.

Where de Valois appears to be different was that from the start she took her training far more seriously than her colleagues. Working as opera-ballerina also gave her new opportunities. With Thomas Beecham she performed in popular theatres, notably the Palladium (opera was performed in music halls as well as opera houses) and also danced at the Royal Opera House, Covent Garden. Again her work with opera ballet combined experiences old and new. At Covent Garden she worked with Belgian choreographer, François Ambrosiny (who had been employed there over a period of three decades) but she also had the chance to arrange her own dances.

In 1921, de Valois courageously put together her own touring group. Is it significant that her group's tour coincided with the Ballets Russes' production of *The Sleeping Princess* at the Alhambra, which opened on 2 November? As one of London's more successful ballet dancers, one might have expected Diaghilev to snap her up at this point. Was her tour already planned when Diaghilev's production was announced? In 1921 did she prefer not to be a part of Diaghilev's enterprise when she would just have been a member of the *corps de ballet*? Might she have preferred to be otherwise engaged? When she was invited to join in 1923 she was, as she said at the memorial service for Marie Rambert, very hesitant. De Valois said it was Rambert saying "just think how much you will learn" that encouraged her to travel internationally with the Ballets Russes for two seasons.[12]

De Valois' tour, performing for six weeks on the Gulliver Circuit of music halls in October – December 1921 is of great importance, for it was the moment when she publicly seized control. It was her first experience as a director/choreographer and she also designed the costumes. I have tracked five of her alleged six dates – weeks performing at Camberwell

Palace (week beginning Monday 24 October 1921[13]) , Holborn Empire
(14 November 1921), Kilburn Empire (28 November 1921), Lewisham
Hippodrome (5 December 1921) and Ilford Hippodrome (12 December
1921). To give some sort of status to de Valois' group it is worth noting
that other Gulliver stars at that time included Little Tich, Derra de
Meroda, Maud Allan, Carlotta Mossetti: in theatrical terms this would be
described as a "number 2" tour. De Valois' creations consisted of a *Pas de
Valse* for seven women to the Blue Danube by Johann Strauss; an *Idyll* to
Edvard Grieg's *Albumblatt No.7*, performed by three of her *corps de ballet*
(Audrey Carlyon, Vera Lyndale and Vivienne Bennett); *The Letter*, a *pas de
trois* to music by Dorothy Foster for Margaret Craske, Noel and Desnaum
and a *Danse Napolitaine* by Roger Desormes for Craske and Desnaum. De
Valois also danced her *Valse Arabesque* to music by Theodore Lack, which
was probably one of her first choreographed solos having been danced at
a series of performances in 1918.[14]

De Valois danced two works, an adagio to Chopin and a Hungarian
dance to music by Wilhelm Kuhe with Serge Morosoff, who also performed a Gipsy Dance solo to music by Camille Saint-Saëns. These appear
to have either been Morosoff's creations or were choreographed jointly.
For the last two dates in December, when Morosoff was replaced by the
New Zealander Jan Caryll, a pupil of Astafieva, these last works were
replaced by a trepak and a version of the Czardas from Léo Délibes'
Coppélia.

 Looking at the composers whose music was chosen indicates that de
Valois' repertoire was very much what audiences would expect, although
perhaps more in terms of a recital than music hall programme. Caryll
described it as being a presentation "ahead of its time".[15] Nevertheless
the music was generally familiar and easy enough for the theatre musicians to cope with. It is, however, conspicuous that de Valois' choice of
music became more adventurous after working for Diaghilev.

Being invited by Léonide Massine to join his group at the Royal Opera
House in 1922 was something of a coup. The group included eleven refu-
gees from Diaghilev's bankrupt *The Sleeping Princess* company with only
four dancers, Massine and Vera Savina (both dismissed from the Ballets
Russes in 1921) and Rita Zalmani and Ninette de Valois not having been
involved in that production.[16] De Valois had been taken under Lydia
Lopokova's wing when she began to take classes with Enrico Cecchetti in
1919. Indeed Lopokova invited her to share her private lessons. However,
in de Valois' essay, "Lydia Lopokova and English Ballet", she overlooks the
fact that they worked together in 1922-23 between the collapse of *The*

Sleeping Princess and the point at which de Valois joined Diaghilev.[17] Instead de Valois placed her emphasis on Lopokova's role with the Camargo Society. Nevertheless, the little Anglo-Russian Companies, which first Massine and then Lopokova put together, also played a role in the establishment of British Ballet and in enabling de Valois to fulfil her dreams.

De Valois was given featured roles in the *divertissement* accompanying feature films at Covent Garden in 1922. Most famously she was Cupid in the solo *Cupidon,* choreographed by Massine to music by Charles Gounod and described by *The Times* as "a trifle".[18] She danced in the Valse and Galop in *Fanatics of Pleasure*, a "Second Empire" ballet to music by Johann Strauss (a forerunner of *Le Beau Danube*) and later in the season was entrusted with a Gavotte to music by Alfons Czibulka which she performed with Errol Addison. De Valois was not involved with the regional tour by the so-called "Massine Quintet" that followed the Covent Garden season but she was invited for occasional weeks at the London Coliseum and was probably one of the larger group that came together again to appear at Bournemouth. She then danced with Lopokova's groups in *divertissement* and chamber ballets such as *Masquerade*. It is interesting that at this point Lopokova felt real *corps de ballet* dancers were what she needed rather than de Valois, yet she found a role for her friend in her little company.

Lopokova brought in de Valois for the revue *You'd Be Surprised* described as a "jazzaganza", the following year. The whole revue, presenting a musical tour of America, appears to have been a muddle and Massine's choreography for the run at the Royal Opera House was not particularly successful. The principal dance number was *Togo; or, the Noble Savage,* in which de Valois appeared as the "negress servant". Significantly for this, as for numbers in the previous Royal Opera House season, designs were by Duncan Grant and the music for *Togo* was selected from *Saudades do Brazil* by Darius Milhaud. This was quite different music to the kind de Valois was accustomed to using. *Togo* only survived a few performances before being replaced and, when the whole revue transferred to the Alhambra, all but one of the dancers were removed from the production. The one survivor, who took over Lopokova's role in *Chicken à la King* and triumphed as the Gramophone Girl, was de Valois. Interestingly, photographs of her in this role reveal a much more sophisticated dancer than the girl of earlier images, suggesting that the experience of working with the star dancers made a real impact and enhanced her maturity.

After *You'd Be Surprised* finally closed in June, de Valois danced again for Lopokova at the London Coliseum but very soon afterwards, in September

1923 she went to Paris to join Serge Diaghilev's Ballets Russes. It really is at this point that de Valois can be said to fully become a twentieth-century dancer. When she left Diaghilev, she looked to new performing arenas and to the establishment of her own school. She was breaking away from the popular theatre and moving into a much more experimental world. Nevertheless, de Valois' early career should not be dismissed and what is remarkable is that she was able to use her early experiences as a foundation for a rich, varied and important career rather than fading into the obscurity which absorbed most of her contemporary British dancers.

Ninette de Valois and Diaghilev

Clement Crisp

The film that David Drew made of Dame Ninette in conversation with himself and colleagues is a unique achievement: it explains so much and we should all take it very much to heart.[1] Dame Ninette's whole career seems to me to have been the absorbing and then the transmission and the transmuting of work that she had learnt from choreographers and particularly from teachers. By the time she joined Diaghilev's company, she was already an established and very gifted dancer with great speed, very good feet; and she was twenty-three, rising twenty-four years old. No novice: she had worked seriously in the theatre since the age of twelve as one of Lila Field's Wonder Children, giving her version of Pavlova's *Dying Swan* at the end of every pier in Britain. She was to write constantly throughout her career about Diaghilev and his influence. What I am really giving here is a selection from her own comments, which seem to me to throw enormous light on what she did from the very beginning.

When joining Diaghilev, she did not audition: she had been noticed in class. She had friends in Cecchetti's class, who were Diaghilev dancers and her entrée into the company in 1923 was absolutely assured: "For the first time in my life I sensed a condition of world theatre. In addition, all Europe was before my eyes."[2] It is necessary to time travel: in 1923 people did not go abroad with anything like the ease and eagerness that we know now, and the whole idea of a European life, a European culture, a European civilisation was certainly different from our understanding and perception today. De Valois continues:

All Europe was before my eyes; its cities, museums, art galleries, its customs and its theatres. Everything merged into a whole – a city's architecture became inseparable from the ballet, and the ballet itself was moulding me as part of a future that was a development of the past. A spirit of tradition was at work, with a heritage so rich that one knew its transplantation to new soil would be possible time and time again. ... Diaghilev respected all people and things functioning in their proper sphere: and as his sense of proportion was as impeccable as his taste, Diaghilev lived beyond the world of his artists. He was concerned with the development of Russian traditions. His strength lay in the fact that his familiarity with the value of the known and the tried was so great that he could advise with conviction and discard with impunity; he could light the path of the unknown and untried with the torch of experience.[3]

This, of course, is one of the vital keys to what she was doing. She already knew a great deal about the various "schools" of ballet. What she did not know was how events might develop, and what developments she could perceive in her own life in a company where she was a much admired dancer.

> To feel one's values and standards undergo a complete change is an extraordinary sensation. It is through Diaghilev that I became aware of a new world, a world that held the secrets of that aesthetic knowledge that I sought, but which showed me that further discoveries would need a divergent approach if I were to attain any knowledge of these principles. In him I encountered a higher form of genius, a state of mind capable of concerning itself with the basic principle of perfect unity in a creative work.[4]

You must understand that she was already a choreographer. Kathrine Sorley Walker's invaluable study of de Valois' created works lists some ten pieces that she made by the time she joined Diaghilev. They were little solos; but, even so, here was not an apprentice creator, here was someone who was mature and, I think, already demonstrating the remarkable intelligence that lay behind everything she did: that sense of value that she found in so many disparate influences: from national dancing, from the Irish Jig up to the most complex works by Bronislava Nijinska, shall we say. We are faced with a mind that was perhaps consciously (subconsciously certainly) preparing itself for something very much larger.

"The main effect of Diaghilev on my dormant creative mind was to arouse an immense interest in the ballet in relation to the theatre."[5] If you think of what passed for ballet at that time, you understand that it had suddenly been made to look totally trumpery by the arrival of Diaghilev's Ballets Russes. The dancing in musical comedies, in music halls and revues, even (dare I say) the free dance that was starting at that time, might be interesting, but it was rootless, it had no soil to feed it. With all this de Valois was aware:

> I further sensed its own single position in the theatre; this in spite of the fact that many of the later ballets (that were produced when I was with

the Company) struck me as of little importance. I had come to one conclusion: the same should happen, along the same lines, and with just such an ultimate goal – in England.[6]

Years ago, talking to her I said, "You must have had an enormous plan; you must have had a great vision." She said: "No, women are housekeepers and I learnt to take every opportunity that was presented." If you examine her career from 1923 onwards, it is a question of seizing opportunities. The great opportunity of course was the encounter with Miss Baylis, of the Old Vic and then the Wells. And then the dancers that came, the dancers that went, and the teachers she could use: everyone and everything she could find. She used what came her way in the most brilliant fashion from dancers and a great musician like Constant Lambert to a young choreographer who had been working with Marie Rambert, Frederick Ashton. She seized every opportunity. She famously once said that it takes more than one person to make a ballet company, but what it also took were the ideas she acquired, the visions which I think she had when she worked with Diaghilev. She also said once that it is very good for young dancers to have two hard years, that is years of really slogging work; and I think, if you examine the listings that both Jane Pritchard and Sarah Woodcock have made of the touring life of the Diaghilev Ballets Russes from 1911, when it was the permanent Company, until 1929, you will grasp de Valois' meaning: years of terrifyingly lengthy tours, long journeys across Europe. (Markova tells of sitting up all night in second class compartments, travelling from Barcelona to wherever the ballet was next due to appear. Getting out of the train and rushing to find rooms. The Hoyer brothers were very good at that, because they would race as soon as the train arrived at the new city to find lodgings for friends, not least the child Markova and her chaperone.) It was a devil of a life, never easy. Even during the First World War the work and the vital creativity in the Ballets Russes continued; and this is exactly what shaped Dame Ninette during her time with the company. Always, there was this sense of something happening, of Europe opening in front of her, no matter what the conditions: a marvel that touched her, educated her.

To de Valois Diaghilev was uniquely both progressive and at heart a great traditionalist:

> It is important to remember that he had made himself the custodian of the highest standard of ballet production in the world, and to complete

his work he had persistently to search for artists adaptable to this particular environment. That those he succeeded with were never a success in other forms of theatrical production, and that time and again since his death they have only succeeded when following his ideals and the life their talents and education had meant them to live, proves that they have only been true to his conception of them. It is correct to say that many, through the original planning of that far-seeing mind, are even now fulfilling themselves in the same direction. Such is the fortunate destiny of those who came under the influence of a man of great vision.[7]

That was de Valois talking about herself: you have to imagine, you have to understand, how she was influenced by this extraordinary creative energy, the sense of the new, the sense of experiment which Dame Ninette never objected to. But remember also that basic belief in a classical academic style and in a vision of the theatre that Diaghilev had had from the very beginning, from the days of *Mir Iskusstva*. And what I think she also acquired in his Company, which was nearly as important as anything else, was her sense of theatrical vision, a vision of theatre as a place of excitement, of decorative and of musical excitement as well as dance excitement. If you examine the list of the ballets that were staged by The Royal Ballet, by the Sadler's Wells Ballet, the Vic-Wells Ballet during her years you have the most sensational list of decorative explorations in making theatrical works. She accepted the idea of employing a Chinese painter (Chiang Yee) to design *The Birds* for Robert Helpmann. Think of Edward Burra's designs for *Miracle in the Gorbals*, for example, or the work that she encouraged McKnight Kauffer to provide for her *Checkmate*. She had a generosity of vision, a vision which was not going to be thwarted – she seized every opportunity as it came to her. This again is something that she owed to Diaghilev.

One of the last subjects that she wrote about was Diaghilev: when Mary Clarke and I had the great good fortune to be working with her while she was preparing her final book about ballet – it was entitled *Step by Step* – we went through her writings, discussing, selecting, and Dame Ninette talked wonderfully. At the end of it she was thinking about a title. She said "What am I going to call it?" I made various suggestions, thrilled by the wisdom and good sense on every page and then said, "You know, Dame Ninette, really what you should call it is *I Told You So!*" and she fell about laughing. But it is true: everything that she writes about her work in her three very important books, everything she observed and guarded and kept as a guide to everything she chose to do, was because she knew – she really did know – what she wanted to do. Though she said that she was only a housekeeper, she understood everything she wanted and she made it all happen. Her final comment about Diaghilev in *Invitation to the Ballet* was one which I treasure: "It was his work and his will that saved him from himself."[8] This was a reference to his sexual liaisons. "But with age, failing health, and the continual financial strain, power waned; the strength of impersonal reasoning became impaired ... His work was done at the time he died."[9] Can we hazard how the Diaghilev Company would have survived following the Wall Street Crash from 1929-1931? It would not have survived, not even in Monte Carlo. And beaten up by hard work and by ill health, Diaghilev died, in a sense when he had to. "His work was done at the time he died and the lull that followed was valuable re-laxation for all concerned. What is happening in the ballet world to-day may ultimately stand as a memorial to the man who succeeded in saving the ballet from itself." As always, she was right.[10]

Evolution not Revolution:
Ninette de Valois' Philosophy of Dance

Beth Genné

Ninette de Valois was one of the most innovative and far-thinking dance theorists of the twentieth century – indeed within the history of dance. She considered ballet from multiple perspectives, attentive to its position within the sweep of history, but also to its moment-to-moment interaction with a specific time and place. And most unusually, she wrote about dance within the larger context of all the arts. Her writings reveal that she was *not* a traditionalist in the dictionary definition of that word – even an adventurous one. *The Oxford English Dictionary* (1983) defines a traditionalist as someone who "upholds the authority of tradition" and traditionalism as "adherence to..., maintenance of, or submission to the authority of tradition, excessive reverence for tradition." By contrast, Madam's view embraced change and welcomed it. She presented a new conception of the role of dance's past and its relationship to the present and future. For her, tradition and innovation were interrelated: dynamic interaction of past and present best promoted dance's growth; dance's future comes through *evolution* not revolution.

De Valois first stated her ideas in an article called "The Future of the Ballet", published in the *Dancing Times* in 1926, and continued in a five part series "Modern Choreography [sic]" in the same magazine in 1933.[1] She elaborated these ideas in *Invitation to the Ballet* (1937) and *Come Dance with Me* (1957), as well as in innumerable talks, interviews, articles and finally in *Step by Step* (1977). Her theories were meant to be embodied in the training and repertory of the Sadler's Wells (later Royal Ballet) School and Company.

It is unusual for professional dancers to publish theoretical writing. Dame Ninette's formal education, of necessity, was minimal: she was self-taught, her education coming, in part, from days in the "sanctuary" of her grandmother's well-stocked library. "How I read!" she remembered. Her tastes ranged widely from the Lilac, Green and Yellow Fairy Books to Shakespeare, Scott, Dickens and Byron (one of her first heroes). She recalls:

I think that I acquired, by the age of ten, quite an astonishing survey of

Victoria's reign through nothing less than the magnificently bound copies of *Punch*... I can still remember staggering across the library to the rocking-chair clutching a volume almost as heavy as myself.[2]

De Valois's grandmother encouraged her reading:

[She] cherished hopes that I would grow up 'clever'.... I faintly sensed this hope on the part of other grownups. I suspect that it was based on the fact that I was plain and inconspicuous next to my very beautiful older sister. [3]

(Family photographs reveal a dark-haired child with a gaze, both intensive and aloof, compared to her blond and more conventionally pretty older sister.) When she started performing, Edris set aside part of her tiny salary to buy books – though she could ill-afford it. "It was no good scolding me; I wanted one day to have my own library, because of the happy hours that a library had already given me."[4]

De Valois also had a passion for writing poetry and prose. She created a magazine of her short stories and staged her own plays for her siblings' amusement. In another time, she would have been a good candidate for university, but it was rare and controversial for women of de Valois' era to go on to higher education. When the family doctor attributed young Edris's restlessness and a tendency to sleep-walk to an "over-active brain", her writing activities were "curtailed".[5] In any case, her family's uncertain financial situation would have made university impossible. Both her father's and her mother's inherited estates were failing, and the situation was made more difficult by the fact that, when she was seven, her parents had separated at de Valois' mother's insistence.[6] Her mother took the children to England and her father, a career army officer, continued his service until he was killed in action in the summer of 1917. Even before then, however, it became apparent that the children would eventually have to make their own livings. De Valois' talent as a dancer provided a solution: her arts-loving mother acquiesced to her daughter's desire to dance professionally, even though it still carried a stigma among people of her class. Her mother decided on the stage name, Ninette de Valois, and she made it her business to consult and cultivate people like Philip Richardson, editor of the *Dancing Times*, in whose pages de Valois received notices from her earliest years.[7]

Despite her lack of formal education, de Valois' dance-writing was lucid and persuasive. It revealed a brilliant, sharply analytical mind at work, able to bring together a wide variety of information and analyse it from a perspective that, even from a young age, was remarkably mature. From the beginning, her sights were set on long-term goals that would ultimately benefit others. She wanted a stable, ongoing institution that could function independently of her, as opposed to an organisation whose survival depended on the nature of her own personality and gifts.[8] De Valois was also keenly aware that she could not do it alone, and made that clear when anyone tried to give her credit for the creation of The Royal Ballet. "It takes more than one to make a ballet company," she would insist.[9] This was not false modesty but a realistic assessment of how institutions are built. She distrusted praise, which I think she read as flattery. When I brought up the importance of preserving her choreography, she responded dismissively, "Oh come on! I'm not *that* good."[10]

Madam's talents as a thinker, writer and speaker (usually off-the-cuff and without any notes) would be key factors in promoting the success of her School and Company. Of course, it helped that she had the kind of upper-middle class accent that, as Shaw demonstrated in *Pygmalion,* could powerfully affect success or failure in the England of her era. But though the accent may have helped, it was what she said and wrote that made people listen or take note.

De Valois presented herself and her theories of dance at a time when women's opportunities were severely limited. Women without property did not get the vote in England until 1931. Though women's colleges existed in Oxford and Cambridge from the late nineteenth century, women were not granted official degrees until 1920 (Oxford) and 1947 (Cambridge).[11] There is a reasonable chance that Madam read Virginia Woolf's *A Room of One's Own* (1929), as she was well acquainted with the Bloomsbury Group through John Maynard Keynes and his wife, Lydia Lopokova. She certainly grew up and spent much of her adult life in the climate that Virginia Wolf describes in her book, a climate in which women had to struggle to be taken seriously as intellectuals, and she may have experienced the kinds of petty humiliations and discriminations that Woolf described at the Oxbridge universities when de Valois worked at the Festival Theatre in Cambridge. Nonetheless, I do not think Madam considered herself a feminist.[12] Still, according to her niece Elizabeth Stannus, she deeply admired and cultivated the company of women who were highly educated and professionally accomplished and was not at all interested in women who did not have careers outside the home.[13] She remained determined to give herself the best education possible.[14] Indeed, de Valois did not just read for pleasure and escape. In *Invitation to the*

Ballet she quotes from Kant's *Critique of Pure Reason* as well as Nietzsche's *Thus Spake Zarathustra*. De Valois' wide reading may have helped foster both her analytical thinking and the confident, even authoritative tone of her writing and speaking, as she strove to become the kind of woman she admired. De Valois seemed to assume that her ideas were worth listening to, and she was determined that readers take her seriously not only as a performer but as someone who had something important to say about the future of ballet.

Despite her confident tone, did Dame Ninette ever have serious doubts about her ability and qualifications? "I kept waiting for them to find me out," she confessed with a rueful chuckle in 1981, when she was eighty-two and had received such high honours as a DBE.[15] Psychologists call this kind of thinking the "impostor syndrome", and it is very common.[16] To proceed with determination in the face of it, however, and surrounded by such low expectations for your sex, is far from common. It takes real courage – especially when you are promoting your ideas to a male-dominated power-structure about an art form that, when she began, did not have the *cachet* of the more established performing arts like opera and "serious" drama.

The subject of de Valois' first major article in 1926 was no less than "The Future of the Ballet".[17] It was an ambitious topic for a dancer in her twenties who had only just founded a new ballet school. *Ballet* to the British public meant the glamorous Russians, not an Anglo-Irish girl named Edris Stannus, who had the old-fashioned French stage name Ninette de Valois and who had made her reputation as a pantomime, musical hall and musical theatre dancer. *Ballet* was associated by the British public not only with Russians but with their largely contemporary repertory of one-act ballets by Fokine, Nijinsky, Nijinska, Massine and Balanchine. British audiences knew little of the nineteenth-century repertory by Petipa and Ivanov or of the French Romantic ballets in which the Russians had once danced, except in the drastically truncated versions offered by Pavlova and occasionally Diaghilev. The full-length *The Sleeping Princess* had lost money and closed after a relatively short run, with audiences and some critics complaining that it was "old fashioned" compared to the one-act modernist ballets to which they were accustomed. Even de Valois had found it hard to see the worth of Diaghilev's nineteenth-century repertory, when compared to his newly-commissioned works:

It took time for me to understand the influence of the classical tradition on the company's work; enlightenment did not come until after I had left, and I had found time to reflect on the whole experience.[18]

In "The Future of the Ballet", de Valois unequivocally presents herself as a modernist. The article was illustrated with a photograph showing de Valois as a barefoot young bacchante clad in a thigh-revealing tunic, head thrown back in a luscious backbend. Although the photo illustrates Fokine's ballet *Narcisse*, which she had danced for Diaghilev, de Valois looks more like a disciple of Isadora Duncan than the young classicist delicately poised on *pointe* in her earlier photos in the *Dancing Times* or the flirtatious musical theatre dancer of the photographs advertising her appearances in West End shows.

De Valois' choreography from around the time of the article was even more avant-garde. After her sojourn with the Ballets Russes, Madam's strongest influences became Massine, Nijinska, and Central European Expressionists.[19] Her work at the Festival Theatre (and later at the Abbey Theatre) reflected the severe angles and compositional tableaux of Central European Expressionism as well as the theories of her cousin, Terence Gray (himself influenced by Gordon Craig's stripped-down, abstract modernist stage designs). Her work at the Abbey Theatre kept up this trend with the increasing use of masks in response to Yeats's interest in Japanese theatre as well as the German Expressionists. The London première of de Valois' vibrantly modernist creation, *Rout*, inaugurated her new school;[20] and in the same issue as "The Future of the Ballet" was an advertisement for the Academy of Choregraphic Art [sic], illustrated by students clad in severe black tunics, kneeling with backs arched forwards, in de Valois' *Rhythm*.

When Dame Ninette wrote "The Future of the Ballet", Romantic notions of "revolution" had a powerful influence on avant-garde artists of many kinds, who felt honour-bound to break from the past and to present the public with continual surprises. For these artists, past and present were perceived as antithetical to one another, one "dead", the other "alive". The past must be abandoned for the future to live. And indeed, the young theorist de Valois started out by presenting herself as a champion of the modern by praising the good influence of "the plastic school on the classic": "The Hellenic School with Isadora Duncan as its figurehead has shown the emotional powers that lie hidden in the theory of broader and freer body movement."[21] But Dame Ninette also offered a new view of the relation of tradition to innovation, of the past to the present, when considering "the contest between the classical ballet of the [eighteen] eighties and the modern choreographical [sic] studies". This "contest" de Valois now addressed not only to provide a vision of the future but also to plead with the "anti-moderns... if not for their co-operation, at least for their enquiry into a matter which they are viewing through smoked glasses".[22] Into a climate of polemics and dissent, she brought reconciliation and a vision that was clear, cogent and historically broad.

Although she applauded the influence of Duncan and the "Hellenic" school, de Valois did not see them as a sole and solid foundation for future growth. For her, the "true" path to the future was being laid out by Diaghilev's choreographers, Fokine, Nijinsky, Nijinska and Massine. Why were they the "true theorists" of "modern choreographical studies"? Her startling answer was that what made the difference was Diaghilev's connections to the *past* – to the so-called "classical" school – as well as to the present.

Here de Valois looks both backward and forward, employing a perspective that encompassed more than just her own lifetime, her own era, by offering a new way of thinking, a new paradigm to apply to the development of her art form. "The modern movement", de Valois insisted, "was not the outcome of a whim or drastic revolution." Nor, she added, did "expansion... spell expulsion [or] construction, destruction...." "No art ever comes to a standstill. Theatre, accompanied by drama, painting and music, progresses steadily through experiment and research."[23] To illustrate her point, de Valois urged a comparison of dance with the history and development of music and musical styles. She quoted her friend, music critic Edwin Evans:

> Broadly speaking each musical style has grown so imperceptibly out of its predecessors that no ordinary intelligent musical mind that could think in terms of the earlier form could find any difficulty in adapting itself to the later. [24]

Thus, like the composer and musician or the playwright and actor, the choreographer and dancer need a thorough knowledge of the historical repertory of forms on which a particular tradition is founded and from which it continues to grow. Hence de Valois stressed the analogy of dance with the arts: just as the actor had to be able to play Shakespeare as well as Shaw, and the musician Mozart as well as Stravinsky, so their counterparts in dance had to be equally at home with both past styles and present.

This, de Valois insisted, was true of the artists of the Diaghilev company, which she offered as a model to the English dance community. "Here" she wrote "we have a repertory company running classical and modern ballet side by side – and what is more important – in many cases blended."[25] As she implied, Fokine, Nijinsky, Nijinska and Massine had benefited from the influence of the modern movement and invented approaches that were as groundbreaking as those of their colleagues outside the ballet: from *Petrouchka* to the *Rite of Spring* to *Les Noces* to *Parade*. However, at the same time, they did not abandon what the "classical" past had taught them. "The teachings of the classic school are the sure and only foundation," de Valois argued, "*limitless in its adaptability*, it consequently proves its power to meet the varied requirements of the theatre" (italics mine).[26]

The key phrase here is "limitless in its adaptability", a phrase which is often overlooked in characterising Dame Ninette's purportedly "traditionalist" approach. For Dame Ninette, the Ballets Russes choreographers had come from a training system that best prepared the body to accommodate the influences and demands of a wide variety of styles, and that gave the dancer's body flexibility, control, strength and endurance as well as the latitude in leg movement that came with the development of turnout. Their school had taught the accumulated wisdom of many dancers and choreographers – French, Italian, Scandinavian – not just one. Thus dancers from the Diaghilev company had a variety of skills to be able to absorb and accommodate contemporary movement discoveries from the barefoot naturalism of Fokine's Duncan-inspired choreography to the spasmodic expressionism of Njinsky's *The Rite of Spring* to the neoclassism of Balanchine, while at the same time they could perform, build on or modify the accumulated lessons of past choreographers and teachers that had been kept alive in the school and repertory they had performed in St Petersburg.

Thus although Diaghilev was perceived by the general public solely as a revolutionary, de Valois saw the bigger picture: "Diaghilev's advantage was that he had a great root from which he could continually draw."[27] In contrast, Duncan and Wigman, while presenting new ways of moving, had limited themselves by rejecting the accumulated wisdom and contributions of past dance makers and teachers. "It would be unjust not to admit that...earnest revolutionary tendencies have most assuredly produced individual artists and minds of importance," de Valois wrote later in *Invitation to the Ballet*. But despite their importance, "the Marie [sic] Wigmans and the Martha Grahams [...] are responsible for 'cults' rather than 'schools', they are concerned with 'sincere but single messages'".[28]

Innovation, de Valois insists, is a natural and expectable outgrowth of a living tradition.

"Root" was a term that kept coming up in my conversations with Dame Ninette. The metaphor of the root and the tree that grows from it shaped her vision of how dance works and continually renews itself. A root is a living thing that must be nourished and cultivated so that the tree may grow and make many branches with many different kinds of blossoms. And to take the metaphor further, my understanding was that Dame Ninette envisioned many kinds of blossoms and fruits – some of which might eventually evolve to be radically different from the fruit of the original species. She spoke of the historical necessity of break-away innovators, but she felt they needed an establishment to break away from: a place and a system that dancers and choreographers could, at various points in their careers, learn from, reject, reinvent, but also return to and renew, adding new nourishment to enrich and strengthen the basic root. She envisioned a school and training that drew not just from the Russians but, as they themselves did, from the French, Italians, and Danish. To this would be added, as it developed, the English school.

In *Invitation to the Ballet* de Valois went further by outlining a more detailed recipe for the relationship of innovation and tradition in a ballet company.

1. "Traditional-classical and romantic works": this first requirement "constitutes the foundation stone, the technical standard and historical knowledge that are demanded as a 'means test' by which the abilities of young dancers are both developed and inspired".

2. "Modern works of future classic importance": "those works that, both musically and otherwise, have a future and that may be regarded as the major works of this generation".

3. "Current works of more topical interest": "sometimes experimental, of merely ephemeral interest and value, yet important as a means of balancing an otherwise ambitious programme".

4. "Works encouraging a strictly national tendency in their creation generally": this fourth requirement is "important to the national significance of the ballet. Such works constitute the nation's own contribution to the theatre and are in need of the most careful guidance of all the groups."[29]

Today, it is the first category that gets the most attention when Dame Ninette is characterised; but in her theories, it comprises only *one fourth* of the balanced whole she presents which, if not maintained within a company's repertory, will render that company extremely limited and result in a general weakness both in execution and creation. When I interviewed her in 1981 it was the balance she was worried about. Where, she wondered out loud to me, were the new works in which contemporary composers, choreographers and set designers collaborated? Choreographers' conceptions (prominently Ashton's and MacMillan's at that time) were likely to dominate the ballets they created, and they were most likely to draw on older musical styles.

Dame Ninette's list also reveals a new attitude toward historical repertory. Along with the modern, the Company must have a selection of historical repertory that is presented in period style. Thus between 1930 and 1939, she set about reconstructing and mounting a period repertory of nineteenth-century works, presented openly and unashamedly in a style as close to the original as possible, and not just as *divertissements* but as part of a dramatic whole, which along with mime, gave a sense of the larger narrative context which the steps were meant to convey. The ballets she chose came from the Franco-Russian repertory: two French ballets (*Giselle* and *Coppélia*), and three from Russia (*The Sleeping Beauty*, *Swan Lake* and *The Nutcracker*). To this end, she hired the Mariinski *régisseur*, Nicolai Sergeyev, who had the Stepanov notation of these ballets; and she brought in Ursula Moreton to teach what she had learned of mime from the Italian school.

But although Dame Ninette's goal was for her dancers to have experience with period styles, she was handicapped by her lack of precisely detailed sources. Although the world of music had developed a detailed system of notation for the performance and preservation of their music, the world of ballet historically had a more *laissez-faire* attitude about preservation and maintenance, preferring, on the whole, the oral transmission of material: license was given to edit and "modernise" steps within limits. Thus the Stepanov notation was closer to an *aide-memoire* (with *port de bras* and other details, for example, only sketchily indicated). The incomplete preservation of period ballets meant that Sergeyev, de Valois and Lambert had to fill in or alter sections that were missing.[30] But, as much as she could, Dame Ninette actively worked to respect the integrity of the choreographer's original conception – even if it was considered "old fashioned". In *Invitation to the Ballet*, for example, she argued for the inclusion of mime, when possible, in period ballets and for its inclusion in her School's curriculum: "There is no better means of ... developing a sense of style and period."[31] The beautiful mime scene in which Odette "tells" Prince Siegfried of her past, that Diaghilev had omitted, was restored in the *Swan Lake* at Sadler's Wells .

Here might be a good moment to compare the attitudes of de Valois' younger contemporary, George Balanchine, who also built a School and Company in a country without an established tradition of ballet. Like de Valois, Balanchine stressed the importance of classical training, the so-called *danse d'école*. Unlike de Valois, however, he did not think that maintaining historical repertory was necessary. His view was a much more drastic, but nonetheless understandable, extension of the more *laissez-faire* attitude towards preservation he had learned as a child, in which the "updating" or revision of an earlier ballet by a new choreographer was permitted. Balanchine wrote:

> Our art of ballet is ephemeral. ...It has only the permanence of a classic vocabulary renewed for every generation of young aspirant. ...The repertory itself is evanescent. ...even the best of them [the historical repertory] deserve to die and let in new vision. I have never considered my own repertory of more than passing interest.[32]

For de Valois, however, there were, and would continue to be, works from every generation, which deserved to be accurately maintained in the repertory. Her model came from the higher status art forms: music, literature, painting and sculpture, drama. As with the orchestral repertory or in an art museum with a modern wing or in a repertory theatre company, past and present would live side by side; these had their innovators and revolutionaries, but the past was also respected and preserved. In this way, de Valois claimed for dance the status of a "high" art in its own right.

She also set out a new kind of goal not only for dance, but for dance's creators. In a sense, this is one of the ideas in which she is most powerfully influenced by nineteenth-century Romantic thought with its "cult of the genius". Choreographers are artists, not just artisans, and their works should be preserved and maintained intact to nurture and delight future generations – works which will not die with their creators, but continue to contribute inspiration to future choreographers. The role of an establishment was, in part, to ensure that outcome by incorporating notation as a part of the curriculum.[33] But Dame Ninette combines this Romantic notion with ideas from other fields. Her use of the word "evolution" can be associated with progressive trends in British intellectual thought of her era. Used most famously in connection with the natural sciences and Darwin's theories about the origin and development of species, "evolution" was a contemporary descriptor of a new and modern way of thinking that had emerged, in part, as a result of the acceptance of Darwin's theories: *homo sapiens* had gradually and over time evolved (through natural selection or "survival of the fittest") from animals. This new paradigm challenged the religious belief that a supernatural and inimitable force had created humans whole and in His image. It was connected as well to writings about social and cultural "evolution" and to the notion of progress through science. Research and experiment, not divine intervention, would lead to a new and brighter future. De Valois' use of the terminology of the natural sciences is unselfconscious, and I do not think it would have consciously entered her head that she was connecting her ideas to scientific thought. Nevertheless, her use of the word "evolution", her metaphors of organic growth, change and expansion into the future, her notion of choreographers, building on past discoveries but making "progress through experiment and research" in dance, all signal her investment in these scientific ideas – and her plans for a future beyond her lifetime.[34]

Her colleagues who shaped their companies *solely* on the revolutionary model and the more "theistic" notion of creation by a single "genius" choreographer faced built-in limits. In that model, destruction comes inevitably with the death of the creator, because adherence to the past, to "tradition", is suspect. To take as an example the brilliant Merce Cunningham: his Company has dissolved after his death; the last-minute creation of an archive of his works is a wonderful thing, but it does not alone ensure continuity. For the most part, his techniques and works will in future be taught in academic settings alongside various modern and post-modern techniques. The ethos of the "revolutionary" model, however, will work against their long term survival, as ever younger faculty and their students, imbued with the ethos of "the latest is best", will tend to reject their own recent past as irrelevant and old-fashioned.

One of the ironies of history is that the work of post-modern choreographers are increasingly finding a home in repertory ballet companies modelled on Dame Ninette's conception of a balanced repertory in which tradition and innovation co-exist happily (Cunningham, Taylor, Tharp and Morris come to mind). Her dancers are expected to use their skills, "limitless in their adaptability", to serve the needs of a variety of styles – both new and old. They are accustomed to a varied repertory. Apart from such companies, there are few modern dance companies in which the interrelationship of past and present – tradition and innovation – are valued and encouraged. Except for companies like Rambert Dance Company and the late-lamented London Contemporary Dance Theatre, the majority of modern and post-modern dance companies adhere to the single-creator model.

Today it looks as though Dame Ninette's theories of evolution not revolution, expansion not expulsion, are widely accepted in both ballet and modern dance.[35] At New York City Ballet, every effort is being made to preserve, revive and maintain Balanchine's repertory (despite his own wishes). Balanchine's own version of *Swan Lake* Act II was, in part, attributable to the public enthusiasm for the historical repertory presented by Sadler's Wells Ballet. Most American ballet companies now include nineteenth-century, multiple-act ballets regularly in their repertory instead of the truncated versions that were the norm in the first half of the twentieth century. Many of these are traceable directly to the influence of the appearances of the first Sadler's Wells/Royal Ballet performances in America and were advised by de Valois' ex-dancers and pupils.[36]

Dame Ninette's understanding of the interrelationship of tradition and innovation was not confined to ballet. Her love and respect for the folk tradition of dances from various cultures was profound and she writes about it extensively in *Invitation to the Ballet*, where she argues for the necessity of the recovery and maintenance of the traditional folk dances of the British Isles, which she saw as a rich resource for British choreographers.[37] As she well knew, Russian and Eastern European folk and social dance forms were already a part of character dance classes in Russia and elsewhere, but to these she added her own nation's forms.[38] In Turkey, she drew upon the traditional line and circle dances of the Middle East.

Drawing from traditional dance sources of all cultures to reconfigure contemporary dance (both ballet and post-modern) is becoming a hallmark of the global age. De Valois' practice again anticipated this development, which in its turn is a further demonstration of her concern to bring tradition and innovation to interact together to produce a new vision. If Dame Ninette were alive today, doubtless she would surprise us with yet new ways of seeing the interrelation of tradition and innovation for the future.

Ninette de Valois, A Woman of the Theatre
A Discussion led by Rupert Christiansen[1]

(Transcript of a panel discussion between distinguished former
ballet dancers, teachers and company directors)

Rupert Christiansen (RC): This panel is meeting together to discuss
Ninette de Valois as a woman of the theatre. It is comprised of Sir John
Tooley (former General Administrator at the Royal Opera House), Maina
Gielgud (former Director of the Australian Ballet and Royal Danish Ballet,
now teaching at English National Ballet), Anya Linden, Lady Sainsbury
(who served under Madam, starred with The Royal Ballet in the late
1950s and earlier 1960s and is now a major patron of the arts), Gillian
Lynne (who danced with Sadler's Wells Ballet all the way through the
1940s) and John Copley (who was told by Madam at The Royal Ballet
School that he was absolutely hopeless and then went on to become one
of the world's most successful opera directors).

A woman of the theatre – I interpret that label in various different
ways. I think there are many implications to it but I would like to preface
this discussion with a quotation from a report in the *Dancing Times* of a
lecture that Madam gave in Liverpool in the late1920s. In this, she urged
all students of the ballet who desire to become choreographers to study
the trend of the modern theatre both in England and on the continent.
Now that is something that she certainly did herself at that time. She
knew all about modern trends in theatre, such as about Gordon Craig,
Adolphe Appia, Max Reinhardt as well as about Diaghilev. And in the mid
to late 1920s, she worked alongside many of the most avant-garde theatre directors of the day, including W. B. Yeats at the Abbey Theatre in
Dublin and her cousin, Terence Gray, at the Festival Theatre in Cambridge, who was, in a way, reinventing the way that Greek tragedy was
staged. Madam wasn't really the choreographer, I think nowadays we
would call her the movement director; she did a lot of work with the
choruses. In that light I want to ask the panel how they feel about her
great ballets in the 1930s: *Job, Checkmate, The Rake's Progress*. They are
very much dramas, aren't they, and as Alastair Macaulay suggests [see
chapter 28] it makes me wonder whether she had much interest in pure
dance. Anya would you like to comment on that?

Anya Sainsbury (AS): Not pure dance certainly; she choreographed to a
minute degree; there was never any doubt exactly what movements she

wanted and there were many, many movements. I can see absolutely how she would have been hugely influenced by Massine because, in my view, Massine's and her approach to choreography seem to be very similar. I think that the ballets she did from *Checkmate* on, stand out as wonderful pieces, beautifully constructed with extraordinary characterisation. We will talk later about pure dance as it comes down to us in the form of *Symphonic Variations.*

RC: She obviously didn't really like *Symphonic Variations* and yet you say when she refers to her own ballets, her technique was purely to concentrate on movement. She wasn't interested in exploring characterisation or motivation or anything like that.

AS: No, and I've been trying to analyse why she got extraordinary performances out of all her dancers in the myriad characters that she created and those characters came from those very movements that she created. They [the movements] were so infused in themselves with the characters, that the dancers could not help but become those characters. She must have been pretty clever in choosing them. She chose Matthew Hart from the School to do The Rake. She saw it was for him. It was her great ability to see the talent in someone, their quality and if they could do the steps, the movements, the gestures and the little expressions perfectly they would be given the character.

RC: Gillian and Maina is that your experience of her as well?

Gillian Lynne (GL): I don't agree with the view that she didn't direct. I thought she was a fabulous director and that her detail, her minute detail for each character, is something I have carried with me all my life. No one has mentioned the fact that that she was a master of making theatre. She made ballets but you could make a ballet and not have a piece of theatre. It could be dull and not interest the public across the proscenium arch. Madam managed the whole lot. I have a quick story about when I was an Angel in *Job*. I was very new and I was so proud to be a body sitting on Satan's chair, we were all on those steps and we were doing those rather strange leanings but because it was such wonderful music and I was new and I was in a ballet, I was just carried away. There was a terrible "Stop" and Madam shouted "Lynne, all we need is a sweet smile. We do not need your whole soul." It appeared to me that Madam had such wonderful humour.

RC: I think Helpmann must in many ways have been her dream performer and she once said, I think in *Come Dance with Me*, that he was the perfect example of an artist who knows the meaning of theatre. Could you endorse that, Maina?

Maina Gielgud (MG): Indeed I have wonderful memories of Steps, Notes and Squeaks [a small touring company led by Gielgud, 1978-1981]when Madam did us the honour of coaching *Checkmate* for Jonathan Kelly and myself and Bobby Helpmann as The Red King. I think my most vivid memory of that is at the Old Vic in the studio upstairs, where so much must have happened in the past and her scolding Bobby for not doing exactly what he should do as The Red King, exactly as the choreography should be.

Anya was saying how it was the construction of the ballets and the spatial awareness that she made one have that was important, the attention to detail. All of those things that she had built up in her own imagination before she even created the works made extraordinary theatre. She didn't allow any leeway. She wasn't going to change any aspect of the choreography just because an individual might feel that it suited them better. That was certainly the case for Bobby Helpmann in The Red King in *Checkmate* at the Old Vic.

RC: For all this great interest she expressed in the theatre and her direct involvement in these theatrical productions, I wonder if later in her life, say after the war, she actually managed to keep up with what was going on in the theatre? We know that she was a great reader, and she wrote some rather good poetry but do we know anything about what her cultural life was like outside ballet? I wonder if she ever went to the theatre, whether she went to the cinema or to the opera? John Tooley is that something you know anything about?

John Tooley (JT): Not really, she had a real capacity for absorbing all sorts of information from all sorts of sources and this is one of her great strengths. Just to go back to the earlier discussion, I think it's quite interesting that in fact, as far as I can remember, all the ballets she created, the really successful ones which we already mentioned, these were not her original ideas. These were proposed to her either by people who had an idea or by composers. Arthur Bliss went to her about *Checkmate*, for example. As she progressed through life with the Company, she was increasingly short of time. The pressures on her were gigantic and often when I talked to her, she was much more interested in literature, in poetry and in writing her own poems. I think she found a tremendous amount of strength in the creative activity of writing poetry. But having said that, she knew what was going on. She may not have seen it directly but she knew what was important and, if she wanted to know more, she could find somebody who knew about it.

RC: It's very interesting, isn't it that she continued to write poetry all through her life but stopped choreographing when she was what, fifty?

JT: That was a deliberate decision, she said at the time that "running this Company is going to occupy all my time, my energy and resources. Something has to go and I'm giving up choreography." That was a deliberate decision of hers.

RC: But she could do that, I feel Ashton couldn't have done that, he was in pain.

JT: But they're totally different people, you can't actually begin to compare what was driving them. As far as Madam was concerned she was driven by this wonderful vision for a permanent ballet company and, by the end of the war, it was also the Sadler's Wells Theatre Ballet, and she knew she hadn't really got time to do any more than try and make them work. And I admired her hugely for this absolute commitment to this one vision. The vision was a realistic one, she knew she wasn't going to get there all the time but she just strove to make the best of it and that took up all her energy.

GL: She was wonderfully helpful to people who were trying something of their own. I made my own company in 1963 and I don't know what age Madam must have been then, but she bothered to come and see it. She wrote to me about it, a wonderful letter full of notes and at the end it said "keep going, lots of love Ninette". She did bother to go and see other peoples' attempts.

RC: So you wouldn't describe her as insular in any way? What about a bit prim, John Copley? I mean ballet companies have an awful lot of goings on, let's face it. Did she ever turn a blind eye to this or cast a cold eye?

John Copley (JC): I don't know. I have just five experiences of meeting her. She saw me fall over in class in a double *pirouette* when I was simply determined to do it perfectly and I ended up on the other side of the room with my legs in the air. I heard this terrifying voice say "who's that extraordinary boy?" Miss [Ailne] Philips said something and she said "Oh, he's very musical you see," as if it was the worst thing you could possibly be. Then she told me I was hopeless and she was having me transferred to the opera because she said: "You'll do better there." She was so right; I wouldn't be sitting here if she hadn't done that.

Eventually, I was stage managing and, because Madam recalled me as being hopeless and falling over, she could not understand how I was suddenly stage manager at the Sadler's Wells Theatre Company. She came on stage when we were doing *Carnaval*, which has wings where you put the lights through but it's a box and it's very hard to light and I was in charge of lighting. She came on stage before the matinée and there were a lot of lamps upstage lighting them from the back. And she said: "Those lamps are in the way of my dancers, move them". And I said: "Well, actually Madam they're lighting". "Move them," she said, so I got a stage electrician to move the lamps. She came tearing round after it had happened and she said, "My dancers are totally invisible". I said, "But Madam you told me to move the lights". She said, "Not those lights".

The most famous story was about a wonderful dancer from South Africa called Bridget Badham, who joined the company in Southsea when Madam had been in Turkey for a long time. She was an extraordinary young dancer and she didn't go into the *corps de ballet*, she went one rank up. So when Ninette saw her for the first time, I was standing there. Ninette came through the door and she saw this girl in a Swanilda Friend costume, which is not *corps de ballet*, and she said "What's your name, child?" and Bridget, who was absolutely terrified, said, "Badham". She said, "What's your name child?" She said, "Badham". She said, "Don't keep calling me Madam, what's your name?" "Badham, Madam."

She said to my partner, who was Stage Manager of the Company in America, at the end of *Swan Lake* Act III: "Mr Healey," she said, "There's a strange green light at the bottom of the backcloth in Act Three." And John said, "Well actually Madam there isn't a strange…" "No, there's a strange green light at the bottom of the backcloth." He said, "Well with due respect, Madam, I am standing with you at the back of the auditorium and I don't think there is a strange green light actually." "Well that's what the trouble is; there should be a strange green light." Well that was put in that night and it stayed in as a strange green light. She was magnificent.

AS: We've all forgotten the question.

RC: Do you think she took a rather prim view of the theatre and its morals?

GL: I've got a reply to that, it's a bit naughty, but it's about when the Company went to the Met. in 1949, our first attempt on the Americas. She got us all together in the Stalls of the Garden and she said, "The girls are all too fat. We are going to the country where the women have the best bodies in the world. You will all go on a diet, you will not eat." She went on with a lot of other things and said: "Finally, I don't want any love making or conjoining from now until we have opened at the Met." She said, "I have done my research and I have found out that an orgasm is the same amount of energy expended as seven games at Wimbledon. I can't spare it." When we got to America, they liked us and they said lovely things about us but mostly they said that the girls look a little pale and wan. So then she came round to our hotel and said, "You must all have cream with your cornflakes". And the other wonderful little story is she kept going round to us saying, "I love this drink called Zup, I really love it, I wish they had it at home, I love that drink." We all looked at each other [bewildered] and of course it was 7 Up.

RC: John Tooley though, do you think she was concerned that the Company was respectable at all times?

JT: I think there is some confusion about this. When she started the company in 1931, she had to struggle to persuade parents to allow their boys to become dancers. She had quite a lot of difficulty with girls too and what she really set out then to do was to make dance as respectable as she knew how. That was really the point about respectability. And those who raised these questions later thought that the idea of respectability had continued too long. But that was thrown out of the window a long time ago and not least with the appearance of Nureyev. This has nothing to do with bad taste; it was the extent to which you could push the boundaries of good taste to embrace more and better dancing. And that was really the point, but respectability goes back to 1931 and the necessity of doing what she had to do. She had a huge struggle; it was a mammoth feat to get that Company off the ground.

RC: Sure, but did she take a close interest in the private life of her dancers? Would she know what was going on? Would she make judgements of it, perhaps haul people into her headmistress's study?

JT: As far as I know, never. I had quite a number of conversations with her and she raised the question with me more than once about the relationships between boys and girls but she would never have ventured into a discussion with a boy or with a girl about his or her relationship.

MG: I used to go and have tea with her when she was in her nineties until almost through to her death. Thinking about whether she was prim and always talked about tittle-tattle in a negative way, when I sat down for tea, she offered me a glass of sherry and the first thing she would say was always, "Now dear, tell me the gossip." She really wanted to know what was going on and I suspect that she knew exactly what was going on at all times.

JT: I think that is true.

RC: This phrase, "woman of the theatre", also has a sort of administrative aspect and I'd like to discuss what one might call her Lilian Baylis side, her management skills. Was she good with money? Was she efficient with legal work? She was a very good, crisp letter writer evidently.

JT: She wrote wonderful letters, yes that is true. She was administratively thrifty and she set all sorts of standards within The Royal Ballet, which were very helpful. But sometimes, and there were others around at that time of the same sort of generation who would take the view of "Oh it's all too expensive, you can't do this, you can't do that". But then when you would agree that something should be done within a budget and, let's say, something additional needed to be produced, if any of us dared say to her, "Sorry but you can't have that, there's no more cash," then that produced a rather different reaction.

I read Kathrine Sorley Walker's biography and the title is *Idealist without Illusions*. That's a wonderful way of summing up Madam. As far as everyday work was concerned she had some problem with names and we used to spend a little bit of time trying to determine what the name actually was, for this she was dependent on people around her. She didn't want to apply herself, she had too many other things to do but it was a huge privilege and joy to work with this quite incredible woman.

RC: And what was she like in Board meetings? Was she collaborative, cooperative, a good colleague or did she just lay down the law?

JT: She'd lay down the law when she thought it was necessary, but equally I go back to that title. She knew sometimes, and she would often say this, "I want to get to that goal. I know I can't get there in a straight line, it will be a little bit wobbly at times." It was the same when Nureyev appeared, *that* was flouting all her rules about recruitment to the Company. But she said, "I can't afford not to have him, can I?" And the answer was, "No, you can't"; and so it went on.

RC: Anya and Gillian, as young dancers in the Company would you have ever gone to see her, if you'd had problems of a personal kind?

GL: I was afraid of her. We were all a little bit afraid of her in the most wonderful healthy way, I mean we admired her, you wanted to sort of fall into a curtsey. I don't think you would have gone to Madam with anything pilfering. But with anything serious, I found that she had a great heart and always listened.

AS: I think a lot of us were terrified but at the same time there was something about her that was approachable. One time, when I was in the Company, I wanted to go and study in Leningrad and I went to see her. She was interested in it, she weighed it up, maybe she had made up her mind before, but in the end I didn't go. I think that there were political reasons and it was probably wise, but she dealt with me extremely well.

RC:　There was no room for argument as a dancer over casting, say? You wouldn't have gone to her about casting?

AS:　I never did, no. I was quite lucky I got some nice things.

GL:　Vera Volkova came to teach quite early on in West Street and we used to sneak out to go to class with Vera because she was so fantastic. Madam was not pleased about that.

AS:　I didn't go!

JC:　I was actually there in one of her thrifty moments. It was the dress parade for *Danses Concertantes* and it was Kenneth MacMillan's first ballet for [Sadler's Wells] Theatre Ballet and was so important. It was designed by Nicholas Georgiadis and Ninette came to the dress parade. And they all came on in these extraordinary costumes by Nicholas Georgiadis. All the ladies had skirts to six inches below the knee, it was Maryon Lane and Sara Neil, Annette Page. Ninette looked at them, she said, "Have you some scissors?" Scissors were brought in and she started cutting the skirts to three inches above the knee, Georgiadis was fainting, Kenneth didn't know quite what to say. She cut them all to the length that they always were for the rest of the ballet's time and she just turned round and said, "They look better and they're cheaper".

Part Two: Teaching

Developing a Training Style:
Ninette de Valois and the cultural inheritance of the early twentieth century

Geraldine Morris

> I don't believe that a period of history – a given space of time... contains within it one 'true' interpretation just waiting to be mined. But I do believe that it may contain within it several possible narratives.[1]

This quotation from a play by Brian Friel sets the tone of this chapter. Like Friel's character in *Making History*, I believe that the history of ballet training in Britain contains many stories. These stories can be told in different ways and I am trying to make a pattern out of the random collection of stories and articles that provide us with evidence of a past training style. I am aiming to pull together that random catalogue of information to make some sort of narrative so that we can understand past aesthetics. The problem of course is that ballet history, and training history in particular, is provided by bodily evidence. Training produces a specific way of moving, while cultural conventions and the social nuances of the era also have a major effect on the trained body.

Dancers from the past had bodies that are unlike those of today and, because of their training, they also moved differently. Two things really make the dancing body: one is the individual and his or her particular talents; the other is that individual's training and performance experience. In the early part of the twentieth century in Britain, there was very little work for the performer trained only in ballet and dancers had to accept work from a variety of places. They were needed in pantomime, in the music hall, in musical theatre, in revue and in the opera. Embracing these genres meant that the demands were varied; but they were highly competent dancers and, I believe, just as skilled as dancers today. Aesthetic values change as do the dancing requirements.

The one place where ballet flourished was in the variety shows at places like the Empire Theatre and the Alhambra. But ballet came to an end at the Empire in 1915; and, although it continued to flourish at the Alhambra during the Great War (1914-1918), there was no significant group of dancers performing ballet by 1918. During the early 1920s the Ballets Russes appeared there and, for a short time, a company headed by

Léonide Massine was also seen, though after 1928 the Alhambra became a cinema. Despite this, there was little need for a dancer to be trained solely in ballet.[2] In fact when Philip Richardson suggested establishing a ballet society in 1917, Richard Crompton, founder of the Imperial Society of Teachers of Dancing [ISTD], was against the idea on the grounds that most theatre managers preferred to engage dancers who could perform in a range of genres.[3]

As a result, in the early 1900s, there was no accepted approach to ballet training and, although there were numerous dance teachers, there was in general no distinction made between social and theatre dance; the division was between amateur and professional dancers rather than between genres. By the beginning of the 1910s, however, there were several respected ballet teachers, not least Edouard Espinosa, Serafina Astafieva and later Enrico Cecchetti. These were London-based and in general did not encourage youngsters. And although there were many dance teachers throughout the country, there was no monitoring body with an accepted code of training, so standards varied.

Yet there was lots of dance: dancing was fashionable, though the recent exhibition of the Ballets Russes at the V & A in 2010 might lead one to think that the passion for dance only started in 1911 with Diaghilev's arrival. Not so, as one dance historian discovered. Plucking a date at random, 1908, she found that it was an exceptionally busy year: Isadora Duncan, Maud Allen and Ruth St Denis were all appearing; ballet was thriving in the context of popular entertainment in variety theatres and in pantomime; the Russians, Lydia Kyasht and Adolph Bolm, were performing at the Empire; and Pavlova danced at a private party for Edward VII and Queen Alexandra; Madame Artemis Colonna the "celebrated Classic Greek Dancer" appeared at the Hippodrome (and the caption to her press photograph, "Classicism Again! Yet Another Barefooted Dancer", shows the popularity of this genre of dancing). There was a diversity of dance styles performed and many of the dancers moved between the different genres. For instance, Edouard Espinosa played Man Friday in *Robinson Crusoe and his Man Friday* and Dorothy Craske, Adeline Genée's *travestie* partner at the Empire, played Crusoe.[4] All of these dancers from Pavlova to Duncan tried to situate themselves within the boundaries of high culture, but the borders between this and popular entertainment were fluid and it was not till Diaghilev arrived with the Ballets Russes in 1911, that ballet came to be considered as a more serious art form. This was because he realised that unless the Ballets Russes performed at the Royal Opera House, alongside the opera, they would not be respected.⁵ By hosting the evening performance at Covent Garden for the coronation of George V, he established the company as both a cultural and artistic triumph.

A little microcosm of history shows not only the place of dance in London during the early part of the century but also its range. And dance training had to reflect this. Today's svelte bodies would have been out of place in this milieu. These early dancers experienced more than one mode of training and this affected the way they moved. The eclectic training styles available and the demands made by a range of different kinds of theatre meant that the dancers of the first twenty or thirty years of the century were individual and far from uniform. In ballet too, the culture demanded artistry and expressivity over technical fireworks and this can be seen in the dances of the Ballets Russes, as the ballets of Michel Fokine testify: Fokine hated turnout and *fouettés*.⁶ There were of course the few like de Valois, Lydia Sokolova, Winifred Edwards who managed to find sufficient training to enable them to work in either the Ballets Russes or Pavlova's company, but these are the exceptions.

Despite a miscellaneous and amorphous group of teachers, there was one body which oversaw standards: the ISTD had been established in 1904, with its express aim of improving dance teachers' knowledge and teaching methods. By 1909, teachers were encouraged to pass an examination, which would reward them with a Diploma. These examinations required teachers to be able to create harmonious *enchaînements*, demonstrate competence in side and centre practice, involving simple steps, and correctly name and analyse steps. Many of the steps had the same terms as those in the *danse d'école* and by 1913 the syllabus required teachers to be able to demonstrate the principles of dancing on *pointe* and to perform "exercises and *enchaînements* on the *pointes*".⁷ But perhaps even more importantly, 1913 saw the publication of Charles d'Albert's *Technical Encyclopaedia of the Theory and Practice of the Art of Dancing* by the society. The book contained amongst other things an explanation and instructions for the performance of "approximately 2,000 choreographical *pas*, 600 ancient and modern fancy dances and 100 ballet dances".⁸ Clearly, there must have been some knowledgeable and conscientious teachers who had a sophisticated background in dance, even if it was not solely for the teaching of ballet. By 1924, the ISTD had become a large organisation, divided into the following branches: as well as the Operatic and General, new branches were formed to deal with a multitude of genres: Modern Ballroom Dancing; Classical; Classical Ballet Cecchetti Method;

Greek Dance – Ruby Ginner Method; Natural Movement – Madge Atkinson Method.

The contribution made by the ISTD has never really been fully recognised and the suggestion that there was nothing of significance before the formation of the Association for Teachers of Operatic Dancing, now the Royal Academy of Dance [RAD], is misleading. Of equal importance was the work of Espinosa, whose major interest seems to have been in codifying the *danse d'école*. In 1909, he began writing a "Technical Dictionary of Dancing, The Theoretical Analysis of the Art of Operatic Dancing [and] the training and reproducing of all the mediaeval dances".[9] He devised a syllabus for his school, entitled The British Normal School of Dancing, which used the French terminology for the steps, printed in front of the English words. As he put it: " The French nomenclature of steps superseded the words "kicks", "twist", "*bas pas*", "stay turns".[10] De Valois was always loyal to her former teacher, acknowledging his contribution to British Ballet and, when as late as 1947 he published over a period of six months, "An Encyclopaedia of The Ballet" in the *Dancing Times*, he dedicated it to de Valois. Like most such works it lists and translates the various steps but gives little idea of arm, head or upper body movement. What becomes clear when reading it is the emphasis on energy. His translations are not of nouns but of verbs. That the ballet step was recognised as an action and not a shape may well have been a feature of the early part of the twentieth century.

So how did these dancers perform? There can be little doubt that because of the stage requirements, right until the end of the 1930s, dancers must have had a style that had something in common with the stage dancing of the era. Most choreographers, including Ashton and Balanchine, made dances for revues and de Valois for plays and operas. So both choreography and training can be seen as a fusion between popular culture and the ballet training and style of the era. But ballet did not exist in isolation and from Russia and throughout Europe expressive modern dance, such as that found in the Ballets Jooss and in the dances of Gretta Wiesenthal and Mary Wigman, was deemed to be as important.[11] There is more than a nod to this genre in de Valois' choreography, particularly in *Job* (1931).

Another early teacher who should not be omitted is Mrs Wordsworth, with whom de Valois had her early training. Her classes followed a specific plan:

The class everywhere followed the plan. We started with skipping...

Skipping was followed by Club Swinging. The class then formed up in twos... March round doing a sort of "goose step" up the centre in twos, divide up in fours. Then we did our spot of dancing, strictly fancy, starting with arm exercises done for some reason with a flower in one hand, and kneeling on one knee. The Steps!... for instance when what we call "Changes" are correctly done, the feet are as close together as possible... In our "Changes" we leapt into the air with, if possible, our legs spread to an angle of a quarter to three. The wider and higher the more Mrs Wordsworth shouted "Beautiful". There was also a sort of *coupé* step we called "On it", done with a high kick in front and back with arms swinging in and out. Our *ballonnés* were taken up to the knee, our Reel steps... were terribly incorrect. Cuts and Shakes all taken as high as possible.[12]

Olive Ripman's description of Mrs Wordsworth's class might fill us with horror but it gave children a real love of dancing; and this approach lasted well into the 1920s, as Leslie Edwards recalled in his autobiography.[13] It did not help much with ballet, he wrote, but it was fun and enjoyed by all. De Valois went on to join the Lila Field Academy, where she performed in a play of Field's called *The Goldfish*. Field was another inspiring facilitator and we should not ignore the importance of these early teachers.

I have looked in some depth at the training styles offered by the various societies in existence during the 20s and 30s.[14] Noticeably in these syllabuses, there is a huge lack of detail, with little on arm, head and body coordination or on the approach to music. De Valois' syllabus is not documented until the 1950s but before that, magpie-like, she employed a range of teachers at the Sadler's Wells School. Pamela May, who joined in 1933, remembered learning with Nicholas Sergeyev, Margaret Craske, Stanislas Idzikowsky and, for a short time Anna Pruzina. Both Craske and Idzikowsky taught versions of Cecchetti's system, while Sergeyev seems to have been working within the old Imperial Ballet tradition. According to May, much of his centre work comprised solos from the nineteenth-century ballets, chiefly *Swan Lake*, *The Nutcracker* and *The Sleeping Beauty*. May did not comment on de Valois' own teaching and it is possible that by the mid 1930s she played a smaller role in the day-to-day training at the School.

The picture that emerges from this examination of the available training during the twenties and thirties is very mixed. Those in de Valois' school generally came with a basic knowledge and received what seems to have been a strong if rapid training before being whisked into the Company; May attended the School for only a year before joining the Company at seventeen. Some, like Fonteyn, were younger. So in general they had four to five years of training before becoming professionals. This compares unfavourably with today's approach; youngsters now are required to have had at least eight years of daily lessons before joining a professional ballet company.

Marie Rambert frequently took older pupils, particularly if they were male. She accepted them at any age, even when they had had no previous training. This probably meant that the ballet dancers of the 1930s lacked the strength of today's dancers and they certainly had less flexibility in the limbs; today's hyperextensions were not valued then. But, in contrast, they had more flexible torsos, an ability to change direction rapidly and faster footwork.

When I looked at the first dance, *Le Baiser de la fée* (1935), that Ashton made for Fonteyn, I felt that to some extent it captured this early style. The dance has a complex floor pattern that spurts in different directions. Beginning centre stage, it has short diagonals from one side to the other and then rushes across the front of the stage. It moves restlessly up and down stage before heading off on a diagonal again. A circle leads into an up-and-down pattern before an opening motif is repeated and the dancer ends, facing upstage, stage left. It is complicated, involves endless weight shifts and rapid footwork, and it taxes today's dancers, who find the speed not to their liking. This gives some idea of the dance style of 1935, and the film *Evergreen* (1934) with Jessie Matthews gives another, yet one which impacted on the ballet bodies of the era. We can see how the dancers looked from studying photographs of the era and glean a little from documentation, but our narrative is patchy and needs more stories.

Somewhere de Valois admitted gearing her training to Ashton's dances. Unlike Balanchine or Bournonville, he did not give classes nor devised a training style to suit his dance movement, so perhaps the de Valois class is the closest we can get to those early years but that was not put in place till the end of the 1940s.

Introduction to the DVD Recording of Valerie Adams Teaching the de Valois Syllabus

Anna Meadmore

This demonstration of de Valois' advanced syllabus work for girls was filmed at The Royal Ballet School, Covent Garden, on 2 April 2011, during the conference *Ninette de Valois: Adventurous Traditionalist*. The class was taught by Valerie Adams, FRAD, who had learnt the work directly from de Valois. The syllabus was originally designed as a guide for teachers, rather than as a system of training for dancers. Adams taught the syllabus for many years to students of the Teachers' Training Course at The Royal Ballet School, whose graduates all have vivid memories of tackling its rigorous demands each Monday morning!

Valerie Adams (b. 1935) had been a pupil of Elizabeth Collins and Vera Volkova before becoming a pupil at the Sadler's Wells School. She joined the Sadler's Wells Ballet in 1953, becoming a member of staff at the School just two years later. In 1956, de Valois asked her to go to The Hague in Holland, in order to found the ballet school at the Koninklijk Conservatorium voor Musik, where she remained as Principal until 1961. She rejoined the staff of The Royal Ballet School in 1962, becoming assistant (to de Valois) on the Craftsman's Course in 1968.

Established in 1964 as a full time teacher-training course, the Craftsman's Course soon expanded from two to three years of study. In 1971 Valerie Adams was appointed Director of the renamed Teachers' Training Course, a post she held for almost thirty years. The closure of the course in 2000 was necessitated by the relocation of the Upper School to Covent Garden. Its legacy was a significant network of 324 graduates teaching around the globe.

In order to prepare the present Royal Ballet School 2nd year Upper School students to learn the syllabus, their teacher Anita Young, a former pupil of de Valois, began to introduce them to the exceptionally intricate footwork and rapid changes of direction, which are a notable feature of de Valois' work. Denise Winmill, a graduate of the Teachers' Training Course herself, then came in to teach the students thirty of the advanced syllabus exercises. Finally, Valerie Adams came in for just two rehearsals prior to the demonstration; the class should not, therefore, be viewed as a polished performance. It is very much 'work in progress' for both the student dancers and their teachers. As time was short, some of the *allegro* studies in the centre are amalgamations of separate exercises.

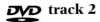 **track 2**

De Valois as a Teacher: A Discussion led by Anna Meadmore[1]

A discussion followed the demonstration of de Valois' syllabus work, which was chaired by **Anna Meadmore**, a graduate of The Royal Ballet School Teachers' Training Course under Valerie Adams, and now Head of Academic Dance Studies at The Royal Ballet School, and Curator of White Lodge Museum & Ballet Resource Centre. Valerie Adams was joined by Julia Farron, Michael Boulton, Henry Danton and Michael Hogan.

All the group had personal experience of de Valois' classes, and while there was much agreement about her distinctive characteristics as a teacher, there were fundamental differences of opinion as to the merits and shortcomings of her pedagogic approach. A brief outline of the panellists' individual relationships to de Valois, her School and Companies will serve to contextualise their various responses.

At the Sadler's Wells School in the early 1950s, **Valerie Adams** and several other students aged about sixteen, demonstrated de Valois' syllabus at her annual Summer Course for Teachers. Later, as a member of the Sadler's Wells Ballet, Adams was encouraged by de Valois to observe her lessons; soon she became a teacher at the School. She taught on the Craftsman's Course (later the Teachers' Training Course) from its inception, working closely with de Valois to develop the training of young dancers whose future lay in teaching.

Julia Farron (b. 1922) was the first scholarship student to attend 'the Wells', joining the School in 1931 and the Company five years later, aged just fifteen. She retired in 1961 after a stellar career, but continued to perform at Covent Garden as a guest artist for many years. In 1964 she began teaching at The Royal Ballet School. She became instrumental in shaping the syllabus of The Royal Academy of Dancing (now the Royal Academy of Dance), and from 1983 – 1989 she was its Artistic Director, then Director.

Henry Danton (b.1919) came late to ballet, and was trained by Judith Espinosa, Vera Volkova and Olga Preobrajenska. He became a member of the International Ballet in 1943, then joined the Sadler's Wells Ballet in 1944. Acclaimed in works by Helpmann and Ashton (notably *Symphonic Variations*, original cast, 1946), he did not enjoy de Valois' style of teaching and directorship, and soon left Covent Garden to work with several international companies, including Petit's Ballets des Champs-Elysées. He now lives in the United States, where he has taught for many years.

Michael Hogan (b. 1928) was fourteen years old when he auditioned to join the Sadler's Wells School in 1942. Taken into the Opera Ballet in 1944, he later became a founder member of the Sadler's Wells Theatre Ballet in 1946. During his time at Sadler's Wells, de Valois would give occasional Company classes, which Hogan much enjoyed. He left the Company in 1952 to join London Festival Ballet as a Principal dancer.

Michael Boulton (b. 1930) also joined the Opera Ballet from the School, in 1946, and became a founder member of the Sadler's Wells Theatre Ballet later that year. After moving to join the Company at Covent Garden, he went on the legendary first tour of the Sadler's Wells Ballet to the United States in 1949. Unusually, he received permission from de Valois to miss her Company classes, which he found impossible to follow; he then became a regular pupil of Volkova's. He later asked de Valois if he could rejoin the Sadler's Wells Theatre Ballet, where he performed Principal roles until his retirement in the late 1950s.

Anna Meadmore (AM): We've already established that the syllabus [we saw in Valerie Adams' demonstration class of the de Valois advanced girls' syllabus] was not intended for training dancers; it was designed to show teachers how to teach.

Valerie Adams (VA): Yes, but it *was* taught throughout the School. I, as a student, learnt it, because people had to demonstrate it every year at the summer course – and I've always said, it wasn't complete.

AM: Watching, I was very struck by your [Valerie's] musicality, and Julia, I think you have mentioned to me you found Madam's musicality…

Julia Farron (JF): It was completely individual, because – to me – she had very little concept of *adagio*. She was a *petit allegro* and an *allegro* dancer herself, and as a teacher she remained the same. I was unlucky in lots of ways, when I went into the Company: she was already running down her teaching in the School, because she had Ursula Moreton to take it over, and she didn't have the time. She was developing the Company and doing her own ballets, so I missed out a little bit there. Then, when it came to this period [of the syllabus being taught in the School], I had nothing to do with it. But now I *see*; in fact I've learnt such a lot about her – and the way she taught us as professional dancers was completely different, because she was anxious that everything was like this [JF makes a brisk "chopping" motion with her hands] because *adagio* was not her scene. If anyone lagged behind [demonstrates a *legato* movement of the arms]: "No, no, no!" I wish I could have learned Madam's syllabus *then*, because this [watching VA teach the demonstration class] was extraordinary.

AM: I think it's important to realise that we are seeing Madam's syllabus through the filter of Valerie Adams' musicality, and there is a difference there.

JF: Absolutely.

AM: You [Julia] did mention to me the word "mechanical", which I thought was interesting, and obviously not at all what you [Valerie] were doing.

VA: Can I just say that, when I was in the School, we only had chords for *adage* [intones plodding, unmelodic piano chords], and I'd come from having a beautiful pianist with lovely *adage* movement, and I thought that every ounce of dance was being pushed out of me. In fact I really felt as though I wanted to leave the School because I couldn't take it; it was ruthless, absolutely! Everybody was taught with a stick. Madam had a stick the whole time; throughout the class [demonstrates banging the floor] you had this thumping going on. And they had different sticks! Harold Turner had this little cane thing, and he used to just flick it to our feet if we didn't stretch them [demonstrates jabbing action] and it suddenly sort of hit us round the ankles.

AM: I can sense that sparked something off in Henry – do you recognise that Henry?

Henry Danton (HD): Oh yes I do!

AM: You found Madam's classes restricting, I know.

HD: Well, I have to talk about myself a little bit, because I was in the army until I was 21 years old; I'd never seen a ballet until I was 19 years old. When I started dancing, I worked with Judith Espinosa first of all: she taught me. My first job was at the International Ballet and I had [classes with Stanislas] Idzikowsky there. I had nothing to do with the RAD [but] I did the exams: Judith Espinosa pushed me through them in one year. I did the whole lot!

So when I came to the Company I had only the background of Judith Espinosa and Idzikowsky. I didn't like the classes at all, because I felt that they were designed to make girl *corps de ballet* dancers; and I wanted to be a boy. I wanted to fly through the air and turn – not do "crochet" with my feet! [indicates *entrechat* action with his hands].

On the ENSA tour we went to Paris and I worked with Russian teachers there, and I thought, well, this is what I want; this is absolutely what I want. So at the end of the Covent Garden season I asked her – I can't call her Madam, I'm sorry, it's impossible for me to call her Madam – I asked her if I could have a year's leave to go and work on my technique, and she wouldn't give it to me; so I just left. So this [the teaching of the syllabus] is all after me, everything happened after my time, so I really shouldn't be here at all!

AM: But we will come on to the particular reason you're here, Henry! That very much echoes Michael's feeling, I think? I believe Madam actually let you [to MB] *off* her classes, because they got your feet in a twist.

Michael Boulton (MB): She did, she couldn't stand it any longer. [General laughter] I couldn't pick it up at all, I just couldn't do it.

AM: You said to me 'I don't think any of us *liked* her classes very much.' [General nodding agreement among the panellists.] Do you think this is a male/female thing?

All: No!

JF: It [de Valois' classwork] *demanded* so much. As a professional dancer, not as a student, you needed to stretch your legs – if you'd done a performance the night before, you were absolutely tired; you'd come in to make your body move again, you *didn't* want to go [demonstrates fast *staccato* footwork, *entrechats* and *battements jetés*, with her hands], and she used to get very cross if you didn't do it.

HD: We were forbidden to stretch.

JF: Oh yes, absolutely forbidden! She also had some mad things: I can remember, when we were in Vienna, and we were doing the usual Madam classes, we [also] had a ballet master at that time (I think it was [Harijs] Plucis); *he* came in one morning, [after] we'd done two performances the day before, and we stood at the *barre* as usual, waiting for the *pliés*, and she said, "Face the *barre!*" and we did a couple of *demi-pliés* and a few rises, and then she said, "Face the front!" and then we had sixteen *grands battements*.

VA: That's right, *grands battements* after *pliés*!

JF: It was tough!

AF: [to MH] Michael, you haven't spoken.

Michael Hogan (MH): I don't feel quite the same way, I enjoyed the challenge that she posed – with her 'aura' [indicates a broad circle with his hands]. She gave a very hard *barre*, a certain [Nicholas] Sergeyev-style *barre*, which I enjoyed very much. She used to become very impatient and irritable with anybody who was off-time, or if anyone was sloppy about finishing an exercise – she would really be angry [the panellists nod in agreement].

Then, of course, she had another side where she burst out laughing at somebody, which would be a disguised form of approval, I think. She'd burst out laughing and say, "No, it's like this, boy." And, as Julia was saying, she didn't like the *adage*, she loved the...

JF: ...knitting! [Demonstrates *petit batterie* with her hands.]

MH: She didn't like *adage*. She used to set very hard Cecchetti adages, which used to twist us around [demonstrates a pronounced use of *épaulement*, using the whole torso], and it certainly wasn't the boys' favourite. But I enjoyed the *batterie*, I always loved the *batterie*. She used to have a particular step which I'd never met before in my life, it was a beaten *frappé* ...

HD: Oh yes, that awful thing... [holding his head in his hands, which produces general laughter].

MH: ... that way going back, and that way going forward, only much faster, much better, with full arms, head and everything, very exact, loved it! [Demonstrates, standing up: a series of double *frappés* on alternate legs, travelling *en arrière* and then *en avant*; arms held in *demi seconde*, or in a low third, and *bras bas*. Evident lean towards the working leg, and use of head and *épaulement*.]

She'd set the boys Petipa-style men's classical work, which I enjoyed very much indeed....[Thoughtful pause.] The outbursts of laughter were always a bit disturbing! [General laughter.]

VA: She enjoyed teaching boys...

MH: Oh she loved it.

VA: ...that was her thing!

MH: I remember some of her classes for the [Sadler's Wells] Theatre Ballet: there was one in 1948, with a now very distinguished person [whom] she had come to see dance [audition] to join the Company. We did a very hard class, a very good class, and I'd enjoyed it. When I went to collect my salary that week, I got 10 shillings extra. So I explained, "You've given me 10 shillings extra." She said: "Madam said you're to have it." So that was excellent. The distinguished person whom she'd come to see in that class was Sir Peter Wright.

AM: That's beautifully tied up!

MH: I first did my audition for Madam on [the] stage of what is now [the] Albery Theatre, in 1942. They set me *enchaînements* and such like. Then they went into conference and, as it was tremendously important to me, I said to her, "Please give me a chance, Madam!" and she *burst* out laughing – which was very disturbing. [General laughter.] She gave me classes with the marvellous Sergeyev.

Apart from those two idiosyncrasies of annoyance and irritation – and laughter – this didn't indicate a very volatile, emotional woman; she had a very calm side too [JF and VA nod in agreement].

AM: That is very helpful, because there's always a counterbalance [needed] whenever you talk about de Valois.

I think it's really important to think about *other* teachers, because none of this exists in a vacuum. There were many other teachers in London, many of whom had studied with [Nicholai] Legat, with [Olga] Preobrajenska; the same teachers de Valois had had; and yet *they* became very different teachers. In fact, many of the Company members – I'm thinking in particular here of Henry Danton and Michael Boulton – 'defected' (if you like) to other teachers. Vera Volkova is a major name here, a student of [Agrippina] Vaganova.

I should mention as well, that there were classes by Kathleen Crofton; she did guest teaching for both the School and the Company from 1960; and Anna Northcote, who had also studied with Legat and "Preo". Also, Margaret Craske. There was Cleo Nordi, another student of Preobrajenska; she was invited to teach at the School, and also taught at West Street, where famously Vera Volkova had her studio. The other important name to mention is Audrey de Vos: Dame Beryl [Grey] was certainly somebody who went off to Audrey de Vos. I'm just opening the conversation, as this is a really interesting group of teachers.

[To MB] I know that you were a huge favourite of Volkova's – you wouldn't say so yourself, but I have been told! [General laughter] So what was it you found in Vera's classes that you didn't find in Madam's?

MB: Vera *understood* the dance ...and she could teach you to do almost anything.

AM: So by implication you feel that de Valois did not teach in a dancer-like way?

MB: I don't think she understood it at all! [General laughter]

AM: Can I just throw that open to the panel?

JF: I think it's not fair to say – you can't say – that one taught and one didn't; they taught in completely different ways. Madam's big thing was speed. Vera came from a Russian background, and they're pure *adage*. I wasn't a pupil of Vera's, but I know well many of the dancers who studied with her, including my own husband [Alfred Rodrigues]. It's a completely different scene. It's not fair to say that one is better than the other, they're better in different ways. [To MH] Don't you agree?

MH: I absolutely agree. She had a style of her own and you just had to adapt to it.

JF: You also had other ballets; you had Ashton for instance. I had Ashton all my career, who was completely different. He didn't use any of this [demonstrates a fiddly *entrechat* action with her hands]. Well he *did*, but he used to say, "You know – how Madam does it!" [General laughter.] We have to take everything that we can get, from whoever is around to teach us.

VA: You went to the person that you felt you needed at that particular time.

AM: Except – the problem was that Madam was not happy about people going to other teachers [general agreement on the panel]. Henry, tell us a bit about your work with Volkova, because you studied with her for many years.

HD: Yes I did. She opened a whole lot of doors up, I mean, some things I'd never seen with anyone else. I used to defect from the Company class, and I was called to the office: "*Why* are you not coming to the Company class?" I said, "I'm going to Volkova", and she [de Valois] let out something which, well, I bet she bit her tongue as soon as it was out of her mouth! She said: "I will *not* have you going to a tuppeny ha'penny teacher around the corner!" [General laughter.] So that was enough for me – I went on going to the "tuppeny ha'penny teacher around the corner". So we just fought the whole time, I'm afraid.

AM: It has to be said, the said "tuppeny ha'penny teacher" *did* teach at both the School and the Company from about 1943 - 50.

HD: Yes, but I want to say something there: I think she [de Valois] let a whole lot of good teachers slip through her fingers: there was Mary Skeaping teaching at one time, Plucis was teaching, Volkova was teaching. *None* of them stayed, and that says something.

AM: Somebody has mentioned to me that Tamara Karsavina was based and working in London.

JF: Yes! My regret was that she [de Valois] didn't ever invite Karsavina to teach – Karsavina had so much [to give]. I only had one occasion when she came: Fred was doing a new production of *Giselle* and he wanted the mime scenes to be refreshed by Karsavina, and he was going to put the mime of the Mother into it. That was a magic day for me. You know, I'd already retired, I was just doing Bathilde. I couldn't believe that this lady hadn't been part of our existence. She was absolutely wonderful, and very old, even older than I am now!

VA: I remember: it was '67 or '68, Karsavina came and took a class, and I can remember her very clearly… yes, I remember her coming.

AM: Why didn't she come more often?

VA: [Regretfully, with a shrug] I don't know.

Michael Boulton subsequently wrote this postscript about his relations with de Valois:

I first met Madam (we always called her Madam – only an older generation called her Ninette) in 1945, when my mother managed to get an
appointment for me to audition for the Sadler's Wells Ballet School. I
knew nothing about ballet – I'd never seen one. I just copied the dancers
at the barre and I was in, with a scholarship. They were that desperate in
wartime!

She was very caring about her students during the War. She had to
close the school at Sadler's Wells for a couple of months and send us away.
There were stories that she would send fresh vegetables to the students,
but we didn't need any because my mother, who housed many students in
Hornsey Lane, kept a big garden with vegetables, rabbits and chickens.

I was taken into the Sadler's Wells Opera Ballet [later the Theatre Bal-
let] in 1946. My first small solo role was in her ballet *The Gods Go
A-Begging.* (Henry Danton gave me my cue to go on.) She came to see us
youngsters perform at Sadler's Wells. She was very particular about how
her choreography should be danced. Later, when I was cast as the Dancing Master in *The Rake's Progress,* I tried to put something of myself into
the role and she wouldn't have it at all. Bobby Helpmann said to me: "You
don't have to do anything in her ballets. Just do the steps as she set them."
And he was absolutely right.

When I was called up for National Service at 18, she got me deferred for
two years to continue my ballet training. Like many others, I used to go to
Vera Volkova's classes in West Street as often as I could. Madam knew and
she didn't like it. But I was very unhappy in her classes. She wasn't a great
teacher, especially compared with Volkova, and the way she used music
was terrible, as far as I was concerned.

Though I wasn't a special favourite of hers, she was always very moth-
erly – she really was. I once had to spend some time in Barts Hospital with
an injured ankle and she used to pop in to see us – Pirmin Trecu was in
with me at the same time. When I eventually had to do my National
Service in the army for a couple of years, she wrote to me several times
just to keep in touch. She asked me to let her know whenever I was on
leave and she'd take me to lunch. On one occasion, Donald Albery was
there and he gave me his card so that I could claim free tickets to any of
his shows.

The day I came out of the army, I was back in the Opera House. It
wasn't long before I was suddenly the only dancer available for the Blue
Boy in *Les Patineurs.* De Valois was watching in the staff box, and after my

first variation, she came backstage, put her arm around me and smiled. I've never forgotten that.

She commanded great loyalty. Pirmin and I agreed that we wouldn't have dreamed of leaving her. I got offers from Rambert, whose repertory would have suited me, but I couldn't do it. As I say, although I wasn't a favourite, de Valois gave me everything – my joy of dancing, of being on stage – the happiest time of my life.

The Abbey Theatre School of Ballet

Victoria O'Brien

In 1927, Ninette de Valois was introduced to William Butler Yeats at the Festival Theatre in Cambridge. Yeats had heard reports of de Valois' choreography for his play, *On Baile's Strand,* in Cambridge and welcomed the chance of meeting the Irish-born dancer. During this encounter, Yeats invited de Valois to help him establish a dance school attached to the Abbey Theatre in Dublin and to choreograph his *Plays for Dancers.* The collaboration would soon result in the Abbey Theatre School of Ballet. This little school created a repertory of ballets, some of which boasted an integration of dance, music, plot and design that were amongst the first of their kind to be created in Ireland. During this time the School also staged regular performances and participated in various theatrical productions with the Abbey Theatre, the Dublin Drama League and the Gate Theatre. The School produced a new generation of dancers, choreographers and teachers during the early 1930s – a period when there was little tradition of ballet or training in Ireland. This essay recounts the history of the Abbey Theatre School of Ballet under the direction of de Valois from 1927 until 1933, including details of the School's premises and facilities, the teachers and teaching styles, its repertoire and performances. The study will conclude by evaluating the accomplishments of de Valois' work at the Abbey as well as the wider legacy of the Abbey School through several of its students.

The Abbey School found its home at the newly opened Peacock Theatre in November 1927. The inveterate Irish theatregoer, Joseph Holloway, was at the opening of the Peacock. An entry from his 1927 journal gives us one of the first records of the opening of the Abbey Theatre School of Ballet, suggesting that it coincided with the establishment of the Peacock, which also provided a permanent performance space for the Abbey School of Acting:

Friday, November 11... A big room in the front building of the Abbey has been converted into a tiny theatre seating 100. It has been named The Peacock Theatre, and seats and decorations have all been carried out in peacock blue – even the front of the building facing Abbey Street has been painted a similar colour. A blue lookout truly, but I hope not

for the little playhouse. A company calling themselves The New Players open the theatre for two nights on Sunday and Monday next with a
play translated from German of Georg Kaiser called *From Morn To Midnight*. 3/6 is the price charged for a seat. The Abbey is also starting a
school for Ballet with one of the Russian Ballet for teacher. It also has a
School for Acting as well – all finding a home in the Peacock Theatre.[1]

The dance studio was located on the top floor of the building. The piano,
played by the pianist Julia Gray, was in one corner, while in another was a
little dance library arranged by de Valois. The books were covered in the
same peacock colours as the theatre, some holding the exotic images of
Diaghilev's dancers.[2] By early 1928, there were approximately sixteen
core students, aged between eleven and thirteen. Classes (which consisted of ballet and character dance) and rehearsals took place two times
a week after school and on Saturdays. The core group was made up
mainly of girls; there were also two boys, Arthur Hamilton and Toni
Repetto-Butler.
    De Valois would travel across the Irish Sea once every three months for
a week or so to teach, set new choreography, oversee the final rehearsals
and perform in productions. The School of Cecchetti was de Valois' preferred system of ballet training and it was elements from this French and
Italian blend that strongly influenced her early teaching in Dublin.[3] The
system of Cecchetti would not have been the only method she employed:
De Valois would have developed her own ideas of dance education and
choreography out of the diverse methods she had experienced; she was
much influenced by the choreographers she worked under at Diaghilev's
Ballets Russes. However, the teachers organised the day-to-day running
of the school, namely: Vivienne Bennett (1927-1928), Sara Payne
(1928-1931)[4] and Nesta Brooking (1931-1933).
    An insight into the School's curriculum can be found in a notice from a
1932 school programme in the Dublin City Archives, which records a
wide range of standards, from amateur to professional dance classes as
well as senior morning and junior afternoon classes.[5] There are also
references to evening classes for "business girls" on Monday and Thursday evenings at seven. The Monday lesson was eclectically classified
as "General dancing with music, Character, Plastic Movement, etc.",
whereas the Thursday session was billed simply as "ballet". Sessions for
"business men" were held on Wednesday and Friday evenings at seven.
While both de Valois and Sara Payne's lessons at the Abbey were freestyle
and not based on examination syllabi, the resident teacher in 1931,

Nesta Brooking, taught the pupils the elementary, intermediate and advanced syllabi of the Operatic Association of Great Britain examinations.[6] Unfortunately, few records of this association's early activity in Ireland have survived, but this research would point towards the fact that the Abbey School was probably the first dance school in Ireland to implement this method of evaluation.[7]

From the references and material available it would appear that fourteen different dance programmes were performed during de Valois' directorship of the School. There were three productions recorded during the first year, four in 1929, two in 1930, three in 1931 and one programme a year for the last two years. Most dance productions opened at the Abbey Theatre on Tuesdays and ran until the following Saturday with one performance a day at 8pm, except for Saturdays, when there would have been a matinée as well as the evening show. The dance performances often shared the billing with a play, performed by the Abbey Company.[8]

The School's repertoire was varied. It was made up of short character dances; longer works, such as *Les Sylphides*; and works that de Valois had staged previously in London and at the Festival Theatre, Cambridge, including: *Rout*, *The Art of the Theatre* and *The Nursery Suite*. There were also dance works which de Valois created specifically for the Irish stage, such as *The Fawn*, *When Philida Flouts Him*, *Rituelle de Feu*, *Bluebeard* and *The Drinking Horn*. We are fortunate to have an insight into these works through two photographs taken of the School's repertoire in 1928: *Rituelle de Feu* (housed at the National University of Ireland, Galway, Special Collection) and *The Faun* (Author's Collection). These two images help us to understand the influences that ultimately coloured de Valois' work in Ireland. In particular, they allow us to see how de Valois drew upon movement vocabulary from modernists of the Ballets Russes, such as a parallel stance, frieze-style lines, sculptural and dense groupings.

As well as the specialised dance programmes, the Abbey School collaborated in plays staged by the Abbey Theatre Company, and of course, in Yeats's *Plays for Dancers*.[9] Significantly, the Abbey Theatre during this time was a repertory company and hence constantly rotating their plays, with some plays being mounted three times in a year on occasion. Interestingly, the Abbey School's work expanded to other theatre companies in Dublin, such as the Gate Theatre, the Dublin Drama League and the Abbey Theatre School of Acting.

The students from the Abbey School took part in what appears to be the School's final production under de Valois' directorship on 25 July

1933. The programme opened with a production of Yeats' *At the Hawk's Well*, choreographed by de Valois, followed by Lady Gregory's play, *Hyacinth Halvey*, performed by the Abbey company; finally, there were two new dance works choreographed by de Valois. The first of these was *The Drinking-Horn*, set to the music of an Irish composer, Arthur Duff, who also wrote the libretto, while the second, *Bluebeard*, was a ballet poem by Mary Davenport O'Neill, performed to music composed by the Abbey's Musical Director, Professor Larchet. The programme was directed by the Abbey Theatre actor, Arthur Shields, and included Ninette de Valois and many of the School's core students as performers.

By 1933, it was evident that de Valois' future lay in England and in her growing reputation at Sadler's Wells Theatre. Ninette de Valois and Lennox Robinson, the Abbey Theatre's Manager, broke the news to the dance students that the School was closing.[10] One student, Doreen Cuthbert, recalled the end of the Abbey School:

> That was it; Ninette de Valois said goodbye and we all went our different ways. It was very sad. We used to have good fun, we were a great bunch.[11]

She was concerned too about the little dance library located in the corner of the studio:

> I went to Ninette de Valois and inquired what was going to happen to the library. There was one book in it, written by Cecchetti, Pavlova's teacher, that I had my eye on... I was dying to get that... So in the end de Valois said, "Let the girls take a book in seniority." I was the first one and got the one I wanted.[12]

Apart from one last piece of choreography for Yeats in 1934, *The King of the Great Clock Tower*, de Valois' work at the Abbey had come to an end.

It is somewhat difficult to evaluate the overall accomplishments of the Abbey School of Ballet, as there is obviously the temptation to compare the Irish school with the success of the Vic-Wells organisation in England. To do so would be unfair. The Abbey Theatre School of Ballet has immense meaning in the history of Irish ballet and it is from the Abbey School that much of Ireland's subsequent ballet history stems. What must be recognised firstly is that the Abbey School recruited, trained and produced an important generation of Irish choreographers, dancers and teachers.[13] In turn they became the key-personalities behind the second-wave of groundbreaking work for Irish ballet. My research has traced the activities of seven of the core students and it is pertinent to summarise their contribution at this point. Doreen Cuthbert, Arthur Hamilton, Thelma Murphy, Cepta Cullen and Muriel Kelly all ran dance schools of their own and, in turn, these five Abbey School students taught ballet to a new generation of Irish pupils. Thelma Murphy opened a school in South County Dublin. Doreen Cuthbert established the Doreen Academy of Dancing in Beresford Place, Dublin, before moving to Kenya in 1952, where she continued to teach dance and is attributed as having introduced the Royal Academy of Dance syllabus to Kenya (*The Irish Times*, 12 March 2005). Arthur Hamilton taught classes in Dublin and in his hometown of Belfast. Hamilton's continuing dance activities in Ireland can be traced until 1959, when he was instrumental in helping to establish the Irish Region branch of the Royal Academy of Dance. Especially significant was the work of Muriel Kelly, who continued the Abbey School of Ballet from the time of de Valois' resignation until 1958; and Cepta Cullen, who established the Irish Ballet Club, also at the Peacock Theatre. Jill Gregory and Toni Repetto-Butler went on to pursue successful performing careers, although both had to leave Ireland in order to do so. Upon de Valois' invitation, Jill Gregory went to London to continue her training, after which she joined the Company and went on to work with de Valois for forty-three years. Gregory's last, and perhaps most important position, was as ballet mistress to The Royal Ballet Company. Toni Repetto-Butler also went to London, where he became a dancer with another Irish native's company: John Regan's Les Ballets des Trois Arts.

In addition to the dancers, teachers and choreographers it produced, it was through the performances staged by the Abbey School of Ballet that Irish audiences were introduced to the art form of twentieth-century ballet. The six years of the Abbey School cultivated an informed ballet audience. From 1927 until 1933 audiences were exposed to dance performances that regularly punctuated the calendar. Through the Abbey School performances, audiences were in step with concurrent choreographic styles and practices that were being performed throughout Europe. Although the Ballets Russes never travelled to Ireland, (and it was not until 1936 that one of its splinter companies performed on an Irish stage), pieces of their repertoire (such as Michael Fokine's *Les Sylphides* and Leonide Massine's *Dance of the Snow Maiden)* were first seen in Ireland on the Abbey stage. In addition, more modern works (such as *Rituelle De Feu, Rout* and *The Faun)* were staged frequently in Dublin. This gave Irish theatregoers an opportunity to see modern ballet works that were influenced by de Valois' experiences of working with George Balanchine, Léonide Massine and Bronislava Nijinska. These productions, which were performed by Abbey School students, would have been the first time that such innovative dance works were seen on an Irish stage. It is of significance that when de Valois returned to Dublin in September 1938 for the first performance by the Vic-Wells Company in Ireland, she told the *Irish Independent* that she believed the work of the Abbey Theatre School of Ballet had "aroused an interest in dancing which has grown steadily and has expressed itself in the attendances we have had this week".[14]

For de Valois, the Abbey School allowed her to experience and develop the various artistic roles of director, choreographer, dancer and teacher. It also prepared her for the different interactions of these roles with other artists, such as dancers, actors, composers and designers. In his book *Ballet*, Arnold Haskell wrote of the importance of de Valois' association with the Abbey Theatre and the Festival Theatre, Cambridge:

> Her work in these theatres, in addition to her experience of pure ballet, decided her future bent. Working with actors unused to movement in the dancing sense, she was compelled to use theatrical production that would be effective. She gained at this time a rare conception of the relationship between ballet and theatre.[15]

De Valois' work with the Abbey developed her understanding of the interdependence of the arts and, as Haskell points out, was the catalyst that crystallised her attitude to dance and the theatre. In summary, her time in Dublin was an important springboard, which helped her successfully to pursue her career as choreographer, artistic director, teacher and administrator for the following fifty years.

It is of note that de Valois remained actively involved in Irish ballet until the mid-1980s. Her patronage of Irish companies such as the National Ballet Company in the 1960s and the Irish National Ballet in the 1980s are testament to her continued interest over the years. What is also of significance is the fact that many of Ireland's dancers, choreographers, directors and teachers throughout the intervening period were trained by a continuous line of educators, all traceable back to the Abbey Theatre School of Ballet. The list of these dance artists is a long one and stretches back to the original inheritors of the Abbey School (Muriel Kelly, Cepta Cullen, Doreen Cuthbert, Thelma Murphy, Arthur Hamilton), who continued the work in the 1930s and 1940s, which was sustained in turn through their respective students during the 1950s (Myrtle Lambkin, Nina Tully, Joan Denis Moriarty, Patricia Ryan), through the 1960s and 1970s (Jill O'Neill, Clodagh Foley-Martin, Deirdre Smith), and indeed up to the present day (Anne Maher, Director of Ballet Ireland; and Katherine Lewis, Artistic Director of Irish Youth Ballet).

De Valois' invitation to Léonide Massine to teach Dance Composition

Kate Flatt

In 1967, one autumn afternoon, the suave, unmistakeable figure of Léonide Massine appeared at the Talgarth Road building of the Royal Ballet Upper School. It was later understood that he had come to meet with de Valois and Ursula Moreton to discuss the setting up of a series of classes on dance composition in relation to his forthcoming book, *Massine on Choreography*. The book, which was eventually published by Faber & Faber (London, 1976), contains notated choreographic studies, with accompanying text, proposed as a theoretical foundation for the study of dance composition. Whatever took place in the meeting with de Valois resulted in Massine arriving to teach a three-week intensive course each term at the Upper School between autumn 1968 and the summer of 1970 to a group of students mainly from the recently set up Craftsman's Course.[1] It seems that Massine's course may have been offered originally to The Royal Ballet but that the intensive teaching Massine demanded was not compatible with Company schedules. De Valois could see value and potential for the School in what Massine was offering and how it matched her own aspirations for a coherent and educated approach to the mastery of movement, in training the understanding of the eye and the body.

Massine's theoretical approach to dance composition, as outlined in his book, was based on the concept of the movement of torso and limbs in space and the notion of degrees or intervals of flexion and extension of body parts from the straight line. He also identified two basic modes of movement between "postures", which he defined as "harmonic progression" and "dynamic evolution".[2] The exercises Massine had prepared and devised for the book explored in abstract dance material the flow of movement in space through angles, dimensions and planes. Throughout the course, students learned to execute a series of solo studies, designed to demonstrate his theoretical principles. Coupled with this were tasks Massine gave to students to create short solo studies on their own bodies. He demanded a high level of accuracy in the execution of the studies, expecting students to aim for clarity and precision in body design. His approach was based on analysis and the importance of reconfiguring material, as a means to the mastery of choreographic craft. He suggests in his autobiography a further rationale for the development of the textbook.

> I have always felt that if music could reach a degree of almost scientific definition without losing the main factor – inspiration – then choreography too could achieve the same degree of definition, and the same artistic standing.[3]

De Valois gave permission for Massine to teach his work within the school, thereby providing him with an opportunity to test and refine the choreographic exercises and examples for eventual publication. It is the aspiration toward a systematic approach, which would have caught the interest of de Valois. The course would have appeared at the outset as a means to not only enable master classes in choreography given by Massine himself but also to develop a pedagogic structure for dance composition with a theoretical underpinnng.[4] [See plates 14 and 15]

Massine, like de Valois, was almost obsessively demanding in his teaching (as in rehearsal) and emphasised the way in which the precise use of the body, and the spatial and temporal properties of movement, created richness of choreographic expression. As choreographers schooled by Diaghilev, Massine and de Valois shared a deep understanding of musicality, theatricality, and choreographic craft. De Valois admired the "intricate and often asymmetrical fusion of body movement with steps" of Massine's character ballets and cited his works from the 1920s as having "immense importance to young artists".[5] De Valois called for a sense of accuracy in choreographic detail from her dancers, and saw it as an essential tool in characterisation. Her own choreography demanded that the dancer should understand what was being danced, and to execute that with clarity, accuracy and coherent precision. Her exactitude as a rehearsal director, of not only her own work but also that of other choreographers, is legendary and impressive. In a filmed recording of de Valois rehearsing the Gambling Scene from *Rake's Progress* with Sadler's Wells Ballet, we see her demanding precise execution of detail for even the smallest role and its place in the action of the ensemble.[6] The ensemble scene could, in other hands, perhaps have easily declined into a semi-improvised mayhem. The specificity of timing, focus and positioning of the body of each dancer defines her choreographic signature and creates the narrative being told with accuracy and clarity. A simple example of Massine's characterisation requiring precise choreographic awareness is the small role of the Shopkeeper's Assistant from *La Boutique Fantasque*.

The character always moves with precise rhythm, using rapid tiny foot-steps, rotating his torso and shoulder-girdle rhythmically back and forth to create flapping arms like an idiotic puppet. Without attention to the anatomical detail, one might miss the importance of the torso movement driving the action of the arms.

Massine's textbook begins with illustrations on anatomy, which are taken almost verbatim from a short manual on the notation system devised by Stepanov.[7] The manual employs anatomical terms relating to movement or action: flexion, extension, rotation, abduction, adduction, inversion, eversion etc. Massine saw potential in the notation system beyond that of recording dances. By understanding the anatomical movement range of the ballet-trained body, it would be possible to realise its creative potential toward making the body a more expressive instrument. Massine made significant developments to the Stepanov three-stave system and its symbols as his theory developed. He added complexity and detail as needed for the adaptations to his studies, especially in recording a much bigger range of movement. All the students on his course learned to read, write and become fluent with this notation system. Massine issued the students with a draft copy of the textbook, which contained a number of studies to illustrate his theories. Each of these required a precise application of geometry, with the notion of dimensions, intervals and degrees playing an important part in not only the writing of the notation but also in the execution of the sequences. In practice, classical ballet principles of curve and line were supplanted by an alternative relationship with geometry. By using an analytical system based on human anatomy and bodily action rather than ballet vocabulary, Massine also proposed a radical approach to the deconstruction of movement in order to realise its creative potential.

Massine was keen to avoid the presentational aspect of nineteenth century classical ballet performance. He instilled in students a much more conscious awareness of the dancer's relationship with space and direction. He emphasised in the creation of his studies, and in his studio teaching, an awareness of the body in three-dimensional space. He would ask students to observe how the quality of the movement and its meaning could be read differently, if facing a different direction. He described these directions as being comparable to tonality and keys in music. He also required a very precise anatomical understanding of *épaulement* and what it actually entails in terms of physical action. He emphasised strongly the use of the upper back and shoulders, as a vital part of the dancer's expressive capabilities. His understanding of use of the arms offered remarkable insight into the expressive potential of invented gesture. He described the arms with their three articulations: wrist, elbow and shoulder, and their movement through rotation, flexion and extension as "the violins of the orchestra". His studies also proposed innovations in the use of floor work as well as introducing material, which explored low, medium and high elevation. The material often took surprisingly imaginative and unexpected twists and turns as students struggled to learn the unusual studies he had prepared, which were not only intriguing, but also technically demanding.

Massine taught these studies in silence and also asked students to compose in silence. He maintained that learning to shape material in time according to rhythmic impulses could only come after mastery and understanding of what was actually going on physically. He did not, at this time, work on the teaching of dance composition to music. Towards the end of the textbook are rhythm tasks, which drew on exercises from composer Paul Hindemith's music composition textbook.[8] Fiendishly difficult as these proved to be as choreographic exercises, they were of great interest to Massine, who was famed for the dynamic rhythmic and musical interpretation in the memorable solos he created on himself. [9]

Students were also given creative tasks, which involved their own choice of stimulus and represented an important aspect of the course. These included short studies just for the torso and head or perhaps only for the arms. He encouraged movement investigation and conscious use of the anatomical understanding gained through his own examples, which students were also asked to reconfigure. The most interesting tasks he gave students were to make studies from the figures in the great Renaissance masters: da Vinci, Fra Angelico, Tintoretto, El Greco and Titian. As a young man, Massine's creativity had been stimulated by visits to the great museums and galleries with an art education given by Diaghilev himself. [10] The tasks involved making accurate notation of postures from the paintings or sculptures and the animation of these, with creation of movement into and out of them. Not only did this encourage observation but it also gave a powerful stimulus for invention. By this means he encouraged an understanding of style and "harmony of expression" as he called it. He asked, however, that the student avoid identifying with the emotional expression in the paintings, in order to observe with clarity how the postures and attitudes offered expressive qualities, particularly in the use of the torso. Further tasks were given to develop solos from a verse of poetry using imagery as a stimulus for creation of short studies in silence.

Once created, Massine would ask students to show their responses to him and then make radical changes, often without discussion and with the tacit assumption that he was "correcting" the work. Pedagogically, current thinking in the teaching of creativity and giving feedback should ideally lead to the student's own discovery as a solution to a creative task. However, his observations, often intuitive rather than following his theory, were always illuminating. His responses to the students' studies were inspiring in how they allowed his own creative, rhythmic and imaginative dynamism to come into play.[11]

De Valois attended sessions of Massine's course quite regularly to watch his teaching and observe the development of the course. She showed a great deal of interest in his analytical approach with its emphasis on spatial orientation, and the specific direction the material was facing. She intimated that it was an ideal tool for training the eye of the rehearsal director as well as developing the dancer's accuracy. She was fascinated by Massine's detailed and stringent use of rhythm in dance writing.[12] It is significant that she supported the course despite the fact that Massine's arrival in the school would have caused major disruption to the programme of study. On completion of the course in July 1970, a final examination was held over which de Valois and Massine presided, awarding certificates, which denoted student participation and evidence of the learning undertaken.

In further recognition of the innovation of the course, the results of Massine's investigation and teaching were documented on 16 mm film. Now in digital format, these recordings from 1969-70 are in the archive of The Royal Ballet School and show students dancing Massine's choreographic studies and their own choreography.[13] Throughout the period of Massine's teaching there were visitors from diverse quarters recognising a need to raise choreography and ballet as an art form to a more academic plane. Apart from a representative from Faber & Faber, visitors included a reporter from the *Times Educational Supplement*, A.V. Coton, the ballet critic, Dame Marie Rambert, and Michael Powell, the film director. Massine was very interested in the developing technology of the videocassette as a recording tool and indeed had it been available then, he would doubtless have recorded all of the textbook examples for an accompanying DVD.

The course of study enabled by de Valois was rich in learning opportunities such as the generation of material, observation and analysis, feedback and discussion. With its intervals, angles and degrees, spatial orientation and rhythmic detail, the framework for choreographic composition offered was replete with rules. Whilst in hindsight, these might appear somewhat obscure, dogmatic and limiting, Massine was at pains to capture for dance the academic authority held by the discipline of music composition. His course provided an opportunity to recognise the significance of change and development in the choreographer's creative process. It was at times an arcane experience as students worked collaboratively with the master in the laboratory of enquiry, developing the studies for the textbook. The results of the work now seem hard to decipher, and the book is devoid of an informative and legible text to support the choreographic examples. Further, these require fluent reading of Stepanov's notation as developed by Massine. The course ended in 1970, but Massine returned to teach and work on the book with Upper School students and Audrey Harman also taught Massine's course material for some years.[14]

In 1973 the annual Ursula Moreton Award was set up to encourage student choreographic endeavour, and in 1975, Richard Glasstone and I were approached by de Valois to set up a new course at the Upper School, which would develop choreographic work in the School on a regular weekly basis. She clearly had identified a need to maintain a culture of creativity in the School and paid visits to these sessions, fostering both the teaching, and students' choreography. From 1987 choreographic work in the School continued to be encouraged, developed and mentored by Norman Morrice, assisted by David Drew. Since 1999 there has been a choreographic course, now a core activity in the classical training at the Upper School, which has been developed by Jennifer Jackson and me, at Gailene Stock's invitation. The course work gives attention to rhythm and phrasing, the awareness of the body in space, pair and group work, and working with music. During the course, choreographic teaching and creative work are connected to classical ballet principles with elements of Massine's approach included. This course content has also provided a foundation for teaching work incorporated into the School's Partnership and Access programme, begun in 2004 to work with primary and secondary schools.

De Valois continued in her retirement years to encourage children at White Lodge to create choreography. The annual choreographic competitions, which take place in the Upper and Lower schools, exist to stimulate ambition and to encourage choreographic talent and endeavour. De Valois set a precedent through her recognition of the importance of choreography as an essential part of the ballet dancer's training and development as an artist. Her enterprising introduction of Massine's work not only encouraged creativity but also acknowledged that any great tradition has within itself the means to develop and move forward without sacrificing the core values of its foundations.

Part Three: Wordsmith

Fiercely Alone: Personality and Impersonality in de Valois' Poetry and Work[1]

Patricia Linton

My first meeting with Ninette de Valois was in September 1964: I was in the graduate class at The Royal Ballet School, which was taught by Madam herself. Nothing prepared me for the first class of the term. Exercise one at the *barre* went well; but for the second, she set eight *grands battements en croix* – then when she saw our agonised faces, she added: "...and repeat it all on *demi-pointe!*" Amidst the audible gasps and groans, I think she was cunningly and mischievously testing our characters and resolve. But to us students then she was definitely formidable, if not positively magisterial.

With successful people, particularly with ones who have had a full life, we tend to see their lives through the prism of their achievements. So much later, when I read de Valois' poems, I was startled. I hadn't really thought of her as ever having been unformed or uncertain, making mistakes or having passions or disappointments. But here, in these poems, there is an inner dimension, quite distinct from her public persona, somebody perhaps few outside her circle suspected.

In the poems, as in her public choreography, there is work that is crafted, disciplined, structured and rigorous, as we might have expected from such a perfectionist. In the fifty or more published poems we also find a whole range of ideas and influences, from Plato and ancient classical and Indian thought, via Christian and Medieval themes and symbols, right up to poets contemporary with her, such as Yeats and Eliot. I'm only looking at a few of her poems in this essay, so that many of her themes, including the sustenance she took from the natural world, will not be covered at all. Nor am I attempting rigorous literary criticism. I just want to bring out the contrast between the inner person and the public figure. As I see it, these poems open a door into another inner, perhaps spiritual world, a world where de Valois sees and seeks a stilled harmony beneath the turbulence of life.

* * *

In looking at de Valois' poems, we can, perhaps, begin at the beginning of her life, which was in Ireland. But, as she tells us in "The Beach of Shells", this life in Ireland was cut short abruptly in a way which marked her deeply:

The Beach of Shells²
(A memory of childhood)

Focused intently now the whole of her eight years…
What magic in the loveliness upturned!
A myriad curved openings, rainbow-hued.
    As sings the sea
    And croons the wind.
A sharp delight is hers as the crackling shells escape
And tumble through her fingers when hard pressed to
Her slender form.

Her child mind does not seek perception,
Blessed as it is to the point of pain,
Yet wildly happy.
The world she knew is blotted out,
There is just herself, fiercely alone,
Alone with God.

If the great beach and its oneness could stay
Forever, and share its thoughts and be her friend,
The sea as well a part of her, forever…

All secrets known and nothing said.

But along the shore she knows a storm will come,
And roughly fall upon the chanting shells…
    One shell she presses to her ear that tells
She may not know such happiness again.

Stilled moment in a heart of innocence.

This poem is clearly linked to her departure from Ireland, with the world she knew quite blotted out. So at the age of seven, uprooted from her idyllic country home for the rest of her youth, she turned her back on this childhood paradise, on a strange, confusing day. As if to emphasise its significance for her, she returns to this experience of childhood loss again and vividly in her memoir, *Come Dance With Me*:

A gardener was cutting a long strip of turf near the top of the centre lawn; slowly and quietly it was rolled. I watched, weighed down with an unhappiness that I could not analyse; I found myself thinking that the turf resembled nothing more than a gigantic green Swiss roll. I knew suddenly that never again, when such things happened to change the visual outlook of the gardens, would I be able to await the why and wherefore of it all, for the great sea was to come between us and the end of the Swiss roll would be someone else's concern.

I did not cry, nor did I ask any questions as to when we might be coming back; I knew the truth and I wanted no comforting grown-up lies. There and then I deliberately tore my heart out and left it, as it were, on the nursery window-sill...[3]

The main theme I am focusing on here is that of loneliness, or rather that of the state of being alone. Being alone comes up in so many of the poems, not as something tragic or as sentimental or nostalgic, but as fundamental to our human reality, and the background against which she forges her proudly determined and solitary way. We have seen this deep sense of being alone in "The Beach of Shells", where it arises from the experience of being torn from her Irish idyll. This unhappy episode seems to have made her determined not to be caught out again by such a twist of fate. Was this experience of loss the source of her self-possession and of her very independent way of thinking? The image she conjures up of this little girl holding the shell tight and seeing the clouds gather is tremendous, as she stands there, indomitable and magnificent: "fiercely alone,/ Alone with God".

This feeling is evoked again in the poem actually called "Alone"[4]:

Alone
Loneliness? It has no real existence,
Just an indulgence that is sought by man.
    Within is everything.
To be alone can be reality,
Divorced from daytime's extroversions.
Tranquil is the search for thoughts that are as shadows.
    "Seek and ye shall find..."

> Find? Yes. Find knowledge that is hidden from
> The earthbound mind.

This poem distinguishes between a commoner loneliness which is a by-product of the hub-bub of everyday life, and a profounder state of being *alone*. Cultivating this existential alone-ness in which you are at one with your true self, is for de Valois an almost metaphysical quest. She says "within is everything", a surprising revelation from a woman who devoted her whole career to performance and spectacle.

As we know, most of her long life was spent in London, in the midst of the bustle of the theatre, the throng of the ballet studio, the maelstrom of administration, the enervating discordance of politics, the distracting tumult of committees. But de Valois – active enacter – was also a witness of the movement of others, standing back to observe "the rat race run... in those globular passages underground"[5] and even the "rough-edged companionship" of the Bull's Head in Barnes where "turbulent thoughts the fumes have bred/ Are trapped as tape-recordings in the brain."[6]

But even in the midst of London a stillness can be found, if you can perceive it. In "The Buddha (In a Museum Garden)" she charts a journey through the apparent disorder of a museum full of shuffling old people, students and noisy children. The journey ends in a garden with a statue of the Buddha: "Hushed in meditation sits the god/ And all is pregnant with arrested thought/ As beauty seeks for wisdom in retreat."[7]

The still inner centre is symbolised here with a physical embodiment and location, but from her own psychological inner retreat, over many years of performing on piers, in music halls, and for Diaghilev, and then in working for W. B. Yeats and in choreographing for her own fledgling Company, and organising it, Ninette de Valois, as she had become, devised and executed a plan. *Her* plan was not merely to form a ballet company or two, (which others had done, and were doing), but to form an Establishment, which they were not doing.

At this point we move away from de Valois as seeker of inner stillness and observer of others, to de Valois as active participant in and courageous creator of this establishment. An establishment in the sense she was after is something which transcends personality; but, like a tradition, supplies the structure, the oxygen and the lifeblood to nurture our true talents. In her own words:

> The whole structure of the venture was deliberately planned to become one of those much derided pieces of architecture known as an Estab-

lishment. The Royal Ballet was never meant to be an isolated personal effort in a particular highly specialised direction. It was to become something that would have a root in the country's theatre; something that the fully-fledged from within its walls might leave to spread their wings elsewhere, and again something to which they could return with their findings, and once more serve and sense the traditions from which they had sprung.[8]

As we see in the poem "Courage", she knew all about the flummery of Establishment; and all those outer forms that would be needed to protect and nurture *her* establishment:

Courage[9]
Tense world that would destroy itself,
We are the dramatis personae involved;
Our minds, encased in double-glaze,
Seek the outsized desk, the padded chair
And air-conditioned suite,
To service gilt-edged courage.

Yet courage sometimes travels inwards
Where a vacuum awaits its industry.
There the great barn of the self can face
The fleeting winds of time's contingencies,
Gales of the world that blow in horizontal lines.
Yet they know the power of the draught,
And courage is a draught.

But *her* courage was not the gilt-edged courage of the board-room; it travelled inwards, so that "the great barn of the self" could face those "gales of the world that blow in horizontal lines". Again she emphasises a positive loneliness and the space *within*, together with the need to clear away what is preventing you from getting to it.

At least, from her inner space, she could always say what she did was hers. What she sought to create in her own ballets and even more in the institutions she founded was something *im*personal. It was something beyond her personality, beyond any isolated personal effort, and greater than all those who sprang from it and spread their wings within it or without, as did so many who worked in her Companies. Indeed, in developing this theme of de Valois' impersonality, there may be something significant in the fact that her most lasting and successful ballets are *Job*, *The Rake's Progress* and *Checkmate.* In two we enter worlds created by other artists, Blake and Hogarth, respectively, while in the third – Noh or Yeats-like – archetypal human tensions and characters, being pulled and driven by a Fate that is not ours to control are represented by the impersonality of chess pieces.

But if de Valois was seeking an impersonality in her own work and, more, in her institutions, this very impersonality was founded on deep feelings within, feelings she continues to explore in her poetry, as we see in "Change":

Change[10]
Change... an earthquake in the mind of man
Of eternity fresh sown
Has no tempi of its own.
The voice of heaven shows its skill
Guiding the rumbles of the will.

This poem is a mere five lines; but as in other short poems, de Valois is touching on big themes, in this case from Medieval and Reformation controversies over predestination. Change seems to us humans to be disjointed, willed partly by us, "an earthquake in the mind of man", but, she suggests here, it is actually guided by God's will as decided from eternity. If we are reminded in this of *Checkmate*, we might also be reminded of Eliot's "time future contained in time past".

But whatever we or de Valois might think about predestination, she was clear that feeling should not lessen with age:

Age[11]
The aged are placed on shelves,
Dim night-lights weeping wax,
Frail biscuit china chipped.

Pills are known to fortify
And help the effort made
To spread thinned peacock tails.

Cut the pills; let life be
More deeply felt, then lived.

We are given here a vivid set of images, sparsely woven, which surely owe something to Baudelaire's "Les petites vieilles". The texture of the poem is as thin as the old themselves, "frail biscuit china chipped". Pills can "spread thinned peacock tails", but it is better to feel and live reality. This is the reality one finds alone and within, as one moves inexorably towards death, a voyage all must make. In "A Voyage", we see de Valois grappling with the awesomeness of that other world beyond this life; but then, hesitantly perhaps, invoking the rainbow, the traditional symbol of the reconciliation of humanity and God:

A Voyage[12]
There is this river that all must cross
With a life-force tide where flickers time,
To the chant of sphere and the dance of stars.
    Yct it may be just a gentle tow
Through the cosmic rays of the rainbow's glow.

Cosmic rays, and rhythms rife before the birth of earth, discernible in the grand sweep of the heavens, and in the transitions through life and death, were part of de Valois' inner landscape, just as they were for Dante in his vision of Paradise. But so was something else, something equally and intensely personal:

Migraine[13]
This pain in the head, so utterly one's own,
Is not the same as in the arm or leg
Which have affinity
With other arms and legs.
But in the head – Oh no!
It is unique, an almost abstract pain
It's so alone.

Dappled fancies; shooting lights; confusion.
There is no way to by-pass
This chaos which so occupies my head,
No outlet for those jostling thoughts that are
Too dead to shape ideas,
Yet too alive for dreams.

Nothing to do. Imprisoned there

The relentless pain circles without purpose
Till, like a wilful child, confused by coloured bricks,
Who topples the bright structure he had built,
My head discards its pictures –
That cubistic array with their painful, sharp edges.

As a balloon deflating with a faint, low sigh
My head becomes aware of weightlessness.
Back comes the urge to fill
This peaceful void with foolishness,
Thoughts heavy with importance, trimmed with fuss.

Good migraine, since you must come again
I would talk with you
And study your reasonings.
But you will wait awhile,
For your return can only be
Through contact with ideas that harass me.

I am told that this is a very apt description of a painful migraine; poetically "good Migraine" has a point, taking us into the inner self she so often sought. Spiritual de Valois undoubtedly was, and it is intriguing how she links spirituality to something as relentlessly and physically inescapable as migraine. But, for all her depth and seriousness, there was also about her a mercurial Irish mischievousness – for not even God has it all, but maybe covets the Earth on which we live and move and have our own type of being:

"He covets the Earth"[14]
"Russell had just come in from a long walk on the Two Rock Mountains, very full of his conversation with an old religious beggar who kept repeating 'God possesses the heavens, but he covets the earth – he covets the earth'." (Yeats)

* * *

Where the peat is sliced as a sticky brown cake
And steams in the trench of a warm earth that breeds
The greenest of green.
When the hills display their haphazard curves

The wild one declaims his suspicion,
As backed by his shrewd yet panicky mood
He continues to raise his keen...

"He covets the earth, aye, He covets the earth"

As he stalks his way through the time-worn climbs
And the sticky peat sucks at his feet,
Comes fear that the turf of the good, green earth
Hordes food for the Garden of Eden.

They claim him to be a real Holy One,
(In Ireland things go to the head)
As many a mystical caper of mind
Has been thought to be wrought
By the Lord's Little People.

So he cries to the sky as the clouds scurry by
Hustled by worrying winds,

"In the name of the Saints, isn't Heaven enough?"

Yet all he could feel was celestial rebuff,
And all he could say with his foresight at bay:

"He covets the earth, aye, He covets the earth."

So the earth has a value of its own, even from God's perspective, but, God being a spirit, will never know exactly what it is that we on earth experience and cherish.

* * *

On this earth, for a driven force like de Valois, there was much to be done. So she took on her public face. But whatever happens in the future with and to the institutions she founded, her poems will remain a timeless testament to that inner self they reveal.

Four Articles for The Old Vic Magazine *and* The Old Vic and Sadler's Wells Magazine[1]

Ninette de Valois

The Ballet in England. [*The Old Vic Magazine*, March, 1928, p.3]

There is so much that one can say about the incomparable subject of dancing that I think an article in the Old Vic Magazine must deal with dancing from the repertory theatre's point of view only.

How much drama owes to the enterprise and uncommercial outlook of the "little theatre" movement everyone is at last beginning to realise, and I am personally convinced that the future of the *best* in ballet will come from a repertory theatre's interest in the dance. In England, especially, this outlook seems to be practical and inevitable, that is, if ballet is to be preserved *at all* in the country.

Grand Ballet, like Grand Opera, means colossal expenditure, and colossal expenditure without a national theatre means the enterprise concerned must run at financial profits, and I have never heard of grand opera or ballet making an impresario's fortune, but rather the reverse.

Therefore I beg of young dancers and producers as a start to concentrate on a "ballet intime". The dancing, choreography, décor, and music may be on a small, but they can be on a perfect, scale. Perfection and taste are demanded if we want the art of Dancing to live and create interest and respect in the minds of the cultured and intelligent public – and they are also the means to impart the right view in the start, to all who do not understand, but are willing to learn.

So with no national trust behind us let us aim at proving our worth to the little theatre movement – and then let us see if they will take us seriously. I think they will, and we well know that if they do it will be a very sincere interest.

The suggested large private sums to be collected and ruthlessly spent on British Ballet at such a moment as the present fills me with doubt – we are not ready for such moves – and a few inevitable failures (as in all such enterprises), would snuff the flame of the candle out very quickly. I don't think a big West-end theatre, with rents, etc., as they are at present, would be a wise place for such an enterprise.

Dancers in England have much to learn. I feel I must say this, and add that I am not with the crowd that says "English dancers only want a chance"; they still want a lot more knowledge as well, especially about dancing in the theatre. The Russian Ballet has shown us the perfect theatre harmony in the art of ballet production – let us never forget this example.

Further, the question of "movement" in plays (especially in the works of some of our present day dramatists), is giving the dancers with a knowledge and feeling of the theatre, an excellent opportunity to play a definite part on the staff of an enterprising repertory theatre.[2]

Ballet at the Old Vic. [*The Old Vic Magazine*, May, 1929, p.3]

With the production of *The Picnic* to Vaughan Williams' delightful *Charterhouse Suite* – the Old Vic appears to be making an effort to give their audience a completely English work. The ballet is slight and produced with due regard for economy. This is a wise policy on the part of Miss Baylis – who realises that if English Ballet is to have recognition on a large scale, it must first prove its worth in a less pretentious fashion. The second production of a ballet at this theatre within five months of its first effort, is extremely encouraging to all concerned. The reception given Mozart's *Les Petits Riens* by the Vic's audience will always remain a delightful memory to the dancers concerned in the ballet. The theatre was quick to show its appreciation of Miss Baylis' new policy – and gave the necessary encouragement for the making of a further effort before the close of the season. Many of the names appearing this time will be remembered by the audience, Rosalind Patrick and the Vic Opera corps de ballet reinforced by others from the Academy of Choreographic Art are dancing. Two of the principal dancers, Miss Ursula Moreton and Mr. Stanley Judson, appeared in *Les Petits Riens*. Miss Mollie Lake and Mr. Harold Turner are newcomers among the principals in *The Picnic*. She is a late member of Madame Anna Pavlova's company and has toured all over the world with the famous dancer. Harold Turner is a pupil of Madame Rambert, who, incidentally, is Mrs Ashley Dukes. Hedley Briggs has this time designed all the costumes.

I remember three years ago watching *The Taming of the Shrew* (with Edith Evans in the cast) from a Vic box. It was a "packed out" matinée, and I was struck at the time with the idea of what a marvellous house it would be for "ballet", and how such a scheme at such a place might develop into a practical possibility. The Vic's management within two years has given English dancers a chance. If dancers give a high standard of work and the audience give their interest and support, the trouble and extra anxiety this new line gives the theatre will be justified.

But the management naturally aims at more ambitious productions in the future. I wonder if the lovers of ballet in the audience realise how much it is in their power to bring these things nearer? Your interest, understanding and intelligent criticism alone can make all this possible and we feel we are right, through the medium of this magazine, to ask for your support, provided you of course feel our productions justify themselves.

There are hundreds of English dancers unable to find an opportunity even to "dance" – let alone make a living wage out of their work. It will be necessary to launch three or four big efforts to cope with the situation. I cannot help feeling that this management means to shoulder the responsibility of one of them, and incidentally one of extreme importance. Most of the big companies we hope to see later will have to tour, not only in England but abroad. A repertory theatre is stationary, the nearest thing we have in this country to a state theatre, and the "Vic" is in our capital. It therefore makes the all-important "experimental" ballet possible for a financial outlay below the average. Not concerned with ballet only, it has other productions which are the attractions to its regular public. Everyone can realise how one enterprise under such circumstances unconsciously supports another.

Giselle [*The Old Vic and Sadler's Wells Magazine*, January, 1937, pp.2-3]

There was a legend in Bohemia, (I was going to say a belief, but as I do not know how much it was believed, I will call it a legend) that certain young ladies were condemned, that is to say they were dead and their souls were damned, and they were condemned at night to leave their graves and dance until daybreak. They were called Willis.

The original title of this ballet was *Giselle, ou les Wilis*. It was written by the great French poet and novelist, Théophile Gautier, on a plot adapted from the German poet, Heinrich Heine, and produced on the 4th of July, 1841, at the Grand Opera at Paris, to music composed by Adolphe Adam. It was first produced in England on the 12th of March in the following year at Her Majesty's Theatre. At this point I consulted my history book and found that Queen Victoria came to the throne in 1837, married Prince Albert in 1840, and two years later this ballet was performed at

Her Majesty's Theatre. I hope you will forgive this piece of history, but it helps to get one's bearings.

While we are still more or less on the subject of these unfortunate dead females, I may say in parentheses that Edward James Loder used them for his finest opera, *The Wilis, or The Night Dancers*, which was produced at the Princess's Theatre in 1846, and again in 1850, and revived at Covent Garden in 1860, and Puccini also wrote an opera about them, *Le Villi*. So that the Victorians were well acquainted with them. I think they are not quite so well known today.

But to return to *Giselle*, the great star was, of course, Carlotta Grisi, and this ballet contained one of her most famous parts. Carlotta had two famous cousins, Giulia and Giudetta Grisi, and their maternal aunt was the famous opera singer, Grassini.

Both Rossini and Bellini took a great interest in Giulia and Bellini wrote his opera, *I Capuleti e I Montecchi* for her and her sister. Giulia later made her first great London success in Donizetti's *Anna Bolena*.

Well, naturally, with such relations as these, Carlotta was taught to sing, but she was not to be a great singer. Fate had ordained otherwise, and under the tuition of Perrot (whom she married), she became the first and foremost dancer of her time. She stood out from her contemporaries most by her exquisite charm.

Carlotta Grisi was also much admired in the part of Esmeralda in a ballet arranged by her husband on Victor Hugo's *Notre Dame de Paris*, for which Pugni, of Her Majesty's Theatre, wrote the music. And since *Giselle* owes something to Heine, we may recall that Mr Lumley, the manager of Her Majesty's Theatre, commissioned Heine to write a ballet. The result was *Mephistophela*, in which Faust is tempted by a female Mephistopheles, who calls up before him the most famous *danseuses* of ancient times, including, of course, the notorious Salome. And also King David dances an impressive *pas seul* in front of the ark. This ballet was totally unsuited to a Victorian audience, and, although Mr. Lumley paid the poet for his trouble, it was never produced.

Perhaps it will have its première at Sadler's Wells, but it would be too rash to prophecy.

The first English Giselle was Markova, who made her first appearance in this role with the Vic-Wells Ballet in January, 1934, at the Old Vic. Three years later, on January 19th, at Sadler's Wells, the same company present the second English dancer to attempt the same role, Margot Fonteyn, the youngest dancer on record, who will make this part the real important event of her seventeenth year.

For the ballerina it is the great test, as both dramatically and technically it demands so much.

The Ballet. [*The Old Vic and Sadler's Wells Magazine, September, 1939, pp.8-9*]

The Vic-Wells Ballet, at present on tour in the north of England, will re-open at Sadler's Wells on Monday, September 18th, their first night programme including *Harlequin in the Street*, *Les Sylphides* and *Checkmate*.

During the coming season the Ballet will give three (instead of two) performances a week, on Monday, Wednesday and Friday evenings and, alternative weeks, Monday and Wednesday evenings and Saturday matinees. Over twenty ballets will be given during September and October. In addition to the three mentioned above, there will be *The Rake's Progress*, *Horoscope*, *Job*, *Nocturne*, *Apparitions*, *The Haunted Ballroom*, *Façade*, *Le Roi Nu*, *A Wedding Bouquet*, *Barabau*, *Les Rendezvous*, *Les Patineurs*, and *Cupid and Psyche*. *Carnaval* will be included in the October programmes, and there will be revival of *Douanes* on October 25th.

* * *

On Monday, October 16th the first performance of *Coppélia* in three acts will be given, preparations for which are already well advanced. In view of the increasing strength of the company and growth of the repertoire, it is intended to devote approximately one out of three programmes to the performance of a classical Ballet in its entirety. The success of *The Sleeping Princess* last season, and the enthusiasm shown for performances of *Giselle* and *Le Lac de Cygnes* in full, indicate that there is a growing public demand for classical ballet; not merely an abridged version of it, but for the work as a whole. And the study of such productions proves to be an invaluable experience in the training of young dancers, whether given a major or minor principal role or a place in the corps de ballet.

* * *

Any habitué of the Ballet must find it necessary to see the full performance of a classical work a number of times before becoming familiar with the details of it. So it may be realised that the full understanding necessary to performance involves a long period of initiation before hand, even by those who may be dancing only a very minor role but whose full co-operation is essential to the entire success of the performance as a whole.

With regard to those taking the principal parts, it will be obvious that a three act or five act ballet calls for a sustaining power which can only be the outcome of a thorough foundation, and of experience gained in roles which, though exacting, do not demand the same degree of endurance.

Because the Vic-Wells Ballet is still in its youth, the approach to the classical works has been necessarily, a gradual one, but it is felt that the company justifies the demands which are being made upon it, and that the public are ready to give their full support to efforts in this direction.

* * *

During September there will be three performances of *The Sleeping Princess*. And after its première on October 16th *Coppélia* will be given on Monday, Oct. 23rd, Monday, November 6th, and at the matinee on November 11th.

In *The Sleeping Princess* a hundred and seventy costumes are used. And in preparation for *Coppélia* the Wardrobe staff are already working hard and craving decisions; the tragedy of completing six costumes in a beautiful shade of rose pink, only to find that salmon pink is essential, is to be avoided at all costs. And the storage and renovation of costumes is an ever-growing matter, in common with most other things concerned with a repertory company.

The Ballet is visiting Manchester during [the] week commencing August 21st, Liverpool on August 28th, Leeds on September 4th, and Newcastle-on-Tyne on September 11th. They finish their tour in Newcastle on September 16th, and open in London at Sadler's Wells on the following Monday.

Writing across the Footlights:
Ninette de Valois and the Vic-Wells community

Elizabeth Schafer

Ninette de Valois was a very versatile and prolific writer; she wrote poetry, memoirs, letters, polemics, apologetics, history and marketing copy. She was able to write imaginatively but also pragmatically and strategically. In this essay I will suggest that a crucial influence in the development of de Valois as a professional writer, that is, one adept at writing for a target readership, was her induction into life as part of the Vic-Wells community.[1] This was when de Valois honed her skills in writing "across the footlights".

When the twenty-eight-year-old de Valois joined the Old Vic community in 1926, that community was well established; it was also looking to expand, as the Old Vic manager, Lilian Baylis, began her campaign to acquire and redevelop the Sadler's Wells theatre in Islington. The Old Vic community constructed itself, and communicated, by means of its newsletter, the *Old Vic Magazine* (hereafter abbreviated to *OVM*). This magazine was usually published eight times during the nine-month season and existed to exhibit "some tangible expression of the interest and affection felt by those before the curtain for those behind and vice versa. It is informal in style and parish-pump in policy" (*OVM*, September-October, 1927). In the rhetoric of the magazine, the Old Vic community consisted of all those in paid work at the theatre, in whatever capacity, plus the audiences who supported the theatre's drama and opera productions; these audiences were expected also to support fund-raising events, to volunteer to help out whenever necessary and to advertise what was on at the Old Vic by distributing green leaflets detailing the season's programme wherever they went.[2] While the Old Vic was located in an impoverished neighbourhood and certainly engaged in community outreach activities, the heart of the 'Old Vic Community' was the Old Vic Association and the Old Vic Circle, that is, what would be seen today as its subscriber base.

There was a clear expectation that *anyone* at the Vic could be asked to write for the *OVM*;[3] those working backstage, front of house and in administration, as well as directors, designers, actors, singers and dancers. Performers in drama and opera wrote about their roles; directors wrote about their interpretations; designers wrote about their vision. A particular feature of the *OVM* is that it gave significant space for women writers, such as Sybil Thorndike, Ethel Smyth, Elizabeth Polunin and Peggy Ashcroft.[4] However, many articles are prefaced by a phrase on the lines of "Miss Baylis has asked me to write some thoughts on ....", that suggests the writers were press-ganged into writing.[5] As a consequence of soliciting such articles, the *OVM* is full of engaged, if often maverick, performance- and performer-centred criticism and histories, an Old Vic alternative to mainstream theatre history, where John Gielgud's thoughts on *The Merchant of Venice* (*OVM*, December, 1932) might appear alongside the results of the "guess the weight of the twelfth night cake" competition; news of recent marriages, births, deaths; and information on how to get tickets for the fancy dress ball. The *OVM*'s pages also include a wealth of short, educational essays on authors, composers, plays, operas, and dances that are about to appear at the Old Vic, partly as an attempt to market specific productions, but also as an attempt to inform and educate: for example, a revival of Philip Massinger's *A New Way to Pay Old Debts*, forty-five years after the last performance of the play carried as a trailer a stage history of the play by John Parker (*OVM*, November, 1922).

From 1920 onwards, the *OVM* always opened with an article entitled "Across the Footlights"; the title epitomises Lilian Baylis's drive to break down the fourth wall in terms of reaching out to the Old Vic audiences and constructing them as a community. Baylis insisted that the, by then, metaphorical footlights had to be crossed by practitioners not only in their performances but also by means of socialising with audiences, signing autograph books and, in the 1920s, quite literally by putting planks of wood across the orchestra pit so that the audience could come on stage for the Twelfth Night party, and eat cake with those who had just performed in that night's show.

This was the community de Valois joined in 1926, at a time when she was beginning to flex her professional writing skills. Evidence of this can be found in the essay she published in February of that year in *Dancing Times*, an essay ambitiously entitled, "The Future of Ballet".[6] *Dancing Times* billed de Valois as "the young English danseuse who has appeared for two years with the Diaghileff Company, and has also danced in the ballets of the Royal Italian Opera at Covent Garden". The essay vigorously defends modern ballet, insists ballet must be studied alongside the sister arts of music, visual art and theatre, and quotes approvingly and extensively from Ernest Newman's *A Musical Critic's Holiday*. Compared with de Valois' later professional writing, the essay is patchy – for example, the extended quotation from Newman is not well integrated – but the writer certainly comes out fighting in the cause of modern ballet. It must have been a few months before this essay was published in February that de Valois had turned her hand to another form of professional writing: the pitch. De Valois wrote letters to both Barry Jackson in Birmingham and to Lilian Baylis at the Old Vic, asking them to consider hosting a dance company in their theatres. Jackson turned her down, but Baylis did not.

The evidence offered by the pages of the *OVM* indicates that, at the time she received the letter from de Valois, Baylis, a former teacher of dance herself, was already exploring how to introduce ballet at the Old Vic. As early as 1924 Flora Fairbairn, who was then running dance at the theatre, had been inveigled into writing an essay for the *OVM*, entitled 'Ballet in England'; this essay is a stirring call to arms, demanding the establishment of a school of ballet that required total commitment from pupils and teachers alike. Fairbairn's students would study 'music, colour, design, history, manners, customs, costumes, dressmaking and above all, stage-craft and choreography' (*OVM*, October – November, 1924). Fairbairn's potentially very expensive vision does not sit comfortably with Baylis' frugal management of the Vic and Fairbairn actually left the Old Vic soon after she wrote this article.[7] The following year Jean Anderton, who was working on dance for the Old Vic opera productions, wrote a brief history of "Opera Dancing" (*OVM*, September – October, 1925). Anderton argues:

> Nowhere in the world is there better material than in our girls for the making of the dancer, and we have the enthusiasm of our audiences; therefore, with the courage and perseverance of those who love their work, the time shall not be far distant when the dancing in opera becomes, not a special feature, but part of a perfect whole.

De Valois' first essay for the *OVM*, entitled "The Ballet in England", appeared in March 1928, eighteen months after she joined the Vic.[8] De Valois takes a different tack from Fairbairn and Anderton and argues that the way forward is to start with a small-scale approach. She stresses the importance of "little theatres" in building audiences for ballet, that is, theatres committed to repertory. She argues that "Grand Ballet, like Grand Opera, means colossal expenditure" and offers this advice:

> Therefore I beg of young dancers and producers as a start to concen-

trate on a "ballet intime". The dancing, choreography, décor, and music may be on a small, but they can be on a perfect, scale.

De Valois specifically cautions against proposals to spend "large private sums" on British Ballet, and claims that looking towards "West-end theatre, with rents etc. as they are at present" would not be wise. This careful approach would appeal to Baylis, who was well known for her antipathy for the West End; she regarded the West End audiences as "bounders", who ought to be spending their money on supporting the Old Vic.

It is important to note in relation to de Valois' first essay for the *OVM* that she had recently given a talk on the subject of "The Ballet in England" to the Vic-Wells Association; de Valois herself, admittedly writing fifty-five years later, constructs this talk as a seminal moment in her career:

> The Vic-Wells Association holds many memories for me, but perhaps the most important is the fact that, at the invitation of Miss Baylis, I gave my first public address in the rehearsal room at the Old Vic. I spoke of the ballet and our hope for the future. I was too nervous to speak without any reference to notes and so I read my message with Miss Baylis sitting there, smiling and nodding her approval.[9]

Baylis regularly used such public talks and lectures as another strategy for ensuring her practitioners at the Old Vic crossed the "footlights" and, while de Valois may have been nervous on this occasion, she soon got accustomed to public speaking: the *Dancing Times* of April 1929 records that de Valois was able to deliver a lecture at very short notice when Marie Rambert went down with 'flu and could not speak to the Liverpool "Dancers' Circle Meeting" on 10 March. And by February 1938 the *OVM* is reporting on "the lectures Ninette de Valois is giving as part of a London University Extension course":

> These lectures, a series of ten in all, will be given weekly in the Association library at the Old Vic, on Thursdays at 6, and the price 10/- for the course is uncommonly modest. Those who have read Miss de Valois' book [*Invitation to the Ballet*], about the success of which both here, and in America she is so modest, will have a foretaste of her quality in a new line of country. At the opening of the course on January 27th the room was overflowing and scores had to be turned away.

While it is clear that de Valois quickly became a strategic, intelligent writer and public speaker, it is possible to see the "adventurous traditionalist" identifying two Old Vic traditions of crossing the footlights – that is, writing for the magazine and giving lectures – that would help hone skills that would be useful to de Valois in the future. De Valois certainly did not embrace all the Old Vic community's traditions; she never threw herself into, for example, judging the costumes at the fancy dress ball as Sybil Thorndike or Edith Evans did. However, in developing her professional writing skills, de Valois was responding and reacting to an Old Vic "tradition" and using it strategically.[10]

De Valois' second essay for the *OVM* appeared in May 1929; "Ballet at the Old Vic" celebrates the Old Vic's production of *The Picnic*, danced to Vaughan Williams' *Charterhouse Suite*.[11] (Though listing the names of the dancers involved and the designer, she modestly refrains from informing readers that she is the choreographer.) De Valois again insists that such small-scale ballets will eventually enable large-scale ballet to flourish, but importantly, in this short piece, she begins the process of creating a history for what was to become the Vic-Wells Ballet:

> I remember three years ago watching "The Taming of the Shrew" (with Edith Evans in the cast) from a Vic box. It was a "packed out" matinée, and I was struck at the time with the idea of what a marvellous house it would be for "ballet," and how such a scheme at such a place might develop into a practical possibility. The Vic's management within two years has given English dancers a chance. If dancers give a high standard of work and the audience give their interest and support, the trouble and extra anxiety this new line gives the theatre will be justified.[12]

Although de Valois grounds this foundational moment in English dance securely in the fabric of the Old Vic building, the Vic-Wells ballet actually used the Sadler's Wells theatre more than the Vic. The Old Vic stage was famous for its intimacy (when alterations were being made to the theatre, Ellen Terry threatened to come back and haunt Baylis, if the circle of the auditorium was altered in any way)[13] but the rake and the splinters did not endear it to dancers. De Valois then goes on to call upon her readership to make "more ambitious productions" happen:

> Your interest, understanding and intelligent criticism alone can make all this possible and we feel we are right, through the medium of this

magazine, to ask for your support, provided you of course feel our productions justify themselves.

The slippage from "I remember" into "we feel" and "our productions" suggests that de Valois was confident that Baylis was completely in support of her objectives.

The tone of de Valois' third *OVM* essay, on *Giselle* (*OVM*, January, 1937), was very different.[14] Although 1937 also saw the first performances of *Checkmate*, and the publication of *Invitation to the Ballet*, de Valois still found time to research and write an essay aimed at increasing interest in her production of *Giselle*, which was opening on 19th January at Sadler's Wells. De Valois looks back to "the first English Giselle", Alicia Markova, "who made her first appearance in this role with the Vic-Wells Ballet in January, 1934, at the Old Vic"; she looks forward to Margot Fonteyn's imminent performance of the role. However, de Valois also writes engagingly about Carlotta Grisi and, less expectedly, of Heine's unrealised ballet, *Mephistophela*, in producing a potted history of *Giselle*, which focuses on the legend of the Wilis and how it made its mark on opera and dance during the nineteenth century. A significant stage in the history of her Company is situated carefully within a larger cultural picture.

De Valois' final contribution to the *Old Vic Magazine*, a piece simply entitled 'The Ballet' (*OVM* September 1939), appears perhaps at a first glance more of a press release for the repertory to be offered in the coming season than an essay.[15] But, viewed alongside the essay dating from May 1929, this shows how over a decade later the Company could within a two-month period call on a repertoire of some eighteen one-act modern ballets as well as three full-length classical works, to which a production of *Coppélia* by de Valois herself was shortly to be added. The essay records a remarkable achievement, though de Valois' own role in the shaping of the Company characteristically goes unmentioned. By this stage Lilian Baylis was dead and de Valois had more managerial responsibility than when Baylis was alive. But over the years, writing for the *OVM*, de Valois had produced polemics, history, memoirs and marketing copy. Her work with Baylis and the Vic-Wells community helped de Valois evolve into a pragmatic and professional writer, as well as an accomplished public speaker, and a practitioner who became skilled at reaching out across the footlights.[16]

Part Four: Company

The Irish and the Italians:
de Valois, the Cecchettis and the "other" ballet mime

Giannandrea Poesio

On 17 January 1954, the Cecchetti Society held a tribute to the memory of Maestro Enrico Cecchetti at the Rudolf Steiner Hall in London. The event facilitated the meeting of artists and pedagogues such as Tamara Karsavina, Alicia Markova, Laura Wilson, Peggy Van Praagh, Margaret Craske and Errol Addison to compare notes on Cecchetti's artistic legacy twenty-six years after his death. Unable to attend, Ninette de Valois, one of Maestro's pupils in London and one the Society's founder members, asked dance historian, Cyril Beaumont, to read the following:

> I was a pupil of Enrico Cecchetti for five years. He was an inspired teacher, a great artist, and possessed of one remarkable quality. He was renowned as a great executive of technical feats, yet he loved, above all, to see grace and poetry in the work of his pupils. Another attitude of his (which I have often, in my particular work, had reason to recall) was his view on young dancers, once expressed to me in the following words: "There is no such thing as a true ballerina under 26 or 27 years of age. But do we know of anything more beautiful and more heartening than to witness those early performances of the potential ballerina?"
>   I wish I could be with you all tonight to pay my homage in person. Instead I ask Mr Beaumont to read this little message to you all - who meet to honour a great professor. English dancers owe him so much for those years he spent in our midst, scolding, praising, encouraging or coaxing as the case demanded. May we not fail to keep alive his memory and his influence.[1]

Four decades later, on 20 May 1992, Dame Ninette was the recipient of the Italian Porselli Award. Once the intimate ceremony held at the Royal Opera House in London was over, she jokingly admitted to having always recommended pupils and colleagues to "study Cecchetti and forget all about it".[2]

A similar, though less humorous remark is reported by Kathrine Sorley Walker in her seminal work, *Ninette de Valois, idealist without illusions*.

According to Sorley Walker, de Valois regarded Cecchetti's method as "important to study at some time in one's career, but perhaps not sufficient on its own".[3] Both statements, which are symptomatic of de Valois' pragmatic approach to ballet training, seem to contradict the content of the 1954 address and could come across as disparaging. Indeed, they have been frequently and erroneously misread as indicative of a conflicting relationship between de Valois and Maestro Cecchetti. Such flawed, superficially hurried interpretations of de Valois' words are indeed disproved by the recent discovery of unpublished letters kept in the private archives of Maestro's grandchildren, Signora Elena Caccini-Cecchetti and the late Professor Giorgio Cecchetti. In addition to confirming the extent of both the friendship and the mutual admiration shared by the Italian Maestro and the Irish ballet pioneer, those writings cast significant light on a little researched chapter of ballet history.

Enrico Cecchetti (1850-1928) had a profound admiration for Ninetta or Nina, as he called de Valois, musing on the conventional associations that name had long had in the Italian theatre and opera tradition since Commedia dell'Arte – the popular soubrette-like stock-character of Nina/Ninetta was traditionally depicted as an ingeniously clever, stubborn and rebellious rascal, who played the ingénue to get wherever and whatever she wanted. Three documents are particularly significant. The first is the draft of a dedication that Maestro wrote on a copy of Olga Racster's book, *The Master of Russian Ballet, The Memoirs of Cavalier Cecchetti* (1922). A meticulously fussy man, Cecchetti kept every draft of all his writings, whether they be original letters, replies to letters he had received, cards, telegrams, postcards and dedications. The inscription, in Cecchetti's distinctive pigeon-French, reads:

> My very dear Ninette, in this book are my memoirs, and I hope in your heart you will always keep the memory of your devoted old Professor Enrico Cecchetti.[4]

The fact that the seventy-two year old Maestro had decided to donate a free copy of the book to de Valois is in itself a sound testimonial of his affection for her. The slightly over-sentimental, though truly heartfelt tone of the dedication is the same as the one Cecchetti used in all his correspondence with his closest friends and relatives, and focuses on a theme – namely the significance of being remembered – that occurred frequently in all the writings of the ageing artist.

The second, and more important document, is the draft of an undated letter to one of Cecchetti's English pupils, Errol Addison, in which Maestro gives a brief account of the activities of his London school during his temporary absence from the UK. According to the syntactically and grammatically uneven English text of the letter – one of the very few in that language – classes at the school in Shaftesbury Avenue were to be run by senior pupils: Ninetta was to be entrusted with the "finishing" class, namely the most important one. (Cecchetti himself had considered his appointment as "finishing teacher" at the Imperial Ballet School in St. Petersburg as one of the greatest accolades of his artistic career.) As explained by Cecchetti himself, such a decision had been prompted by the Maestro's profound admiration for de Valois' teaching abilities.[5]

Finally, the third and arguably most revealing letter reads:

My very dear Ninette,
It is *a truly long time*[6] since I received your letter with the enclosed photographs, cherished souvenirs of our farewells at Montecarlo. They are well shot, they gave us immense pleasure and we would like to thank you.

Soon you will finish your engagement at the Coliseum and will take some holidays. Have you decided whether you would like to come to Italy with Margaret?

If yes, please do let us know, so that I can make sure I will be able to meet you in Turin.

I have some news for you, very good news and, at the same time, not so pleasant, as this winter I will not come to Montecarlo! I have been appointed Professor, Director of the Dance Academy at La Scala Theatre.

So, starting from the 1st September I will be in Milan for 10 months every year. For an old artist to be able to end his artist career as Director of the Dance Academy at La Scala is the supreme honour...

I know my dear Ninette that such news will cause some upset to you and to my other dear pupils, but I also know that you love your old dear Maestro and that you are not selfish. On my part, I can reassure you that the honour bestowed upon me by La Scala will not make me forget my beloved students, and that I will be very happy and proud if, from time to time, they came to Milan to pay me a visit.

Dear Ninette, please pass our regards to the whole of the Diaghilev company, and to all our friends in London, particularly to Mr Richardson, whom I'd like to thank for sending me The Dancing Times regularly; I'd be obliged if you could pass the good news and if he could publish something about the great honour that has been bestowed upon me [...]

I send you my most loving wishes and please embrace everyone on our behalf.

Your old, affectionate

Professor Enrico Cecchetti[7]

The letter is one of only four on the same subject: the others had been written to three of Maestro's closest friends, namely Sergei Diaghilev, Cyril Beaumont and Farfa – the nickname Cecchetti had chosen for his former pupil, Luigi Albertieri, an eminent dance teacher in the US. The fact he had entrusted such news to de Valois dispels any doubt about the closeness between the old Italian artist and the founder of The Royal Ballet.

On her part, de Valois too wrote affectionate letters to the Maestro, although she never indulged in copious details about her work and her life. The most poignant is the one she sent shortly after Giuseppina Cecchetti's death, on 23 October 1927, penned, in a grammatically not so fluid French on the letterhead of the Academy of Choreographic Arts in South Kensington:

My very dear Maestro,

I cannot find the words I'd like to send. The sorrow, the sympathy which all of your pupils feel for the most beloved Maestro and all we have lost with the death of Madame – who was so good and so much loved by everyone.

But it is to you Maestro, so dear, that I send my heart, which, together with my thoughts is only for you at this time.

Yours always devoted

Ninette. [8]

The kind, heartfelt words of appreciation of Madame Cecchetti match the devotion that the Cecchettis themselves had expressed in their 1925 letter. Still, de Valois' recollection of Madame Cecchetti prompts questions concerning the extent of both the professional and personal relationship the two women might have had. The role that Giuseppina Cecchetti played within the activities of her husband's school in Shaftesbury Avenue in London remains to date a poorly documented, grey area of ballet history. According to both Cyril Beaumont and Errol Addison, Madame Cecchetti always kept a vigilant eye on the pupils' progress and was always very keen to provide extra help in making them rehearse the most difficult exercises in a little room adjacent the dance studio.[9]

The late Laura Wilson, who had studied with Cecchetti in London and danced with Diaghilev's Ballets Russes under the name of Wilson Olkina, recalled that:

> Madame Cecchetti frequently taught ballet mime after Maestro's ballet class, either for sheer personal fun or upon the request of some dancer attending the school. She insisted a great deal on facial mime, which had to accompany every single movement of the arms and the hands. She could express joy and horror in a vivid, memorable way, and there is no doubt she could have been a great silent movie actress, had she wanted to.[10]

Indeed, Giuseppina Cecchetti had been a well-respected mime dancer in her performing days and her silent acting abilities had often been praised by the international press. As "prima mima", she had appeared at La Scala Theatre in Milan in the highly successful *Amor* (1886). In St Petersburg at the Mariinsky Theatre, she created the role of the Queen in the original production of *Sleeping Beauty* (1890) and that of Countess Sybil in the *première* of *Raymonda* (1898) among many other roles. Finally, her artistic versatility had been exploited by Léonide Massine, who created for her the role of Marquise Silvestra in *Les Femmes de Bonne Humeur* (1917) and of the Russian Merchant's Wife in *La Boutique Fantasque* (1919).

As reported by Sorley Walker, one of the aspects "of ballet performance that was prominently featured" in the curriculum devised by de Valois for her early dance academy was traditional mime:

> De Valois decided to take class herself with a remarkable teacher, Francesca Zanfretta [...] She was a superlative coach for mime and not only de Valois but Ursula Moreton gained greatly from her tuition. At Moreton's request, Sheila McCarthy wrote down what Zanfretta taught. This was handed on in its complex and fascinating details to the Vic-Wells Ballet and its successor companies.[11]

Zanfretta's mime, however, had little in common with that known, practised and taught by the Cecchettis. Born in Mantua in 1862, Zanfretta had been trained at La Scala theatre at the time Enrico and Giuseppina were already touring the world as two much-praised professional dancers. Although this is not the appropriate context to embark on a discussion concerning the historical fallacy of the existence of a much idealised nineteenth-century "Italian school" of dance training and making, it is worth mentioning that the choreographic traditions within which the Cecchettis had grown artistically in the first decades of the second half of the nineteenth century, differed greatly from those that had rapidly developed only a few years later in the newly unified kingdom of Italy. As a student at the prestigious academy in Milan, Zanfretta was brought up artistically in line with the precepts and the aesthetic of an artist and choreographic school that had little to do with that the Cecchettis had professionally matured within before leaving Italy. As far as mime was concerned, at La Scala Zanfretta had been taught "scenic poses", or conventional theatre gestures by Serafino Torelli, a former actor and author of a celebrated manual of gestural acting for thespians, opera singers and dancers.[12] Although Torelli's expressive and narrative gestures drew upon the well-established gestural tradition of the Italian Commedia dell'Arte, like most Italian theatre practices of the time, they had little in common with the principles of gestural acting codified and taught, earlier in the same century, by Antonio Morrocchesi, the author of *Lezioni di Declamazione* (1832), which was considered by many as the ultimate and final expression of the developments of the Commedia dell'Arte tradition.[13]

Not unlike many other contemporary mime theorists, Morrocchesi too had been inspired by Johan Jacob Engel's major work on theatre gesture, *Ideen zu Einer Mimik* (1799). In his *Lezioni di Declamazione*, which includes 40 drawings illustrating different gestural actions corresponding to particular emotions, situations or narrations, Morrocchesi, like Engel, advocated a non-schematic approach to gestures, which left ample space for the actor's own interpretative and improvisational abilities. Such versatility and free-agency were abhorred and refuted by Torelli, who believed that the universality of the language of gesture adopted by the Commedia dell'Arte actors stemmed from the constant reiteration of rigidly set conventional poses.

Morrocchesi's principles were well known to both Cesare Cecchetti, Enrico's father, a celebrated mime, and to his close friend Marino Legittimo, who taught mime at the short-lived dance academy in Florence, directed by Giovanni Lepri. As one of Lepri's private pupils, Enrico is more than likely to have complemented his "refining" classes – which included 15 minutes of "gesturing" anyhow – with Legittimo's private tuition. Thanks to the influence of his father and the teachings of

Legittimo, he acquired unique acting skills, which he combined with equally unique technical feats, in a truly innovative way for a nineteenth-century *premier danseur*.[14] It is not surprising, therefore, that he made history with the creation of mime roles such as that of the villainous protagonist, Diavolino, in *La Fille du Bandit* (1888), Carabosse, the wicked fairy, in *Sleeping Beauty* (1890) and the Charlatan in *Petrouchka* (1911). Still, he only taught mime for a brief period at the Imperial Ballet School in St Petersburg between 1892 and 1893, and always delegated the teaching of that art to his beloved wife.

Giuseppina too was a pupil of Legittimo, for she had enrolled as a student at the academy in Florence in 1864, from which she graduated six years later, shortly before the celebrated institution was closed down for political and administrative reasons. She too, therefore, belonged to that essentially late Romantic school, which prioritised the interpreter's own subjective response to given principles over a mechanical reproduction of set gestures.

The reasons that led de Valois to choose Zanfretta's mime instead of pursuing and perpetuating the Cecchettis' "other" mime, remain open to speculation. It is possible that de Valois never had the chance to learn directly from Madame Cecchetti, or ever asked to be coached, and that, by the time she devised the curriculum of the academy no one else was around to pass on those teachings. But it is also possible that her choosing a mime syllabus that stood out for less interpretative subjectivity was determined by the same pragmatic approach to training dancers, mentioned earlier. It is thus possible that the way she felt about Cecchetti – whom she referred to as "an artist-teacher as opposed to a pedagogue"[15] – informed also her views on both his mime abilities and that of his wife as a mime teacher. What Giuseppina Cecchetti taught was not wrong, but, as reported by witnesses of the time such as Mark Perugini,[16] could not be easily passed on, given both the complexity and the elusiveness of a language that relied so much on subjective reading and even improvisation and was so clearly rooted in long-lost theatre traditions. Zanfretta's less flowery and subjective approach, on the contrary, could be easily codified in a set of readily transmissible principles, as indeed happened when Ursula Moreton asked Sheila McCarthy to write down the various gestures. A comparison between those notes and the few existing examples of mime passages notated by Cecchetti himself - namely those from *Catarina, La Fille du Bandit, Coppélia*, Carabosse's "prediction" scene from *The Sleeping Beauty* and *Amor*[17] – clearly highlight the differences between the two mime languages.

Although the basic nature of the conventional gestures and, to a certain extent, their dynamics are similar, though never identical, the Cecchetti/Legittimo/Morrocchesi approach tends to fill the musical phrase with a considerably complex and varied amount of movements. The mimed phrase, therefore, relies on the combination of set, conventional gestures and non-set or codified linking ones, the creation of which is left entirely to the inspiration and artistry of the interpreter. This is particularly evident when comparing what has survived in The Royal Ballet's repertoire as "Carabosse's prediction" in the Prologue of *The Sleeping Beauty* and the detailed indications given on the same passage in both the notated *repetiteur* score for the whole ballet by Nicholas Sergeyev[18] and, more significantly, Cecchetti's own notes.[19]

There is little doubt that Zanfretta's less subjective and much more memorable gestures were ideal for the syllabus of a newly founded academy that aimed at training new generations of dancers, whereas the Cecchettis' mime remained too much within the sphere of the refinement classes only seasoned artists could attend. De Valois' choice, therefore, was not dictated by disrespect towards the old Maestro, but by pedagogic acumen – not to mention that she was fully aware of the fact that the British, unlike the Italians and the Russians, have always had problems with picturesque, expressive gesticulations. Interestingly, when she oversaw the stagings of classics such as *Coppélia* and *The Sleeping Beauty* – namely the two ballets in which Cecchetti had been actively involved, whether as reconstructor, a performer, or both – de Valois kept the mime passages but "adapted" them through the Zanfretta tradition, creating a splendid historical and artistic hybrid. It is a hybrid that, together with many other aspects of her choreographic work, remains testimony of her inventive genius and artistic pragmatism and, in a rather odd way, can be regarded as a unique tribute to the Italian ballet tradition. Or should we say "traditions"?

Interviews with Ron Smedley and Simon Rice on the teaching of folk dance and national dance at The Royal Ballet School

Libby Worth

Ninette de Valois was unequivocal in her belief that "all the ballet's funda-mental dance steps are derived from the folk dances of western Europe. There can be traced, from the Basque country to the highlands of Scot-land, not only the steps, but the very style of the classical dance".[1] Given her curiosity about the integration of national dance steps within differ-ent styles of ballet and her preoccupation with the development of an English ballet choreography that would draw on national dances, it is not surprising that she introduced teaching of national dance to The Royal Ballet Schools. Led by Douglas Kennedy,[2] the programmes of teaching began in the late 1950s, but Kennedy's original anticipation of conflict that might arise in attempting to introduce such a contrasting form of movement to students of ballet was in danger of being realised. In an early class he describes how it was difficult to encourage sharing and on "the basis of their natural everyday behaviour ... [to] try to build the folk-dance 'body' technique". He recalls that "When I saw anyone gazing at themselves in the mirror I turned them round to gaze at someone else".[3] As suggested by this comment he was particularly concerned with how to teach students not only a different type of step but a different way of learning "starting from 'inside-out', rather than from 'outside-in'".[4]

In the following interviews, two subsequent teachers of national and folk dances at The Royal Ballet School, Ron Smedley (1969 – 1989) with the late Bob Parker and Simon Rice (2008 – current) reflect on their contrasting experiences of de Valois' experiment in bringing such differ-ent forms of dance together. That this curriculum initiative has continued for over fifty years is in itself testimony to its value, but still, as Kennedy found, the combination of such different styles provokes challenges, alongside positive and to some degree surprising outcomes for the stu-dents. Through his extensive experience within the English Folk Dance and Song Society from 1947, Smedley is able to provide the long view of working with Royal Ballet students at White Lodge and their connections with traditional dance festivals and events. Not content to lose such out-lets once in The Royal Ballet Company, a number of male company dancers led by Guy Niblett and Jonathan Burrows set up their own Morris team, "The Bow Street Rappers", and continued to entertain audiences abroad at official embassy engagements, in the street and at more traditional festival gatherings in the UK. As a Royal Ballet student, company member (1982 - 1992), a member of the Bow Street Rappers and now visiting teacher of National and Folk dances at White Lodge, Rice brings a double perspective to his reflections on the importance of maintaining these elements within the young ballet students' curriculum.

For logistical reasons the interviews with Ron Smedley and Simon Rice were conducted separately a short while apart. The summary below focuses primarily on their teaching and experience of folk dance with students of The Royal Ballet Schools, but inevitably their answers included wide roving reference to the many changes taking place in national and folk dances within the UK, reflecting the shifts in attitudes towards, for instance, women and girls participating in Morris dance, resurgences in folk dance popularity driven by Royal involvement (the 1951 photograph of the then Princess Elizabeth and Prince Philip square dancing in Ottawa caused a sensation), or links with rock and pop music or currently the flash mob clog dance that took Newcastle shopping centre by surprise in 2010. As de Valois had appreciated on many occasions, the building of a folk and national dance repertoire allowed students at The Royal Ballet Schools an opportunity to perform in the midst of many other dance teams drawn from around the country, particularly at the Royal Albert Hall Folk Dance Festivals.

DVD track 3

The Folk Dance recording and commentary could be viewed at this point. It consists of Ron Smedley and Simon Rice introducing and discussing several dances performed by students from The Royal Ballet School (The Jig and Rapper Dance by Year 10 students from White Lodge and the Clog Dance by Year 11 students also from White Lodge). The musician is John Graham an accordionist, and since he was a boy, the musician for the Headington Quarry Morris Dancers.

* * *

Libby Worth (L.W.) When you began to teach with Bob Parker at The Royal Ballet School on Saturday mornings, what was the initial reaction?

Ron Smedley (R.S.) We realised that we were teaching people who did not want to be taught, absolutely no question of that. They were courteous in an icy manner; I'm talking about the slightly older boys now, the little boys did what they were told, but the dominant older boys did not want to do it. I spoke to Richard Glasstone who had come from the Turkish Ballet and was teaching the senior boys ballet. I said to him that we were having this uphill struggle and that, if this continued, it's only fair that we resign because we are not going to get anywhere. He agreed that the boys did find it hard work and the words "and pointless" were not uttered but were understood. But we persevered – and we didn't resign. Twenty years later we *retired.*

L.W. All the students were training to be professional ballet dancers, so what do you think the content of these folk dance classes contributed to their training?

R.S. The short answer is, I have no idea; we just did our job and we did it as well as we could. I think what we did on the Saturday mornings, once we had got it going and without ever losing any discipline, became like a sort of youth club. The boys used to come early because there was always one of us teaching and one of us sitting out, so they could chat and tell you their problems. So it was a nice relaxed atmosphere, which could not have been part of a classical class because that was just too important. Therefore they were dancing for the fun of it. On the other hand it was not just silly nonsense. They knew that what they were doing was actually quite demanding. I remember a Yorkshire boy, saying "Oh, this is so hard". There was a satisfaction in it after the pressure of the other dance and then of course you dance in a group, whereas when you start off learning ballet you don't get into a group of dancers. The tight form of the Rapper Sword Dance (see DVD) for instance is real group work; when they go wrong, they can get really cross with each other.

L.W. You are completely reliant on each other, on everybody performing perfectly, otherwise it will all go wrong.

R.S. Yes, and each boy has a different dance, a different track, but up to a point that's true of the Morris too. Step dancing is solo. Also you are very much into the music and into the rhythm; and, if you are not rhythmic, it will show up. Dame Ninette says so herself in her writing, it shows up very quickly. She used to enjoy coming [to see the classes] when she'd retired and thought we were doing well.

L.W. Did these classes help teach those who were rhythmically weaker?

R.S. It couldn't have done them anything other than good. We didn't shout at them or anything, but yes: I remember a lad who went on into the company and he found rhythm very hard but went on to a perfectly respectable career. And the folk dance can have done him no harm. We realised quite quickly that there was material that could be put on display by both boys, and boys and girls together, in situations where the classical dance was not appropriate as it was too theatrical or required a proper setting. Whereas this could be done anywhere, in local village halls, so we did quite a lot of that, including taking the students out of the country to folk festivals. We had invitations to dance in Israel, Portugal (twice) and in France.

L.W. So it had a complete life of its own in terms of performance?

R.S. Yes, there's an organisation called CIOFF, which in French is the Conseil International des Organisations de Festivals de Folklore et d'arts Traditionnels, and we were asked to go to CIOFF festivals and also to Portugal for a festival entirely for young people. It was a marvellous experience and terrific training for what was to be part of their lives.

L.W. Then you had the Bow Street Rappers. How did they emerge?

R.S. Very early on we had a wonderful first year: you know, years have a personality all of their own, and some were keener than others, although none were a problem. One week, Bob wasn't there, we were in the salon and this was the first time I was going to meet these new boys, the door burst open and in fell these puppies [imitates small boy's voice] "Oh whamy, whamy, we'll wallop these sticks. Oh this is going to be fun". I said to Bob later, you wait till you see the new first year and they were keen. We took them to Bampton and they had lessons from the Bampton boys[5] ; all sorts of things like that. And they included Jonathan Burrows, Guy Niblett and others. Jonathan was the one who took it to the deepest level and has used it as a choreographer. There was something in it that went deep into inner self, the Englishness of it and the quality of the dancing. Even when he was working hard he was a member of a Morris club. Guy Niblett was very keen as well and, when in the company, he overheard in the office a discussion on what to do in China at occasions when the Chinese do Chinese dance at receptions; he said that, if you get wardrobe to cooperate and get a small sum of money, we'll buy some rapper swords and we'll do the Rapper Sword Dance. I think that they had kept an interest in it when they were part of the upper school even though it hadn't been part of their repertoire and they kept it going. They made up the name of the Bow Street Rappers, but they did a lot of other dances as well. If they could, once a year certainly, they would go to the Morris Ring meeting with lots of clubs. They didn't practise enough to be really good and they knew that, but they were good enough. They could do things like put a couple of double *tour en l'air* in just for fun; and the other Morris clubs you might have thought would say, "Show offs"; but they didn't;

they said, "Oh that's terrific fun". They formed the group in 1983 and they did something for me for television in 2003 so the Bow Street Rappers lasted for twenty years. They kept it going during their professional careers. So there's Stuart Cassidy being Romeo in the matinée and then outside doing the Morris in the street and then back again being Romeo – oh it's wonderful. I don't think any other professional company in the world has ever done that. It's finished now, and people still ask where the Bow Street Rappers are?

L.W. De Valois placed such importance on the inclusion of folk dance in the ballet students' curriculum for reasons you have discussed, but she also anticipated it filtering into the choreography for the company, as one of the means to create an "English" style. Have you seen this happen?

R.S. I remember Frederick Ashton coming to Cecil Sharp House to research for *La Fille mal gardée*. There is the famous clog dance for Widow Simone and nobody knows where the steps came from, there are all sorts of theories... Then there is the maypole group dancing that is all quite good fun, but I don't think that Fred was keen on English Folk Dance really. I think Jonathan [Burrows], David Bintley and William Tuckett were the three choreographers that used it [the folk dance teaching]. David Bintley was the most accepted, but he was never a pupil of ours, although he was a member of the Bow Street Rappers. But they loved it and it was nice that they loved being street dancers, nothing precious about it.

L.W. De Valois writes about the English style being neat and quick. *Neat* doesn't seem quite the right word in relation to the folk dance element?

R.S. Well, one of the old traditional Morris dancers used to say "plenty of brisk and no excitement". In other words it's cool, but with no showing off. I hope it stays part of their training.

* * *

L.W. In your role as a student learning folk dance at The Royal Ballet School, what did you gain?

Simon Rice (S.R.) I was taught by Ron and Bob so I've known them for quite some time and they were great teachers. They were with us all the way through the school and again when we were within the company and performing with the Bow Street Rappers, being a diplomatic body within a diplomatic body when we went on tour and when we were dancing in the streets when in the Eastern Block or in Russia. It was great for them and great for us.

I think that from an early age you get used to working in different dance styles, particularly if you come in at the age of 11: you come in for a year, you acclimatise yourself doing ballet every day, which is something you haven't done before; and, when you study the Morris dancing, you are already learning a new way of working and adjusting your mind accordingly. And it's much more casual, the atmosphere and the energy is not so contained, it's a little wilder, it's fun. And I think that, considering you are going to go on later in life and learn a lot more styles of dance, whether you are working with contemporary dance or with classical dance, I think it's good to be learning from an early age how to adapt your mind to learn new dance forms. The other part of course is that when you are doing ballet, it's all about being in the air, whereas when you are working with Morris, it's all about being earthy and into the ground. You have this alien style that you are learning, which is a lot of fun.

L.W. Did the Bow Street Rappers come out of the Company or was it part of the School?

S.R. They came directly out of the company, which is quite unusual as we were already pretty busy, but there was a desire and I think that came through Jonathan Burrows and Guy Niblett wanting to set up a group. They knew a number of us would be up for doing it as well, so we ended up with six or seven people from the beginning. So, as well as having our ballet repertoire we also had our Morris dancing repertoire that we took with us.

L.W. So did it stay the same people or change over time?

S.R. It changed over time. The original group was Jonathan Burrows, Guy Niblett, myself, Stephen Beagley Anthony Dowson and Mick Coleman was always kind of there as well. He would come along to rehearsals, ready to step in and he was one of The Royal Ballet's top dancers. Then it changed over time obviously with people coming and going within the company and of course they were still teaching the folk dancing in White Lodge, so you always had fresh people coming in and rejoining.

L.W. How long did it keep going?

S.R. I've spoken to Ron about it because I left around 1992-93, but he seems to think it was very solid for about ten years, which was about the time I left. But it was in and out for another ten years; Stuart Cassidy and people like that were within the group. So probably within the last ten years it's petered out a bit more. We're hoping now that with the fresh crop in White Lodge learning the Rapper Sword Dance perhaps a similar thing might happen later, if that is what they want to do.

L.W. Turning now to your experience as a teacher, you've been teaching at White Lodge for how long?

S.R. About three years. There were a few other people before me after Ron and Bob. I think it had quietened down a bit and I was asked by David Yow.[6] I think he was concerned that it was going to stop completely.

L.W. Had you taught this kind of dance prior to teaching at White Lodge or was it new for you as well?

S.R. It was pretty new for me actually and that's why I took a while to think about it. I had often been asked to teach ballet and I just didn't feel I had anything to contribute that someone else couldn't offer. So when I was asked about the folk dancing I thought well this will be great because I will learn something in the process, because I have to learn from Ron and hopefully there is a two-way learning process going on as then I'm teaching the students.

L.W. Do you feel the students gain a lot from learning the folk dances?

S.R. I think they do in terms of how they use their minds; that is probably the most important thing. If they are learning, as we were, from eleven years old to work in different styles, that's going to be hugely beneficial for them and that will only accelerate as they get older. And I've heard some of the teachers say that actually the boys' ability to learn is slightly above that of the girls. I think that the Morris dancing has something to do with that; it's such a different skill compared to learning ballet.

L.W. You are teaching students a range of different dances: the Morris, the Rapper, the jig and step dance, all of which presumably demand different skills?

S.R Yes: for a start the Morris is more earth-bound than ballet. You do propel yourself into the air, but the earth is the important thing, whereas in ballet you're just constantly trying to escape gravity. Clog dancing has a very different skill factor. We get boys coming in and they have obviously done tap dancing and they take to the clog very quickly. I had one student in particular, now in year eight, who had never done tap, but who is absolutely phenomenal in his ability to pick up clog dancing. It's a really difficult thing to do. Ballet is a totally different form to tap or clogging but, because he's already used to using his mind in a particular way and adapting, I can see his mind working and he's up already with the other students who were tappers. And of course the rapper sword dancing is particularly about team work; when there are five of you working that closely and that quickly together, every moment has to be right. With the boys that I've been working with in year ten, you reach the point when you have to drill them because they have to understand what makes this particular dance work. Of course team work is exactly what they are going to need when they work in a corps de ballet. They are going to be spending a large portion of their lives working in this way, so the sooner they get to learn that, the easier for them. They can step into a corps de ballet and become an asset. Rather than learning the trade, they know it already.

L.W. It's a different kind of teamwork, isn't it? Performances seem to be such fun, so there's a kind of pleasure in the way they are working?

S.R. Yes, it's exactly the same kind of thing that we had when we were in the company. We would be doing various roles and would have different statuses within the company and yet when we came together as a rapper team we were equals. I think these students already have a sense of that. Basically, they are competing with each other in the school, they are friends but they compete with each other. But when they come into something like the rapper, they become equals and they can have a sense of joy at being equal with each other and learning exactly the same things and making it a team. I think they enjoy that as much as we did.

L.W. Both you and Ron have suggested that learning these dances can help students improve their sense of rhythm and musicality. Have you experienced this in your teaching?

R.S Yes, it's interesting that Ron said that he noticed the students who struggled with musicality. I never really had any concept of that, that children would struggle with musicality, because most people I come into contact with have an innate sense of musicality. It was absolutely true that in the same way as people can struggle to perfect their technique; this is another skill that they have to understand. They have to learn how music works and of course that becomes more complex and sophisticated the older you get. There were definitely students who struggled, but I think that the struggle came from learning a different kind of movement as well, at the same time. If you think about [folk] music, it's quite basic, it's quite repetitive but, not only are they listening to unfamiliar music, they are learning brand new steps. It's not so much that they are unmusical, but that they struggle to put the two together. You have different types of students; you have the students who push forwards and the ones who sit back. Those who sit back also sit back on the music, so you have to propel them a bit further forward to get *with* the music. There's a psychological element involved as well, I think, but certainly when you put the two aspects together, the dance and the music, it's not easy and definitely something they have to learn. Once they get past the first year it's rare to see a child who struggles with the music. They spend their whole time listening and working with music; it becomes an innate skill for them.

L.W. When I spoke to Ron about the teaching of folk dance to girls in The Royal Ballet School, he gave a history of why certain ceremonial dances were traditionally assigned to men and boys. He addressed the complex history of the development of folk dance and folk dance revivals in the UK and the way that views have split and altered regarding women's and girls' involvement. We do not have the space to develop this complex theme, but Ron was keen that the girls gained experience of national dances and he and Bob taught mixed classes during one of their sessions on Saturday mornings. As the current teacher, what is your view on the inclusion of girls in the folk dance teaching at White Lodge?

S.R. I have no problem with women doing whatever they want to do in dance: it's absolutely fine. And folk dance is not different; it's the richer for it actually. There are some fantastic women's Morris teams. I did a rehearsal with a team who are a very good rapper side and I've also been to watch them. Some of the best teams come from Scotland and are all women's teams. In terms of muscular development for young girls at White Lodge, I would have my doubts as to whether it is a good thing. It's an important stage in their development and ultimately they are going to be ballet dancers so you have to think of it in those terms. I can't think about it in just folk dance terms, it would be wrong; and even when we work with the students I'm always thinking does this work for them as ballet dancers not just as folk dancers? We have the case sometimes where we have dancers who may not be doing the style in a relaxed enough manner. They spend their whole time in ballet bolt upright, stretching their spines towards the sky; and what they do with us is totally different, relaxing the spine. But you have to remember that the children are growing and to do a relaxed dance just makes them look weak. So we spend time making allowances for them and maybe working with them so their backs are strong, because it helps them perform better. In that way they are getting benefits in both areas. I'm a firm believer that we are not just teaching folk dance, we are teaching skills that can help them in ballet and other forms of dance as well. I think that they have to work hand-in-hand. I am teaching girls for the summer school this year [2011] that is being held at White Lodge. So the teaching of the girls has already started and I just need to think about the best thing to teach them, whether it's going to come from the Morris repertoire or whether it's going to come from something slightly different.

L.W. Ninette de Valois considered UK folk dance important for the development of English Ballet – that is the development of an English style or form of ballet. What are your thoughts on the relationship between folk dance and the development of ballet in this country?

S.R. I do not think (I'm happy to be proven wrong) that ballet and Morris dancing particularly work together in a choreographic capacity. I haven't seen it work; and even if I were to try it myself, I think it would take a great deal of thought to do it properly. In terms of contemporary dance I think it might be more possible to free things up a bit more. But in ballet you have got such a strong and rigid technique and in its own way Morris dancing is like that as well. They are somewhat conflicting, for me personally.

L.W. Yes and there aren't that many examples of choreography for ballet that do include both.

S.R. Well, the obvious one is *La Fille mal gardée*, which is the one that is always cited; but they are very rare. For me, the one that works really well is *Hobson's Choice* [by David Bintley]; but there are not that many examples where you would say you have to do folk dance because of these ballets. I think folk dancing has its own benefits and is beneficial to ballet in other aspects, not just because we do these ballets.

L.W. So for you the value in learning folk and national dances lies in the way the process helps to broaden your mind and accelerate the ability to adapt to different stylistic demands?

S.R. Yes, I think it's important for the students (and I'm looking retrospectively as well) that they can learn different styles of dance from a young age. When they become adults they will be learning various contemporary dance forms, modern forms or choreographing in new ways, moving into new ideas of moving. And of course there are many balletic styles as well, as you can see moving round the world. Certainly as an individual, I don't believe I was that quick in learning when I was young and I still struggle with things now; but being able to have that within my schedule every week, learning something different from an early age, can only be of benefit. The fact that they are learning Morris dance and many other dances from eleven years old opens their minds; they develop this capacity to learn like sponges, they soak everything up. I think Ron's view is that, if you are going to do it, you should do it properly or not at all. I certainly understand that argument, but then you have to look and say, well these are not *folk dancers*. They *do* folk dancing, but these are ballet dancers; and actually it is a good part of their training to learn as many aspects of dance as possible; in that way with the amount of our dancing – the stick dances, the handkerchiefs, the clog, the rapper, the jigs, so many different types – they are going to be reaping the benefits for many years to come.

L.W. It makes them versatile.

S.R It does. If you think of individuals who have come out of The Royal Ballet Company, they can use all the skills: Jonathan Burrows, for example. They can use those skills in other areas and most of them are very successful. Russell Maliphant is another. Sylvie [Guillem] is from France, but she's worked in the same way: she's come from a big institution and moved out and is working with mind and body in different ways. You can really foresee a time where dancers will be doing everything, every type of dance you have and also many other skills. I see it's there, it's already happening. They may not even be called dancers in the future; there may be some other word for these people who have this extraordinary capacity to learn many things, many different types of physical training, and incorporate it into their work. It's a very exciting time actually to see things opening out.

L.W. Do you think we might see a group similar to The Bow Street Rappers come back?

S.R. Well, we already have the "White Lodge Rappers", it would be up to them if they wished to continue, and if they did, what name they gave the side. I think it's a seed that we'll plant, but I wouldn't want to push anyone into something they didn't want to do just for the sake of tradition. The students are very busy, but those boys seem to enjoy it and the Rapper is the big dance of the year, and all the years want to learn it. I know the feeling I had from dancing it; and it's fantastic in terms of the teamwork. You go beyond thinking, you slot in, your mind is on this pathway with four other individuals and it's a great experience to have. The chance has been given to them, if they wish to take that up. The other possibility of course, if they are not too busy, is it could happen in the upper school. But I think that that is the most difficult place for it to happen, their learning becomes quicker, everything accelerates and they are getting ready to audition for companies. There is usually a year or two when you join a company like The Royal Ballet where you are kicking your heels for a bit, learning the ropes, then that's the time they could take it on. I would be happy to teach them, if it's something they wanted.

L.W. Are these dances shown within folk events or festivals, like once they were at the Royal Albert Hall, or does this tend not to happen anymore?

S.R. Ron's on to me on that one already; he's not one to miss an opportunity! I have actually talked about it with a couple of friends who do the festivals, and they would be really interested in getting the students from

White Lodge. If they could have an opportunity to perform in places like the Albert Hall or elsewhere, I think it would be great for them, just to be performing; it doesn't matter what dance they are doing. They get plenty of opportunities to do ballet from White Lodge upwards, but to be performing something like the Rapper – people love that dance. We are looking to having the White Lodge Rappers involved in a Rapper dance competition which would be a great experience for them.

L.W. To see other people bringing different folk dances must be very interesting as well.

S.R. Well within White Lodge they are already learning a lot of national dances. But to get together with other groups, perhaps from around the world, would be fantastic for their education. There are lots of people to consult about this; but the earlier we can get them on there, the better. If we were to get the eleven-year-olds doing a stick dance at the Albert Hall... Fantastic! But the Rapper is the one to bring the house down; that would be a great one to use. The other thing that I think is great that seems to be happening at the moment is people are starting to play with the original form, so that it has a chance to expand. The choreography that we have now is much more sophisticated than it was thirty or forty years ago. I think it is great that people are working choreographically to enable folk dancing to move on in the future. It will not just be something traditional, it will blossom into other forms, which means it will survive traditionally and in new ways. I think Ron is a staunch traditionalist, but I think even he would say in the end that this is a good thing.

De Valois and Labanotation

Ann Hutchinson Guest

The focus in this article is on my experience of de Valois' remarkable organisational ability and attention to detail, both quite extraordinary. But first, a little background: I had met the Laban dance notation system early on in my dance study and became quite proficient at it. Notating takes time – as does writing a letter, a music composition or a book. Was there another system that was quicker or easier but also as flexible and capable of detail? What else existed?

This led to my investigating both historical and contemporary systems. My research covered eighty-six systems since the fifteenth century. Of these I studied twenty-seven in detail and made translations of eight. I published two books on the subject: *Dance Notation: the Process of Recording Movement on Paper* (1984) and *Choreographics* (1989), a comparison of thirteen different systems.

In 1947 I met Balanchine who became interested in and studied Labanotation with me. He understood the basis of the system and, after three lessons, he notated the theme step from his ballet, *Theme and Variations*. In 1948 he asked me to notate his Bizet ballet, *Symphony in C.* Following this, I persuaded him of the extra value derived from notating during the creation process. For his ballet *Orpheus* I was there notating from the beginning. I notated for him during the next twelve years, when he considered a work important enough and had the money. People did not realise how strapped for funds City Ballet was in those days, which was why his ballets had no scenery and very simple costumes. Each season was launched on credit.

By early 1954 de Valois had heard of Balanchine's use of notation and came to visit me at the Dance Notation Bureau in New York. In London, *The Times* of 2 April 1954 contained the announcement that Labanotation was to be taught at the Sadler's Wells School. In October 1954 I was in London and had lunch with de Valois at the Nag's Head. We discussed plans, ways and means, to introduce Labanotation into the curriculum of the Sadler's Wells School. Looking back, I now realise that I should have also talked business and pinned down more details concerning the job.

De Valois had already given much thought to her dance notation plans. The first three school year groups were to have short sessions on notation at the end of their ballet class, three times a week. The next three forms would have longer sessions and the senior students would be given an hour and a half twice a week. The plan was for the members of staff at the School and also members of the Company to start taking classes. De Valois gave me a copy of the ballet syllabus, which I at once translated into Labanotation in preparation for its use. (See material included at the end of this chapter.) The whole programme would go into effect as soon as the Labanotation teacher arrived.

One of our teachers, Iona Mackenzie, a Canadian with a strong ballet technique, was interested in the job. We were concerned when no written contract was forthcoming, but were told that Covent Garden Opera House worked on verbal agreements. There was also a slight hitch in that de Valois took Mackenzie's interest in the job to mean that she would be paying her own fare to England, whereas I had stipulated that the fare be paid by the Opera House. Before the programme could get started, we were informed that, because the School roof was leaking, two studios were out of commission and so the notation programme had to be postponed.

Early in September 1955, I received a phone call from de Valois, who was in New York at the start of the Company's USA tour. She apologised for the delay in getting the programme started and said, "But we are definitely going ahead". She added, "I feel I should tell you that a member of the Company has developed a notation system, and I thought we should give it a trial".

I replied, "I think we should look into all new ideas". To which she responded, "Oh! I am so glad to hear you say that, *but we are definitely going ahead with Labanotion*". Five days later I arrived in London. A notation colleague phoned. "You had better sit down," she said. "Yesterday there was a Covent Garden press meeting at which Rudolf Benesh, taking advantage of de Valois' absence, announced that his notation system had been *officially adopted by the Sadler's Wells Company.*"

De Valois returned two months later to face a very awkward situation. I met with her. "What is going on?" I asked. She was very embarrassed. After collecting her thoughts, she said, "In France they have a dance notation system, don't they?" I replied, "There is the Conté System, but it is hardly used." "Well," she said, "they have their system in France, you have your system in America and we will have ours here!"

"But Madam," I replied, "what if every country had a different music notation – there would be no exchange, no sharing." She waived that aside: "I want something quick and easy for my Company, a British system." That statement echoed what Philip Richardson, then editor of the *Dancing Times*, had said in 1936 after our German colleague, Albrecht Knust, had given a talk in London on the Laban system. "This has been most interesting," Richardson said, "now we should have a competition for someone to design a British Dance Notation System."

In 1955 the English dance world was disturbed about the notation situation but no one felt they could challenge de Valois, so as a result nothing was done. From 1955 on, no comparison of systems was made, no trials. A few were suggested, but Benesh refused to take part. De Valois had made her decision and could not go back on it. There are, in fact, more details to this story but, in total, it still boils down to a political decision.

What if de Valois had carried through her plan with the already more highly developed and established Labanotation system? With her forcefulness and influence we might now have generations of dance-literate dancers. We have some examples of such integration in the States. The Philadelphia Dance Academy, which featured modern dance, saw that all staff members were familiar with Labanotation. Starting with eight-year-old children, it was used throughout the School. If a movement was not understood, the teacher would grab a piece of chalk and write on the green wall what the students were doing and what the movement should be. Before class, a movement phrase would be written down on the board for the students to study: "We are going to work on this today, so take a look now." Books at different levels were published to support this curriculum. This education produced a thirteen-year-old student who notated her own choreography and performed it at a concert with the Philadelphia Orchestra.

The Hartford Ballet School also adopted Labanotation into the curriculum, all the teachers being familiar with this system. To begin with, the eight-year-old incoming children were divided into two year groups: one group had the notation integrated in the daily teaching of ballet, the other did not. At the end of the year, the question was: did the Labanotation group lag behind the other group in their ability in ballet? Not at all, the children had a clearer understanding of what they were doing, as well as being able to read notation. For this programme a special notation ballet book was produced, which the children could take home.

This programme progressed well, until teachers had to be replaced, and new teachers were not willing to learn the notation. It is my experience that teachers encountering Labanotation prefer to dismiss it. It is too difficult, not needed, not for them. They do not understand the process, the value, the movement investigation and the understanding that learning Labanotation entails.

At the Royal Academy of Dance, during my twenty years teaching there, I heard teachers discuss the need for sessions on movement analysis. They were not aware that this is what takes place in the notation class. Take the correct articulation in performing a *glissade*. It is a seemingly simple step – basically a step followed by a closing – but the footwork is difficult to master in detail.

With de Valois' plan for the staff to study notation, there would have been a *common language, a common movement analysis* and *understanding*. Where this situation existed in certain USA colleges, it has proved valuable both for teachers and students.

And so in 1955 the pieces fell into place. De Valois had the vision to have a notator attached to the Company, an example that was to be followed around the world. She also twisted the Arts Council's arm to get money for the Benesh Institute. Balanchine, even if he had had the money, never had the vision to understand the value of referring to dance scores during rehearsals.

To conclude, when I married Ivor Guest and moved to London, I dreaded running into de Valois. When it happened at Covent Garden, she came towards me, extended her hand warmly and said, "How nice to have you here with us." A fearsome lady? Yes! But also a gracious lady.

Coda

In preparation for establishing the study of Labanotation at The Royal Ballet School, de Valois provided me with copies of the classroom syllabus for the *barre* work and also the centre practice. I then translated these into Labanotation in anticipation of their use by the teachers, students and children. The resulting sheets still exist in my library. Here are three examples showing the correlation between syllabus and notation scores.

SADLER'S WELLS BALLET SCHOOL 1.

ELEMENTARY ROUTINE SIDE PRACTICE

For children between 8 and 10 years side practice should be from 1st and 3rd positions. Pliés should always start in the 1st position. The development between 9 and 10 years decides when the pupil can get into 5th. (In 5th the heel is to touch the joint of the big toe, and not the tip).

Later, when the pupil is more advanced, pliés can be executed from both positions of 4th (open = 4th opposite 1st; and crossed = 4th oppo- site 5th; avoiding the effacé position), as well as in 5th.

The arrangement of the side practice should be such that the student commences with the small work, progressing to the high work at the end. The 3rd or 5th positions are used throughout, according to age and standard. The arm is left down at the side for all ground work, and bent across the chest for raised work.

Whenever an exercise is commenced from one position and then re- peated from another there must be a complete break between the two, and the feet placed in the new position.

The Elementary Side Practice has been divided, and the exercises marked "A" are for beginners. Exercises marked "B" should not be attempted until those marked "A" have been thoroughly mastered.

mpo

1. Plié

      Absolute beginners are to do pliés facing the barre

    "A" In 1st, 2nd and 3rd. (one set in each position).
    "B" In 1st, 2nd and 5th. (one set on each side).

$\frac{3}{4}$

      2 demi-pliés (2 beats each) ⎫
      1 slow full plié (4 beats) ⎬ 8 beats
      In 1st, 2nd, 3rd or 5th in front and behind.
      (The 4th position is not used until later).

2. Battement Tendu

    "A" En croix from 1st with straight legs for 8 beats (2 sets), and
        with demi-plié for 8 beats (2 sets). (Only one set of each
        for beginners).

$\frac{2}{4}$

    "B" En croix from 3rd or 5th with straight legs for 8 beats (2 sets),
        and with demi-plié for 8 beats (2 sets).

        (It is recommended not to use a demi-plié in this exercise for
        the first few months of training.)

9 & 10½

Sadler's Well. Ballet School

List of steps covered by the various forms.

FORM I

Barre
Plié
Battement Tendu
Battement Glissé
Rond de Jambe à Terre
ent Frappé — Assemblé Soutenu
Battement — Rond de Jambe en l'air
Battement Retiré
Developpé
Demi-rond de Jambe
Grand Rond de Jambe
Grand Battement
Battement ~~Developpé~~
Battement en Cloche

Centre Practice
All barre exercises plus:-
Temps Lié with Chassé Foundation
Temps Lié with Pas de Basque Founda
Pirouettes en dehors from 2nd and :
Pirouettes en dedans from 2nd and :

Adage 4 Arabesques (Russian)
Attitudes
Developpé in 8 positions of t
Demi-rond de Jambe (unch
Grand rond de Jambe

Petite Batterie
Changement Battu
Entrechat Trois devant and derrière
Entrechat Quatre
Royale ouverte
Royale Fermée

Preparatory Point Work
Relevés and rises in all positions
Echappé relevé to all open positions
Retiré relevé - devant derrière and passé
Picked-up pas de bourrée X
Posé

Allegro and Steps
Changement
Soubresaut 5
Saute in all positions
Echappé sauté open & closed
Assemblé - devant, derrière
over, under, en avant,
en arrière and de côté
Assemblé - coupé.
? Retiré sauté
Sissonne - ordinaire, pass
fermée en avant, fermée en
arrière, fermée over, fermée
Jeté - petit, ordinaire, and
grand jeté - surplace, en a
en arrière, de côté and by ½ t
~~The~~ Grand jeté en avant
~~Ballotté~~
Ballonné sauté
Pas de chat
Temps Levé
Glissade - devant, derrière
over, under, en avant, en a
Pas de bourré - devant, derriè
over and under with front o
back foot - en avant, en arr

SADLER'S WELLS BALLET SCHOOL

Plies in 1st., 2nd., 3rd., & 5th.

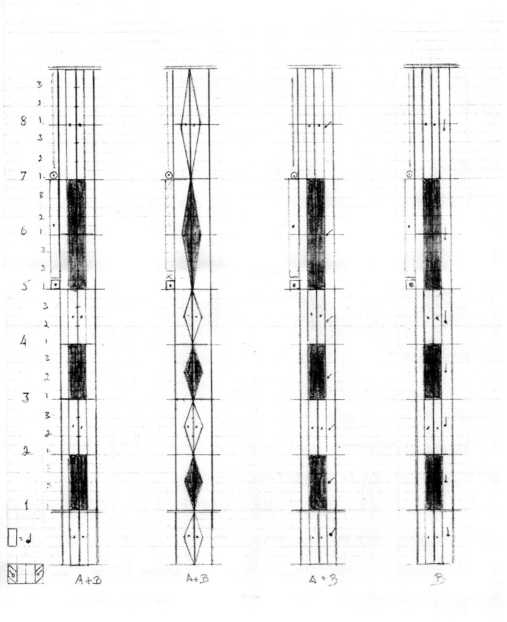

De Valois' role in the development and dissemination of Benesh Movement Notation

Robert Penman and Victoria Watts

Victoria Watts: Robert Penman and I independently proposed chapters on the topic of de Valois' support for dance notation but from quite different points of view: Robert as a lecturer in dance and in this context Secretary to the Benesh Institute Endowment Fund; myself as a notator and doctoral candidate in Cultural Studies, whose research looks at changes in embodied subjectivity as revealed through changes in dance notation. In order to avoid repetition in the areas where we overlapped, we have combined our work into one chapter. Robert addresses why de Valois was committed to adopting a notation system and why she chose Benesh Movement Notation (BMN) over any possible alternatives. I address the significance of this choice for the successful development of BMN.

Before getting into the meat of our discussion it is worth taking a moment to address the inevitable questions about relevance. What value is there in dance notation in an age of cheap multimedia? I always have to address this question when I present my research, even when I am not making any kind of argument about contemporary uses of notation. The arguments have been well rehearsed[1] but I will bullet point some of the more common ones here.

• The written score is always accessible whereas film and video formats are frequently rendered obsolete by new technologies
• Notation does not 'show' the dance but rather provides a set of instructions on what to dance
• Film and video capture performance whereas notation aims to record choreographic intention
• Notation is not hampered by choice between camera framing close-up detail or overall stage picture
• Learning from video requires awkward right-left reversal that is avoided by notation
• Notation can show detail of contacts and support for partnering and depth of spatial patterning more clearly than video
• Notation score can be appended and updated whenever changes are made or alternatives put in place for different casts.

Even if it were the case that notation has become obsolete or that it never was up to the job of recording choreography, Robert makes the case that notation was very important to de Valois.

Robert Penman: My interest in this subject was sparked by a particular letter that I received from de Valois in 1988, when I was briefly the Secretary and Archivist at the Benesh Institute in Margravine Gardens in West London. De Valois was on the mailing list. She wrote that she was glad to receive the good news about BMN from a newsletter that we had sent out. She then commented that at the time (in the early 1950s) it was really a very difficult decision, whether or not to choose "the established German system" by which she meant Labanotation, or the new, untried British one, her description of Benesh Movement Notation. From her comments I draw certain obvious conclusions. First, de Valois was convinced about the importance of notation to her dance company. There was no doubt in her mind, she was going to have to choose a notation system to record her Company's repertoire. The choice was simply about which one.

This commitment to notation of any kind was in itself unusual. It was not completely unheard of, but against the tide of dance history and culture in the twentieth century. None of the other major players showed any interest in notation. Diaghilev, Balanchine, the two major Russian/Soviet companies, the Paris Opera, the Royal Danish Ballet were all by and large notation free zones. In modern dance – apart from Laban himself – none of the leading choreographers faithfully adopted or promoted the use of notations systems in the way that de Valois did in the 1950s. Although Massine and Nijinsky had both experimented with their own forms of notation, neither had taken root to become established or widely used systems. I think I am right in asserting that de Valois was exceptional in her use of notation.

Second, de Valois' choice of a notation system was, at least in part, influenced by nationality. Strictly speaking, the authors of the two notation systems that she had in mind were both descended from families in Mitteleuropa, sons of the old Hapsburg empire; but to de Valois, Rudolf von Laban and Rudolf Benesh and their notation systems were clearly distinguished by nationality: one was German and one was British. To what extent her decision was influenced by that is hard to judge at this distance. The Sadler's Wells Ballet toured extensively and was seen as contributing to the war effort. She chose to use British dancers after the war. So, her choice of a British notation system would at least be consistent with her overall management of the Company. Ann Hutchinson Guest, was, understandably, disappointed by de Valois' decision.[2]

In opting for Benesh Movement Notation de Valois knew that she was taking a calculated risk. Her letter to me reflected the anxiety that she felt about the decision. The system that she chose to use was new and had never been put to the test. It was a risk. Her relief was palpable: BMN had proven to be a robust and effective system.

VW: When I first learned the basics of Labanotation and BMN, each system was presented to me as though it were fixed. These are the symbols, these are the rules, this is how you read them, and this is how you apply them when writing. As I advanced in my studies, I discovered that neither system was immutable: both were subject to review, adaptation, and modification. I suppose I had imagined that dance notation systems were purely the product of their inventors' ingenuity and that they emerged, fully formed, ready to be offered to a largely ambivalent dance world. This view of the invention of dance notation makes it possible to believe that these taxonomies of symbols are adopted or rejected, based on the inherent merits of the particular system, and it perhaps fuels the wholly unhelpful debate about which system is better: BMN or Labanotation.

I suggest that dance notation systems are better understood as visual-kinaesthetic practices shaped by their users, by the institutions in which they are used, and by the dance forms they document. To use a bodily metaphor, the Benesh system was still a mere skeleton when Joan and Rudolf Benesh presented it to de Valois in 1955. They had already spent nearly eight years working on the development of what they hoped would be a "complete, feasible and practical" system.[3] In choosing this skeletal system over the more fully-fleshed Labanotation, de Valois provided an opportunity for meat and bones to be added and for the integrity of the system as a whole to be tested in professional circumstances.

Teething problems were worked out as early choreologists such as Faith Worth and Elphine Allen recorded new works and established repertoire at The Royal Ballet.[4] Problems or questions about the theory that arose from work in the studio, along with suggestions for their remedy, were referred back to Mr. Benesh for final judgment. Although the Beneshes envisioned a general dance notation (the curriculum of the early training course attests to this), there is no doubt that the ballet context in which the system was used affected the development of BMN. Early exposure to the rigours of professional use ensured that BMN became a robust tool, fit for purpose in the professional dance world. If de

Valois had not decided to adopt the Benesh system for use by The Royal Ballet, it seems unlikely that BMN would have developed any further at all.[5]

This institutional support was crucial for providing the context in which BMN practitioners had the opportunity to test the system's assumptions and develop its theory and application accordingly. Such support ensured that BMN spread throughout much of the ballet world. The relatively rapid spread of the system was due, in part, to its use for recording repertory by Sir Kenneth MacMillan and Sir Frederick Ashton and for recording a number of The Royal Ballet's legacy ballets: versions of the classics received from the Russian repétiteur, Sergeyev, and shorter works created for The Ballets Russes. If companies abroad wanted to stage an authoritative *Sleeping Beauty* or the latest hit by MacMillan, it was most expedient to send the score and the Company notator to set the dance and to have the choreographer come in for the last few rehearsals to coach and polish. Having seen how efficiently new repertory could be transplanted within companies, and having seen the vibrant creative relationship between Monica Parker and Sir Kenneth MacMillan, ballet companies in Canada, South Africa, Australia and Europe soon began to appoint their own company notators.[6] This in turn presented further opportunities for the BMN system to be tested, challenged and developed in relation to the movement experiments of other choreographers.

De Valois' choice of Benesh over Labanotation was decisive in establishing BMN as a credible notation system. However, had she chosen to adopt Labanotation, we might now find a more unified field of dance notation. Energies expended on a notation "turf war" might instead have been spent promoting the use of notation in dance more widely.

RP: Ninette de Valois leaves the dance world with some intriguing and challenging questions. First, why was she committed to the use of notation in the way that she was? The answer must lie in part in the origin and development of her Company. She and Frederick Ashton had made new works for the fledgling Vic-Wells Ballet in the 1930s, but she had ambitions that went beyond that, ambitions to build and perform a repertoire that reflected the great canon of European theatre dance, as she understood it, and in doing so to assert her own company's bona fides and status. And so Nicholas Sergeyev was summoned from Paris to teach *Coppélia* in 1933, and then *Giselle*, *Swan Lake* and *The Nutcracker* the following year, and finally *The Sleeping Beauty* in 1939. His productions were based on the Stepanov notation scores that he had brought with him from St Petersburg, so a form of notation had become essential to de Valois' ambitions for her Company. She and Ashton may have "filled in" the missing details and assisted in the staging of these productions, but she had witnessed the way in which choreography had been captured in a notation system and then passed on faithfully to a future generation of dancers.

In re-staging these nineteenth-century ballets, she challenged the traditional attrition rate, as new work is constantly lost. Today, choreographers, or their legatees, are busily setting up foundations to preserve their legacy, and all sorts of strategies are being devised to achieve that end. De Valois addressed that crucial question well before she retired. To have done so in the way she did showed remarkable perspicacity and bold leadership.

Today, I have with me my Grade 1 Certificate in Benesh Movement Notation, which I gained while I was a pupil at The Royal Ballet School, at White Lodge. Now, either de Valois was wasting my time, simply keeping me out of mischief, or she intended that her dancers should at least read notation and in that sense be literate – like musicians. That has not happened and I believe I am right in saying that The Royal Ballet School has now dropped notation from its curriculum.[7]

Despite the invention and development of workable notation systems, dancers, generally, still do not read notation of any description. It is perceived to be a specialist skill in which dancers are dependent on experts. The dance community has maintained an oral culture; dance works are still inherited body-to-body, dancer-to-dancer in the studio. This dependency has consequences: dancers have to be shown or told what to do and then they have to remember it and reproduce it faithfully from memory. The advent of viable notation systems has not changed or challenged this traditional approach in most dance companies. Indeed, this applies equally to the world of dance scholarship, where only a minority of dance scholars read and use notation regularly in their work.

But why should anyone bother with dance notation – and this is the provocation of de Valois' legacy – when there is nothing published to read? There are hundreds of BMN scores, but they are all in private libraries, and the guardians of those scores often seem too anxious about copyright, which has frequently been cited as a barrier to publication.

Indeed, nearly sixty years since its invention, Benesh Movement Notation itself has yet to be definitively published as a complete system. There are some introductory guides to it but nothing that provides a full account of BMN as a whole system. If usage bestows meaning and currency to language, as Wittgenstein argued, it must be true that usage will validate, maintain and develop movement notation systems, as Watts has outlined. The good news is that the Benesh Institute, now based at the Royal Academy of Dance, is about to publish the system in its entirety online. I would argue, however, that it is only meaningful to do so, if there are scores to read. This remains both an elusive possibility and a challenge.

Will the advent of digital technology – the possibility of reading not only the entire BMN system but also scores on-line – offer a solution that has so far eluded the dance community? Is a form of Kindle or IPAD technology the key that opens the door to the benefits of BMN, the viable notation system that de Valois bestowed on the dance world? The cost of any other forms of publication would appear to be prohibitive, given the limited market. But these new technologies may have the potential to transform the use and application of movement notation – an opportunity not to be missed.

Benesh Movement Notation and Labanotation: an overview

Victoria Watts

DVD track 4

Readers are encouraged to watch the recording of a student performance of the extract being discussed and notated, while they are reading this chapter.

A multitude of dance notation systems were invented in the twentieth century but of those only three have established any traction within the dance community: Benesh Movement Notation [BMN], Eshkol-Wachmann Notation, and Labanotation. Each offers the notator a particular conceptual framework for analysis and documentation of human movement. As discussed in earlier chapters, de Valois considered adopting Labanotation for use by her ballet companies before she opted to throw the weight of her support behind the then untested BMN. Here I illustrate these two systems and, rather than drawing a comparative analysis between the systems, I give a brief description of the key features of each.

I notated a short phrase, and the transition into it, from The Betrayed Girl's solo in *The Rake's Progress*.[1] These are not authoritative score excerpts: rather these are first impression drafts, as such incomplete, taken from my observation of the video of Nicola Katrak's performance.[2] I have not aimed to capture all the nuances of the performance but rather to provide an outline of the movement in terms of body design and timing. The level of detail in each extract is roughly equivalent, although different features of the movement come to the fore depending on the system I have used. For example, in the BMN score the flexion of the wrists in bar two is more striking than the flexion of the elbows during that same movement. By contrast, in the Labanotation example, the contraction of the arms and the orientation of the palms of the hand are made more explicit. In either instance I could add more detail to highlight wrist flexion in the Labanotation score or orientation of the palms in the BMN score. Any errors in these examples should be taken as the fault of the notator and not as flaws in the systems themselves.

It is immediately apparent that the BMN stave is modelled on that used for music. It is read from left to right and divided into bars just as you would expect. Here, I have indicated a time signature of three beats per bar. Three areas of the stave are used for distinct types of information about the movement being analysed and documented. In broad terms, information about body design and body action are shown on the five line stave itself; information about rhythm, tempo, phrasing and dynamics goes above stave and information about direction, location in space and travel go below stave.

The five horizontal stave lines refer to planes at floor level, knee height, waist height, shoulder level and top of head. You can see above that I have marked off the top stave with dotted lines as well as with bar lines at the beginning, middle and end of the stave. I have included them so that you can see how the notation is organised into 'frames' of movement, much like the frames of filmstrip. It would take too many words to describe the whole of the phrase I have notated here, but it may help to know that the first three frames of the first bar shows the dancer standing in 5th position, right foot in front, palms of the hands on the waist. She then turns her head to look right then left. The final frame of this bar occurs on the "and" count and shows the preparatory action into the step and turn that starts the phrase on count one of the following bar.

The edges of each frame mark the extent to which a straight leg can extend sideways from the body and the centre of the frame relates to the centre line of the dancer's body. On the two bottom staves I have not included these guides. Hopefully you can see how easily the eye adjusts to reading the notation in frames quite automatically.   The horizontal lines of the stave and the vertical reference of centre line and frame boundaries provide a grid upon which the extremities of the limbs can be marked to show body position. The depth dimension is indicated by use of one of three basic signs (a horizontal dash – level with the body, a vertical tick – in front of the body, a dot – behind the body). It is not easy to see those basic signs in this example, because they have been combined with other signs to indicate wrist direction and flexion.

The various positions that can be plotted from frame to frame are animated by the use of movement lines and step, jump and slide lines. Movement lines show the path a limb may draw in space when moving between positions. I find the idea of key framing from animation quite useful here. It is not that BMN prioritises static positions over fluid motion but rather that the positions marked within frames serve as anchor points to help reader and writer orient themselves within the ongoing flow of movement action.

The Labanotation below shows exactly the same phrase of movement as the BMN. This score should be read from the bottom of the page to the top. These staves are also marked off into bars, which I have numbered to the left of each stave. The three slightly heavier stave lines help orient the reader's eye to the vertical columns of the stave. The centre line bisects the dancer's body and also serves as a time line. In general the length of the symbols indicates the length of time taken to complete the actions they describe. Thus, for Labanotation time is visualised as an ongoing flow whereas in BMN that same flow is implicit. Due to the complexity of the movement recorded here, the basic signs within Labanotation that indicate direction and level for gestures and steps are hard to pick out amidst the array of other symbols that either modify this information or add detail in terms of specification of body part, limb flexion, rotation, and hand-to-body contact.

Broadly speaking, on the Labanotation stave, symbols plotted to the left of the centre line refer to actions by body parts on the left of the body and symbols on the right of the centre line refer to actions by body parts on the right. For fundamentals such as gestures of the legs and arms, there are dedicated columns. In my example, the arms are written in the third column out from the main stave lines. Gestures of the legs are written in the column to the inside of the main stave lines. The head is always written to the far side on the right whereas information about room facings is placed far out to the left.

I am often asked which system I think works better and about the proc-

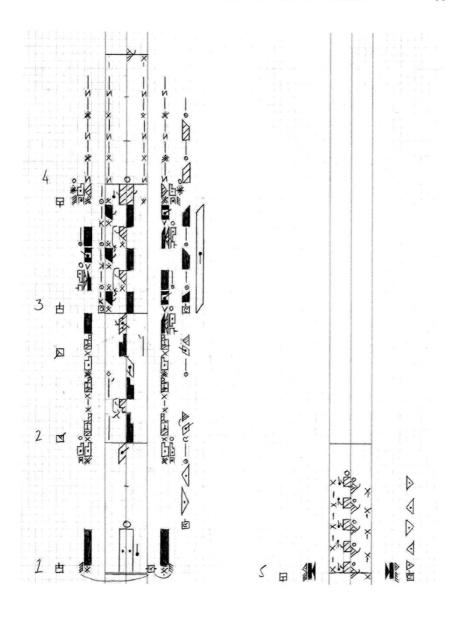

ess of translating from one to the other. I have no preference for either
system although there are aspects I find more straightforward or simply
remember more clearly in each. For example, I find it easier to analyse
and describe floor work in Labanotation yet prefer to tackle complex partner work using BMN. I think this may have as much to do with my own
attributes and understanding as a notator and as a dancer as it does with

the innate capacities of the systems. I was talking with Liz Cunliffe recently, Director of the Benesh Institute, and she mentioned that she thought one of the key differences between the systems was that Benesh choreologists generally strive to write the minimum necessary, stripping out any redundant information that can be inferred, whereas Labanotators aim to specify every detail, preferring to double up information in belt and braces fashion. The extreme of either of these approaches would lead to unreadable scores—too little detail for the score to be read by anyone other than the notator herself or so much detail that the score becomes impenetrable and mitigates against any interpretation by the dancers. Having always worked across the two systems, I bring a little of the BMN commitment to economy to my Labanotating and a little of the belt and braces thoroughness of Labanotation to my choreology. Even with this hybrid approach to notation, the act of translating a score from one system to another is complex. It is not possible for me to read a score in one system and then just jot it down using the alternative symbol system of the other. The terms of the description differ so radically that I must always make recourse to my own embodied understanding of the movement and begin my analysis from there.

There are several books available that explain the fundamental principles of each system in much more depth. However, notation is a practice and its theory is learned best when encountered in an environment in which the nuance of the movement analysis entailed can be understood somatically. To gain a meaningful understanding of either BMN or Labanotation I would recommend enrolling on a short, or a distance learning course. More information on learning BMN or Labanotation can be obtained by contacting The Benesh Institute in London (020 7326 8035) or The Dance Notation Bureau in New York (+1 212 571 7011).

Benevolence in Ballet – The Philanthropic Legacy of Dame Ninette

Clementine Cowl

2011 saw the tenth anniversary marking Ninette de Valois' death in 2001, aged 102. What is less well known, but equally interesting is that she died on 8 March, which is International Women's Day; a global day celebrating the economic, political and social achievements of women past, present and future. De Valois' achievements are legendary. For instance, it seems certain that de Valois' early years in theatre were a driving force in her desire to improve conditions for dancers. As de Valois writes: "When I look back on those wasted years between tcn and fifteen I feel only a renewed anxiety to leave English dancers with some security and definite standards", [1] which of course she achieved through the setting up of The Royal Ballet and The Royal Ballet School. Records suggest, however, that her involvement in dancers' welfare extended beyond this, and that she was also instrumental in improving conditions for dancers in other ways. It is likely that without de Valois, The Royal Ballet Benevolent Fund (hereafter RBBF), an organisation which has been able to support legions of dancers over the years, would not still be in existence today.

The RBBF is fortunate to hold the records of the many meetings held over its history, which are a fascinating insight into another aspect of de Valois. From the records that exist, it seems that in 1936, a fund was established, called the Vic Wells Ballet Fund (later to be called the Sadler's Wells Benevolent Fund), to help the struggling Company at the Sadler's Wells Theatre surmount its financial difficulties. It is likely that this fund was set up after the success of the Camargo Society, which, as de Valois records, had come into being after a suggestion by Philip Richardson and Arnold Haskell. [2] Eventually, the Camargo Society was wound up after five years. [3] The Vic Wells Ballet Fund started life almost immediately, after a suggestion again by Haskell. RBBF records suggest that Haskell chaired Vic Wells Fund business, with a sub-committee of Lilian Baylis, Ninette de Valois, Constant Lambert and Frederick Ashton, with Lambert also having been a member of the Camargo Society. Other individuals de Valois had met along the way were to play a part in the fund's success – as de Valois got nearer her dream of having her School in the Sadler's Wells

Theatre, she recalls: "I then had to produce some accounts and seek an interview with Reginald Rowe, the Acting Governor of the Old Vic."[4] No doubt due to his financial acumen, after that, Rowe was invited to become a valuable committee member of the Vic Wells Ballet Fund; for instance records show that on his advice £1,000 worth of Defence Bonds (about £35,000 in today's money) were bought in 1942 to boost the rapidly growing assets of the organisation.

It is interesting that, although de Valois was involved in the early days with the Vic Wells Ballet Fund for fairly practical motives (to help the Ballet Company, and the School), she can be seen over the years to develop a real commitment to the fund's charitable objectives. Records suggest that in the early days, however, de Valois and the rest of the Committee were concerned with a really rather robust fundraising and publicity strategy in order to raise funds for the Company's productions.

A primary function of the fund was to organise the annual gala (usually attended by the Queen) to both showcase new work and raise necessary funds for the Company's expanding repertoire. This included printing leaflets, posters and souvenir programmes for the gala on May 10, 1938. Records show that the Vic Wells Ballet Fund assisted with the production of *The Sleeping Princess* (which later on became one of the cornerstones of The Royal Ballet repertoire) with a grant of £300 (£15,500 in today's money) made to the Company in 1938 for that express purpose. However, this was on the agreement that an acknowledgement of the fund's grant should be put in all *The Sleeping Princess* programmes, as well as a mention of the fund "on all ballet nights".[5] Grants were made to the Company as and when needed; The Vic Wells Ballet Fund guaranteed, for instance, the Company's 1939/40 winter season at Sadler's Wells, as well as replacing costumes and scenery lost during the tour of Holland during the war.

De Valois herself seems to have had a particular fondness for the galas, as she writes about the gala in 1956: "In March the annual Sadler's Wells Benevolent Fund performance holds a very special gala. The Queen, the Queen Mother, and the Princess Margaret are all present; in one of the intervals Her Majesty receives every member of the company and staff who has served the Sadler's Wells Ballet for twenty years."[6] Although galas were the main fundraising activity, another favourite way of fundraising for the Vic-Wells Ballet Fund in the early days was to hold private views (to which the press were invited) with a rapidly growing collection of pictures and stage designs which the fund had acquired. In 1942, the fund bought Rex Whistler's designs for *The Rake's Progress*, along with many other purchases over the years, which are still in the RBBF's ownership.

Nowadays, the items of the RBBF collection are in two locations; some are housed at the Royal Opera House, with others on permanent display at White Lodge. It was exciting that in 2011, elements of The Royal Ballet Benevolent Fund design collection were on show at the Royal Opera House, as part of the exhibition entitled, *Invitation to the Ballet: Ninette de Valois and the Story of The Royal Ballet*. Once again, the Rex Whistler *Rake's Progress* designs were to be seen, as well as designs by Piper, Armstrong and Burra.

Arts Council funding in 1945 to the newly formed Sadler's Wells Ballet, the newly-formed Sadler's Wells Opera Ballet and the Ballet School meant there was no longer the need to support the Company's artistic programme. It is at this point that the fund began its "second life", as it were, when the present charitable aims really took off – a decision, it seems certain, which was suggested by de Valois. As the RBBF records show: "Miss de Valois said that in view of the grants to be made by the Arts Council to both Companies and the Ballet School, she thought that the fund should be used in future for charitable purposes only, as it would no longer be required to encourage and aid the work of the ballet artistically and academically."[7]

De Valois certainly seemed to develop a sense of social justice and a notion of philanthropic values after returning from America. This probably reinforced for her the belief in a School where those dancers who displayed a high degree of ability should be given a chance to benefit, regardless of ability to pay. After the second Company visit to America, and seeing the building legacies created by the great philanthropists, she wrote: "When first in the States, I was fortunate enough to come across Carnegie's essay on 'Wealth': it was this essay that lit up my understanding... ."[8]

It seems certain that de Valois wanted to play a very active role in the new charity's activities. Many of the early grants from what was, at that point, called the Sadler's Wells Benevolent Fund, were to assist dancers who were employed by the Company. These grants in essence covered loss of salary whilst the dancer was unable to perform. (In fact since the early days a few grants had been made to dancers with injured knees or sprained backs.) The Fund had also sent grants to male dancers serving overseas during the war. However, it is interesting to note (given today's preoccupation with appearance) that many of the early grants were for cosmetic work, particularly teeth, also for growth hormones, to enhance the appearance of Company members! In addition, the fund continued to give support to The Royal Ballet School students until 1966, when the creation of The Royal Ballet School Endowment Fund made this a less pressing concern. For instance, following the success of the 1953 Gala (*Homage, Daphnis and Chloe* and *Coppélia*) which raised £3,357-1sh-7d (£68,887 in today's terms), a cheque for half the sum was given to The Royal Ballet School.

By 1951, it was recognised that some former Company members who were facing difficulties since leaving the Company would benefit from additional financial support. This was the beginning of an entirely new way of supporting former dancers, which continues to the present day, although the Royal Ballet Pension Scheme, established in the 1960s, has made the lot of some dancers in recent years much easier. In 1956, after the granting of the Royal Charter to what became The Royal Ballet and The Royal Ballet School, the Fund became The Royal Ballet Benevolent Fund. Galas certainly continued into the 1970s, and the RBBF always gratefully received any other donations from well wishers. The RBBF was finally registered with the Charity Commission in 1966.

In 1980, a few months before her retirement from the fund, de Valois drew up a paper of Policy Recommendations (of which there is still a copy) many of which would be relevant today. She also appears to have possessed a genuine concern for the dancers who needed help; minutes record her visiting Company dancers in hospital. At one point, ambitious plans were drawn up to provide a house in Barnes for ex-dancers to share once their dance careers were over, although sadly this never came to fruition. Over the years, the RBBF has been able to reach out to more and more dancers, extending far beyond the original grants made only to Royal Ballet dancers.

The Chairmanship of the RBBF is now in the hands of the capable Dame Beryl Grey; she was one of the eight young ballerinas at the 1956 gala mentioned with such fondness by de Valois. Stories of de Valois' sternness are well known, and yet this remarkable woman probably did more to improve dancers' conditions than anyone else. As a trustee for forty-two years, Dame Ninette was the longest standing Board member; she became patron after retiring in 1980.

Part Five: Turkey

Ninette de Valois' Turkish Adventure

Richard Glasstone

I was privileged to witness at first hand something of the miracle de Valois was able to achieve in Turkey. My own time working with her there lasted mainly from the mid to the late 1960s; but Madam's Turkish adventure started long before that. It was in 1947 that the Turkish government first invited Ninette de Valois to explore the possibility of establishing a ballet school in a country with no tradition and very little knowledge of classical ballet.

On her initial visit to Istanbul, Madam (accompanied by Joy Newton) visited a number of local primary schools, explaining the basics of ballet to teachers, parents and pupils. Auditions were held and eighteen girls and eleven young boys – aged between seven and ten years – were selected as the nucleus of the first Turkish vocational ballet school. This was housed in Yeşilköy, a suburb of Istanbul, and was officially opened on 6 January 1948.

For the first few years of its existence, the Turkish State Ballet School was directed by Joy Newton, more or less on the lines of the Sadler's Wells School. The curriculum combined general education with ballet training and both residential and day pupils were accepted. By 1950, the original intake of twenty-nine children had expanded to over one hundred students and the school was now moved to Ankara, the state capital, to become a department of the State Conservatoire of Music and Drama, with the students following a full-time educational programme from primary to high school level. Joy Newton was now succeeded first by Beatrice Appleyard and then, later, by Molly Lake and Travis Kemp, who were to remain at their posts for some twenty years, training a whole generation of fine dancers.

In 1957, the first graduates of the Turkish State Ballet School were to form the nucleus of what was eventually to become the Turkish State Ballet Company, housed at the Ankara Opera House. In 1960, Robert Harrold staged de Falla's *El Amor Brujo* for the fledgling Company; but their real debut as a classical ballet company came the following year, with Ailne Phillips' staging of the full, three-act *Coppélia*. Following this, the Company now embarked on an extraordinary decade of rapid development and remarkable artistic achievement.

Whilst the school continued to produce a steady supply of increasingly able young dancers, the Company itself was directly controlled by de Valois. Having retired as Director of The Royal Ballet Company in 1963, Madam was now able to devote even more of her time and energy to nurturing her "Turkish baby". She visited Ankara regularly to plan and supervise the Company's progress, entrusting its day-to-day running to a succession of British teachers, ballet masters and choreographers, including at various times Claude Newman, Ailne Phillips, Nancy Hanley, Gordon Aitken, Joy Newton, Dudley Tomlinson, Andrée Howard, Richard Glasstone and Alfred Rodrigues. In her book, *Step by Step*, Dame Ninette states that "We can claim, in the Turkish State Ballet, the first national ballet in Europe to have its foundations laid in England."[1]

A list of some of the works staged by this Company between the early sixties and the early seventies gives us a picture of de Valois' achievement. After *Coppélia* came *The Sleeping Beauty*, *Giselle*, *Swan Lake* and *The Nutcracker*. In 1962-63, Andrée Howard staged three of her ballets for the Company and, during the next two or three seasons, the repertoire was to include Fokine's *Les Sylphides*, Ashton's *Les Patineurs* and *Les Rendezvous*, as well as MacMillan's *The Burrow* and *Solitaire*. De Valois had already mounted *The Rake's Progress* for her Turkish dancers – declaring their dramatic interpretation to be among the finest she had witnessed – and was later to give them *Checkmate*. But her ambition was to see the Turks develop their own indigenous dance style and repertoire.

To this end, as an example of the type of new work that could be created in Turkey, Madam choreographed *Çeşmebaşi* (*At the Fountain*). Set around the fountain found on every Turkish village square, and using the music of Ferit Tüzün's *Anatolian Suite*, de Valois set out to demonstrate how, using Turkish themes and music, and drawing on the rich and varied language of Turkish folk dance, a truly indigenous ballet could be created. The première, on February 17, 1965, was a turning point in the Company's development and was to show the way forward for future local composers, choreographers and designers. De Valois herself was characteristically modest about her new ballet, referring to it jokingly as "my bastard *Petrouchka*". But her ingeniously structured choreography had real vitality and charm and included a choreographic gem in the duet for traditional Turkish shadow puppets.

It was still to take one or two seasons for the first young Turkish choreographers, Oytun Turfanda and Duygu Aykal, to make their mark; but meanwhile, de Valois created a new ballet to a score by another Turkish composer, Nevit Kodalı's *Sinfonietta*. This was a pure dance work – something unusual for de Valois – but its purpose was didactic: to show

Ninette de Valois in *Oh! Julie!*
(*Photograph by Bassano Ltd. Private collection.*)

MISS NINETTE DE VALOIS

SUPPORTED BY

SERGE MOROSOFF

AND A

BRITISH CORPS DE BALLET

IN

DIVERTISSEMENT

1. Pas de Valse ... ... *Strauss*
   A. CARLYON, M. CRASKE, V. LYNDALE, V. BENNETT,
   G. NOEL, D. DESNAUM, L. BENTLEY.

2. Adagio ... ... *Chopin*
   NINETTE DE VALOIS & SERGE MOROSOFF.

3. Danse Napolitaine ... ... *Desormes*
   M. CRASKE & D. DESNAUM.

4. Valse Arabesque ... ... *Lack*
   NINETTE DE VALOIS.

5. Gipsy Dance... ... ... *Saint-Saëns*
   SERGE MOROSOFF.

6. An Idyll ... ... *Grieg*
   A. CARLYON, V. LYNDALE, V. BENNETT.

7. The Letter. Pas de Trois ... ... *Dorothy Foster*
   M. CRASKE, G. NOEL, D. DESNAUM.

8. Hungarian Dance ... ... *W. Kuhe*
   NINETTE DE VALOIS & SERGE MOROSOFF.

**DANCES BY THE CORPS DE BALLET ARRANGED BY
NINETTE DE VALOIS.**

DRESSES DESIGNED BY NINETTE DE VALOIS.

**ADAGIO AND HUNGARIAN DANCE ARRANGED BY
SERGE MOROSOFF.**

Divertissement insert from programme at Holborn Empire for the week commencing Monday 14 November, 1921. (*Private collection*)

Ninette de Valois & Noreen Feist

Ninette de Valois and Noreen Feist with Lila Field's Wonder Children. (*Photograph by Hana. Private collection*)

Early years to 1935

Entrance to the exhibition, *Invitation to the Ballet: Ninette de Valois and the story of The Royal Ballet,* mounted by the Royal Opera House Collections at the Lowry Centre, showing images of the child and the adult de Valois. (*Photograph by Ben Blackall*)

The *pas de trois* from Frederick Ashton's *Les Rendezvous* (1933) with Ninette de Valois flanked by Robert Helpmann (standing) and Stanley Judson. (*Photograph by J.W. Debenham © Victoria and Albert Museum, London*)

Robert Parker in the role of Satan from De Valois' *Job* (1931), The Clore Studio Upstairs, ROH, 2011. (*Photograph by Patrick Baldwin. The Royal Ballet School Collections, White Lodge Museum*)

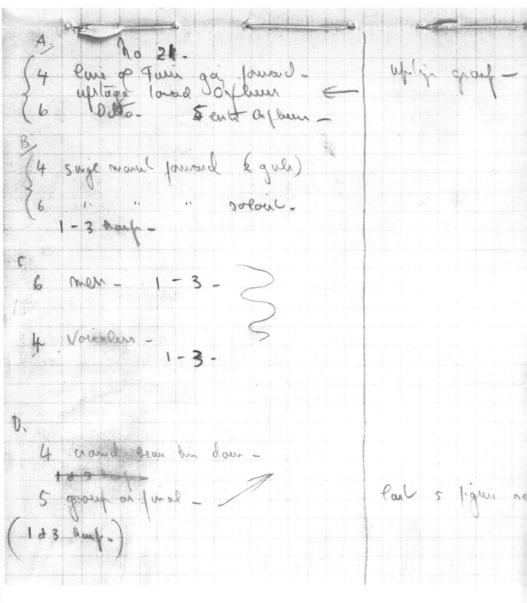

A page from de Valois' Choreographic Notebook for *Orpheus and Eurydice* (1941), illustrating her comments about organising a notebook, see p. 157. The left-hand image gives de Valois' analysis of the music, while the right-hand image shows her choreographic notes with an accompanying sketch of a climactic grouping where Orpheus in Hades is carried aloft by the Furies; the inset photograph shows this moment realised in performance. (*Notebook from The Royal Ballet School Collections, White Lodge Museum. Photograph by Gordon Anthony © Victoria and Albert Museum, London*)

tail group —

gradually built up —

2

Orpheus and Eurydice (Scene II)

Pauline Clayden as the 'Promenade' Girl with Gordon Hamilton as the Lepidopterist in de Valois' *Promenade* (1943). (*Photograph by Gordon Anthony © Victoria and Albert Museum, London*)

Valentino Zucchetti as Vestris in de Valois' *Every Goose Can* (1981), The Clore Studio Upstairs, ROH, 2011. (*Photograph by Patrick Baldwin. The Royal Ballet School Collections, White Lodge Museum*)

A 2nd Year Royal Ballet Upper School student as Will Mossop in David Bintley's *Hobson's Choice* (1989), The Clore Studio Upstairs, ROH, 2011. Simon Rice cites *Hobson's Choice* as one of the clearest examples where folk dance and ballet worked well together, see page 114. (*Photograph by Patrick Baldwin. The Royal Ballet School Collections, White Lodge Museum*)

Ninette de Valois with Margot Fonteyn and the Turkish Ambassador in the grounds of the Turkish Embassy c. 1957-1960. (*The Royal Ballet School Collections, White Lodge Museum*)

Marguerite Porter being coached by Ninette de Valois (1966). (*Photograph by Snowdon, Camera Press, London. The Royal Ballet School Collections, White Lodge Museum*)

Two photographs of Léonide Massine teaching Dance Composition at The Royal Ballet Upper School in 1968. (*The Royal Ballet School Collections, White Lodge Museum*)

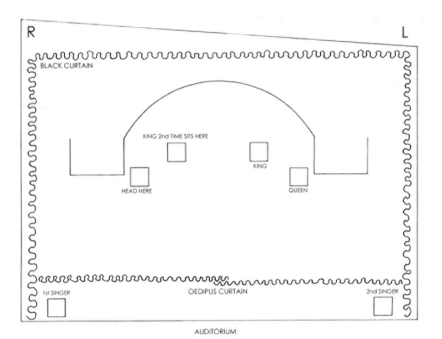

R   L

BLACK CURTAIN

KING 2nd TIME SITS HERE

KING

HEAD HERE

QUEEN

1st SINGER

OEDIPUS CURTAIN

2nd SINGER

AUDITORIUM

Cast line-up for the Abbey Theatre production of *The King of the Great Clock Tower* in July, 1934. (*Private collection*)

Top left: Transcription by Rosie McGuire of the floorplan of the setting for the Abbey Theatre production of Yeats's *The King of the Great Clock Tower* (1934). The actual set was designed by Dorothy Travers Smith but the sketch, to judge by the handwritten annotations, is by Lennox Robinson. (*Copied to scale from a loose sheet inserted into the National Library of Ireland's manuscript, NLI 29,550[2]. © Rosie McGuire*)

Bottom left: Yeats's sketches showing the evolution of the "thrones" for *The King of the Great Clock Tower*. (*Verso of page 9 of the typescript, SIUC 76/ 1/7. By courtesy of the Special Collections Department of the Morris Library, Southern Illinois University, Carbondale*)

Ninette de Valois at home in Barnes, c. 1975. (*Photograph by Richard Farley, by kind permission of the photographer*)

the Turks yet another way of using indigenous talent. For the same 1966 programme, Madam encouraged me to choreograph a ballet to a score by another Turkish composer, Bülent Tarcan's *Hançerli Hanım* (*The Lady with the Dagger*), a tale of love, murder and mysterious visions, set alternately in old and new Istanbul.

De Valois was also determined to develop new, young Turkish stage designers and she set her sights on Osman Şengezer. Guided by her, his first major commission was to design the sets and costumes for my staging of *Sylvia* for the Turkish ballet's twentieth anniversary. This was the first three-act ballet to be created on the Company and Osman's designs for this ballet were to launch his career as Turkey's leading stage designer. His work, not only for ballet, but also for opera and all forms of theatre, has been acclaimed both in Turkey and abroad and he is the first to attribute the seeds of his success to de Valois' early mentoring.

Parallel to her efforts to foster local talent, Madam continued to broaden the Company's horizons. In 1968, two of John Cranko's ballets, *Pineapple Poll* and *Beauty and the Beast* were staged by Pamela Chrimes and the following season Alfred Rodrigues mounted his *Blood Wedding* and *Three Sisters*. This was to be the first of several seasons devoted to Rodrigues' ballets, culminating in his fine staging of *Romeo and Juliet* in 1972.

De Valois' ultimate aim was to train a full Turkish staff capable of eventually running the ballet company without a foreign ballet master or resident choreographer. During my time in Turkey, it was an important part of my brief to assist Madam in training such a staff. By the time I left Ankara, in June 1969, the Company had an excellent ballet mistress in Oya Gürelli and a fine teacher and *répetiteur* in Tenasüp Onat, as well as a Turkish choreologist, Suna Eden. Sait Sökmen had staged the first ballet by a local choreographer, soon to be followed by several important works by Oytun Turfanda. By the early 1970s, de Valois' task was complete. The Company was now directed and staffed by Turks who, as dancers, had all come up through the school that Madam had founded way back in 1947.

In so many ways, this was a parallel achievement to what de Valois had created in England: a National Ballet Academy (with full-time education and dance training); a professional State Ballet Company with an international repertoire; the nurturing of indigenous choreographers, composers and designers; the training of a fully professional staff; and the creation of a ballet audience which, today, supports *six* full-time ballet companies and several smaller modern dance groups. All this in a country with no previous interest in ballet. Arguably an even more impressive achievement than her magnificent British one!

Anyone who experienced de Valois as the martinet she was known to be in England would have been astonished to see her in operation in Turkey. Although ever practical and pragmatic, her relationship with her Turkish dancers was almost that of a jolly mother figure. They were enormously fond of her and, although they respected her, they were never in awe or frightened of her, as were so many of her British dancers.

When groups of Turkish dancers came to London to study here on British Council Scholarships, Madam always took a personal interest in them, arranging medical appointments, enquiring after their marriages and their children, and there were always parties for them at Madam's house in Barnes to introduce them to dancers from The Royal Ballet. The contrast between how they and the Turks reacted to de Valois was remarkable, with Madam laughing and joking with the Turks much to the astonishment of the local dancers! She often declared that there was something about the Turks that reminded her of her native Ireland – hence her special affection for them.

Politically, the British Foreign Office was always anxious to support de Valois' work in Turkey, if only to keep the Soviet Russians out at the height of the Cold War. From a geographical point of view, it would have made sense for the Russians to be involved in ballet in Turkey, their next door neighbour; and I remember their cultural attaché's indignation when it was the British who first staged *Swan Lake*, that most Russian of ballets, in Ankara. More than once I heard de Valois joke about being "a sort of Mata Hari figure", determined that the communists should not get a foothold in Turkey.

Indeed, it was not until the mid-seventies that (for various political and economic reasons) the Russians did begin to infiltrate the Turkish ballet scene. They found there a fully professional Company, with dancers who were technically accomplished, extremely musical, and particularly expressive in dramatic roles. Seldom have I seen as moving an interpretation of The Rake as was given by Hüsnü Sünal, and Meriç Sümen's Giselle was good enough for her to be invited to dance it in Russia.

When I returned to Turkey for a second time, in 1993 – this time to work for two seasons with the Istanbul rather than the Ankara Company – the most striking change I encountered was in the growth of a number of dynamic contemporary dance ensembles. Their genesis dated back to the early seventies. By then, Istanbul – thanks largely to de Valois' pioneering work – had become a touring destination for many foreign dance companies. This was to lead to a number of Turkey's classically trained dancers becoming interested in other dance disciplines.

Notable among this new generation of dancers was Duygu Aykal, a young woman with a very personal and original attitude to dance. De Valois soon spotted her potential and arranged for her to study in London with Leonide Massine, who was directing a Dance Composition Course at The Royal Ballet School.[2] This was eventually to equip Duygu for the more analytical approach to choreography, which was to underpin her seminal work as the pioneer of new dance in Turkey, with its focus on subjects such as problems of urban life. De Valois' legacy was now moving in a new direction.

De Valois' Turkish adventure had succeeded against what must sometimes have seemed to be almost insuperable odds. There had been endless battles against Turkish bureaucracy, with all the artists employed as civil servants; compulsory military service regularly decimated the ranks of the male dancers; currency regulations hampered the importation of *pointe* shoes; and establishing discipline among a group of people for whom many aspects of a Western work ethic were alien had been no easy task. For a quarter of a century de Valois soldiered on, earning no money and often little thanks for her endeavours. But hers was a mission and nothing deterred her from fulfilling it.

In her memoirs, *Step by Step*, de Valois recalls that, as a child of about ten years of age, she was asked to dance in a London drawing-room for the entertainment of a visiting Persian Prince. "He gave me a dancer's charm, an exquisite tiny gold coin that had engraved on one side (in Persian) the words, 'Allah guide thy feet'. They were guided to the shores of Asia Minor in no uncertain terms, some thirty-five years later."[3] And with what extraordinary results!

Dancing Across the Bosphorus: An Introduction

Anna Meadmore

Levent Kurumlu completed a postgraduate degree in film studies at Bristol University, and currently teaches Cultural Studies at the Mardin Artuklu University, Turkey. While researching the history of the vibrant Turkish ballet and modern dance scene of the early twenty-first century, he developed a fascination for Ninette de Valois, both as a personality and as a cultural phenomenon. His film, *Dancing Across the Bosphorus*, traces de Valois' professional and personal relationships with the Turkish Ballet, its dancers, and with Turkey itself. It was four years in the making, and was first shown at The Royal Ballet School on 2 April 2011. The film was subsequently shown later that year in Istanbul and Ankara on 3 and 23 November respectively, at two major conferences which celebrated Ninette de Valois as the Founder of the Turkish Ballet, hosted jointly by the State Ballet Companies and Conservatoires of Istanbul and Ankara.

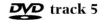 **track 5**

Part Six: Choreography

Six Essays contributed to Dancing Times in 1926 and in 1933[1]

Ninette de Valois

The Future of the Ballet[2]

[*Dancing Times*, February 1926, pp.589-593]

I hesitate to write in too authoritative a fashion of the ultimate issue of the contest between the classical ballet of the eighties and the modern choreographical studies. But I claim to have had the good fortune to study the theory of this much discussed subject, and for this reason I can safely say that the future of ballet in its modern form will be assured, provided sufficient encouragement, study and practical criticism are forthcoming. I also dare to hope for and prophesy a revival of the more dramatic form of ballet. Of course the only creative works that can be considered seriously are those of Fokine, Nijinsky, Massine and Nijinska. I put them in the sequence in which they made their appearance in the world of choreographists. Nijinsky has been lost to the world of art through ill-health – but we still have the remaining three and they are the only three that can be looked to at the moment for clear theoretical explanation. Apart from the visual proof, the depth of their work is shown in each artist's extraordinary hallmark of individuality. They have each treated numerous ballets of diverse subjects and periods – embued the same with the necessary character – and yet the production has always been stamped by his or her individual expression.

The true aim of modern ballet is a serious practical effort to extend the authentic methods of the classical ballet. It is to forward and expand the possibilities of the art of dancing in harmony with the other arts of the theatre. No art ever comes to a standstill. The theatre, accompanied by drama, painting and music, progresses steadily through experiment and research. It has its lean years, but we have abundant evidence of years of plenty. Are we not also of this progressive theatre? Ought we not also to accept and apply the same lines of thought and action to the advancement of our own work? It is difficult to go far into the matter in a short article, but, for a simple example take the close relation of dancing to music through its rhythmical movements, and to painting through form and design. The dance cannot exist in its complete form without the direct co-operation of these two, therefore the evolution and research work that continue without cessation in the worlds of its most influential sister arts ought to find a sympathetic echo in its own world.

For the last fifteen years we have had numerous theorists whose work has resulted in productions both good and bad. Dancers and dance students are now entering a new and important era – they are to be faced with the most serious task of all, that of establishing and safeguarding the methods of the true theorists on a solid foundation. Everyone knows what happens when an express train runs off the lines – the same disaster awaits an advancement in art that is not treated with intelligent care. The three theorists I have mentioned have countless imitators springing up on all sides, but they do not want imitators: they want disciples. One must see that the sincere work they have done towards the progress and expansion of ballet will not be swamped in time either by (a) enthusiastic but fundamentally inexperienced artists, or (b) the criticisms of those who have no real understanding of the aims and efforts of their more advanced contemporaries. (Class (b) is sometimes excused as being "old-fashioned". This is most unfair to our great dancers and teachers of a past generation whose indisputably thorough technique is and always will be the basis of all first-rate modern work.)

In order to obtain adequate support it is necessary to show that the present movement is not the outcome of a whim or drastic revolution, that expansion does not spell expulsion nor construction, destruction. The student of the future will have his time fully occupied with his studies so enlarged; he is not asked to give up anything of his past work but his co-operation is asked for in the present world of progressive art in its entirety.

Those ill-used terms "temperament" and "personality" (vaguely flung at young students as the only necessary appendage to their technical knowledge) might well be removed and the following practical studies substituted: (1) a sound body technique of expressive movement; (2) a wider and more sensitive mental outlook through general study, which will lead to an increased interest in the pictorial and rhythmical construction of the dance. Thus emotional understanding becomes subconsciously developed, surely a more successful method than stereotyped mannerisms.

Discussing the ballet as a complete theatrical art, there is no question that the teachings of the classic school are the sure and only foundation – limitless in its adaptability it consequently proves its power to meet the varied requirements of the theatre. But the Hellenic School of Dancing with Isodora Duncan as its figure head has shown the emotional powers that lie hidden in the theory of broader and freer body movements. The influence of the plastic school on the classic has been greatly felt – and the result has been most satisfactory.

A close study of all literature dealing with the arts separately and the theatre in general (which, by the way, should be an essential part of the curriculum of every student) will show that we are not alone in our troubles – classicism, romanticism, realism, and lastly expressionism, have all held their universal sway. The isolation of ballet from all these innovations is unwittingly to put it on an inferior plane and turn it into a cramped and limited affair. One of the many works of the moment that should have a place on the bookshelf of every dancer is Ernest Newman's *A Musical Critic's Holiday.* It covers a long musical period and everything in the book can be digested by the dancer and transferred into his world of thought. The following extract will give a brief idea:

As with the vocabulary of art, so with its forms. Broadly speaking, each of these has grown so imperceptibly out of its predecessors that no ordinary intelligent musical mind that could think in terms of the earlier form could find any difficulty in adapting itself to the later. Vocal music has gone step-wise from the simplest folksong to the subtly unsought songs of Hugo-Wolf, and from the most primitive piece of "imitation" to the intricate voice weavings of the madrigal. Instrumental music has gone step-wise from the primitive dance tune, with its simple balance of parts to the fugue of Bach, the symphony of Beethoven, Brahms, Franck and Elgar. Opera has progressed step-wise from the *Euridice* of Peri on those still earlier quasi-dramatic tentatives of the sixteenth century with which modern research has made us acquainted, to the opera of Verdi, of Wagner, of Strauss, of Mussorgsky, of Debussy. In none of these instances has progress consisted of anything but putting old material to new uses expanding it as was necessary.

As an ex-member of the Royal Italian Opera, Covent Garden, and the Diaghilev Russian Ballet, I can claim the experience of both classical and modern productions, and I can vouch that the amount of hard work, concentration and understanding necessary for the execution of the modern is by no means below the standard required for the purely classical.

The working hours of the Diaghilev troupe are six per day permanently – this is increased up to nine whenever necessary (which is very often).

The four months' season at Monte Carlo has the opera ballets attached to the ordinary routine. Every day throughout the year the morning lesson prior to rehearsal commences at nine o'clock and attendance is compulsory. This routine is kept up for ten months out of each year – and includes Sunday performances when abroad. Here we have a repertory company running classical and modern ballet side by side – and what is more important – in many cases blended. Hard work and keen competition are the order of the day – there is never any finality, always new ballets, new music, new décor. The success of this ballet is due to its unfailing enterprise, and all its established productions are the work of the four artists I have mentioned. I have purposely drawn attention to the amount of serious work that is carried on behind the scenes, to sober the students who imagine Rome was built in a day, and fail to realise that even the greatest work of art has its flaws, to stimulate the anti-moderns, and to ask, if not for their co-operation, at least for their enquiry into a matter which they are viewing through smoked glasses.

Modern Choreography
I. Introductory. [*Dancing Times*, January 1933, pp.434-437]

Sometime ago I made a statement in a lecture to the effect that the old ballets, in comparison with the new, were infinitely more simple in structure and required less rehearsing. I want to make it clear that I was alluding to the choreographic and musical side. Virtuosity in the older ballets is, in a sense, on a higher technical plane. But it often consists in the execution of certain recognised technicalities, and is therefore removed from choreographic criticism as we know it today.

The main difficulty attached to the production of these ballets nowadays lies in the result of an economic warfare that has not left the theatre untouched. One reads so often of dancers "failing to give the true Romantic illusion". Here the fault is not psychological, but practical.

Simplicity characterises the steps and figurations of the recognised classical ballet. They are executed in numbers of anything from sixteen to thirty-two dancers, and originally devised for theatres of the Paris Opéra dimensions. Even on a smaller scale the mind recalls Covent Garden, Alhambra, Empire, etc.

Theatres, unsubsidised, with the rivalry of the cinema, do not and cannot exist solely for the presentation of such ballets nowadays. Even State theatres are in a precarious position, whilst the end of the regime of ballet at the Empire and Alhambra mainly consisted of one ballet supported by what amounted to a variety bill. Even the "grand ballet" consisted of three or four famous dancers surrounded by a "corps" that were by no means trained dancers in the real sense of the word. The ballets were definitely "spectacular". I distinctly remember seeing Kyasht in a "ship" scene (I think it was *Round the World*) which might have been a scene out of *Cavalcade*. Also *Midsummer Night's Dream*, a curious mixture of song and dance.

When we present such works as [*Les*] *Sylphides*, etc., at Sadler's Wells Theatre, many suggest I should cut the number of dancers down. I agree in theory, but I find from a production point of view that ballet suffers greatly from curtailment. Simple figurations cannot afford to be still further simplified, nor can groupings, demanding a certain number of dancers, be altered out of all recognition. From time to time, the occasion will arise for us to present such ballets in a sufficiently large theatre (Copenhagen gave us one opportunity), therefore I prefer, as we have the number of dancers, to keep the tradition of these ballets going in their full choreographic figurations. The dancers must be prepared to put up with a certain lack of space and the adverse criticism coming from those who have a right to express their reaction.

The true history of choreography is just the history of the theatre influencing another of its important arts. Choreographically, I prefer to study the prints and books that tell the story of the earliest Court ballets, those examples of formal classicism that correspond with the period of Handel, Bach, etc.

In such times the art of virtuosity had not reached the pitch it had by the middle and late nineteenth century. But the "theatre" was taken seriously and was remarkably alive. The music` had not become, as later, a slave to the dance. It had not reached the stage when producers actually were in a position to demand so many bars for a certain step, or when ballerinas were permitted to remove a favourite "variation" from one ballet into another! (This is, to my mind, as incredible as if John Gielgud, going straight from his success as Hamlet at the "Vic," to play in *The Good Companions*, had recited "To be or not to be"...in the middle of the latter). In fact, ballet had not reached the point when good composers were generally writing for it. But even this burst of virtuosity, and the accompanying harm it did choreography, had its point. It raised the "standard" of execution enormously.

In many nineteenth-century classical ballets the music is of such a mechanical form that, choreographically, it could only inspire spectacular figurations devoid of the most innocent complexity, or, at the most, a series of brilliant *enchainements* for the principals.

In the later Romantic Ballet we have Fokine producing pure classical ballet to the best of the Romantic School of Music. Virtuosity is at a lower ebb, production, both musically and choreographically, at a very high one.

We go back to the earlier Romantic era, and look at *Giselle* or many others familiar to those who remember Pavlova's repertoire. In *Giselle* we have music that does not stand any analysis, and its influence can be traced in a lot of the ensemble work. But the virtuosity demanded of the principals is of an extraordinarily high order; there is also a simple and beautifully constructed dramatic story, and a sense of the theatre running throughout the entire two scenes. How great it might have been if it could have reached all the standards by which it is possible to judge a ballet nowadays.

"Ballet", *i.e.* "dancing" from the purist's point of view, is inseparable from music. "Dancing", *i.e.* "movement" from the choreographist's point of view, is inseparable from the theatre. The growing realisation in the theatre of the importance of unity is being felt by the choreographer of today.

Every choreographer should have some knowledge and interest in play production, and work, at [the] same time, under a producer whose productions demand choreographic treatment.

Some of my most valuable experience in the past has come from working at the Festival Theatre, Cambridge, during the first four years of its existence, also the Abbey Theatre productions of W. B. Yeats' *Plays for Dancers*. Coming straight from the study of ballet pure in the Diaghilev Company, I was faced with the demands of the theatre dramatically. The productions of "The Japanese Players," "La Compagnie des Quinze," and the present Festival Theatre Company, are the works which our young dancers and choreographers should see whenever possible, if only to make them realise the use of the dance in relation to the drama.

The Festival production of Ashley Dukes' *One More River* was the best example of this kind a dancer could wish to see in England today.

It is impossible to underestimate the importance to dancers of this side of their work. Speaking generally, English dancers have no love or understanding of the theatre. It is here Miss Baylis has done so much at Sadler's Wells. Young students at "The Wells" live in a theatre atmosphere. Some time ago I came across three or four children in the ballet school discussing some production. Further enquiries elicited the fact that it was not one of our ballets which was the subject of lengthy criticism, but the current Shakespearian play. Between classes and rehearsals, throughout the day, you will find groups of young dancers listening to the rehearsal of play or opera.

I have touched on these matters in my introductory note because, subsequently, these articles will be dealing with the more practical side of ballet production, the work the Vic Wells demands of me.

But I can only state the case as experience has made me feel and understand. Creative minds do not necessarily agree in theory, nor do they work along the same line of action. But I think they have some rules in common that are often overlooked.

Coming from a dancer whose country has no tradition of ballet behind it, those who have known the luxury of the state theatre, and who have grown up with every advantage round them, may find these articles rather out of place. But short of a great inheritance, it is better to be born empty-handed.

English dancers and choreographers lack tradition and experience, which will naturally lead to many mistakes, but we are also able to benefit from the mistakes of the past. Lack of money in these days makes extravagant experiments out of the question. Hardship, if it wins through, leads to tremendous efficiency – an efficiency and solidity that money cannot always achieve.

Modern Choreography

II. [MUSIC] [*Dancing Times*, February, 1933, pp.549-552]

In the following article I propose to consider modern ballet from the musical point of view. Music still remains an essential component of choreography, and the major influence of the pure form of ballet.

The ever-recurring argument dealing with the comparative merits of modern ballet music and that of the older school is rather confusing.

The later Diaghilev era may seem to us dated. The implied criticism, although true in a sense, is a little unjust. It was a period of small works. Expressionism, one of the most abused movements of the drama, is not regarded by discerning critics as a failure because it has not survived in its entirety, and for the same reason the ballets of the above period should not receive unduly detrimental criticism. Small movements are as much the result of some universal psychological outbreak as are big ones. When such movements, however slight, affect the minds of some of the cleverest creative artists, something of importance survives and is added to the history and progress of art in general.

In England music and ballet of today receive, generally speaking, two forms of dramatic criticism.

(a) "Later Diaghilev" and therefore good. This form of criticism comes from the young man whose experience of ballet started and finished with that particular period. It is his only standard, therefore his attitude is understandable.

(b) "Later Diaghilev" and therefore bad. This criticism comes from the honest die-hard who hated this particular period because the perfection of sumptuous pre-war works (resulting from years of tradition) satisfied him greatly. The war, giving him other things to do, checked the progress of his critical facilities regarding the change in ballet, or worse, made him entirely nationalistic in his outlook. So he gives it up, and talks about the past, but perhaps with more gusto than when it was the present.

The modern ballet that is worthy of serious criticism is the one which shows itself sensitive to the laws of tradition, indifferent to temporary fashion, and courageous in revolutionary experiments.

Although the choreographer, in the first place, is subjected to the style of the music, I think it is a mistake for the composer to have anything to do with the stage presentation. Of all the units that go to make a ballet production, the composer has the least theatre sense. I do not mean lack of taste, only ignorance of theatre production. After all, there is nothing in the handling of an orchestra or the atmosphere of an orchestral pit to develop this particular faculty. Further, the actual composition of music is far more abstract than the composition of ballet.

There are two things a young choreographer to-day should try and develop: a sense of the mood and period of the music, and a knowledge of its pattern. Formerly the first was the only essential musical gift a choreographer needed. Melody was predominate in early ballet composition, the phrasing and time signatures of a simple form. But this lack of stimulation had the effect of gradually diminishing the dancer's musical concentration and analysis. Such subjects as the piano and eurhythmics were not so easy to learn thoroughly when I was a child as they are now. I can only claim the simplest tuition in both directions. But I know enough in theory about a printed piece of music to go up to the piano and unravel technically something I cannot altogether trust my ear to do for me. I have found even this slight knowledge invaluable when composing ballets to difficult modern music. Yet there are many dancers and teachers who do not realise (particularly if you ran a fairly big company with little time for production) that it is absolutely essential to make a *corps de ballet* regard themselves as another orchestra, and to give them, at the start, a *mental* picture of their music, and allow their own intelligence to develop the *oral* appreciation gradually at later rehearsals.

Therefore a system of counting should be worked out according to the "phrasing" of the music. Lack of melody, odd bars, frequent changes of time signatures, are all common pitfalls of modern composition, and the dancer has not the music in front of him to refresh his memory. Counting to a steady time signature is not always advisable, because it is often just a time signature and bears no relation to the actual pattern of the musical phrase, which may start on the last beat of one bar and end on the first of another.

Of course this system can be very abused through ignorance, lack of a natural musical sense, or the simplest knowledge of musical technicalities. But I do not force such methods on my company blindly. Unless unduly hard pressed, I show them what is happening, and why the "counting" must vary in places. They know how many bars are allotted to each choreographic movement, and what they are counting to each bar. Therefore any slip at an orchestral rehearsal is not in the least upsetting to them. The same rule applies to a "pause" or "rest". They are always warned which it is. Constant Lambert (who knows something of the trials of ballet conducting) has often asked me "if I would like a certain pause to be given the value of a full bar's rest". I know many dancers who would not understand what he meant.

On the page in my note book facing the one with my choreographic notes I write my corresponding music notes. The pattern of the two coincide. The printed music is marked off in the same way, so a sudden change of pianist does not give any trouble. I find this method forms a framework that time does not easily shatter, or quick production and insufficient rehearsal leave little but chaos when it comes to a revival with many changes in the cast. Further, it is a "fool-proof" method of dealing with difficult modern music, and the fact that not every member of the corps de ballet has a highly developed musical ear.

There is also the difficulty of the orchestral version, generally to be faced in one rehearsal. Counter movements are often introduced into a score, melodies non-existent in the piano. The dominant piano melody in the full orchestral version may have become entirely subordinate to another. It is always advisable, if working on a piece with two distinct movements, to go over the score with your conductor and find out what will eventually predominate. Nijinska works from the score. *Les Noces* had no piano version for one pianist. It was played at performances (apart from orchestra and chorus) by four pianists, each at a separate keyboard. We always had to rehearse with a pianola. Nijinska had a score with the ballet worked out on it. I have heard it said her work on this particular score was a masterpiece, but I never had the privilege of seeing it. *Les Noces* was by far the most interesting modern work I have ever danced in. It was, musically speaking, terribly complicated, and demanded intense concentration from beginning to end.

It has been said that these views lead to a mechanical effect, killing the spirit of the music, etc. But this is not a very sound argument. Analysis kills the spirit where the abilities are limited, and bores those who lack interest, concentration and discipline. Artists who aim at real efficiency are able to survive any work in detail, and enjoy the spirit of it all afterwards. To me this criticism is as illogical as the reason given against the Cecchetti system of numbers to ensure symmetrical line, namely, that it is unnecessary, as many good dancers have never heard of it. But it is wise to bear in mind there are some fortunate mortals who know nothing of the dentist's chair, yet this does not put them in the position to help their less fortunate companions.

I know too well how irritating it is to hear a dancer counting blindly, ignorant of the form of the work, and making no effort to listen to the music. Only by listening can the light and shade of music penetrate, and tone is as much a part of the ultimate musical picture as the phrasing and technical points one analyses at the beginning. This is proved by the fact that no analysis is satisfactory until each section has been listened to many times.

The general standard of ballet production these days may be modest and mounted on very economical lines, but I think it aims high in its ideals. In England it is good, if still immature in its execution. English girls make an excellent *corps de ballet*; they are impersonal, and know the necessity of a production being successful as a whole. This is an essential spirit in modern repertory ballet.

When in Copenhagen I had a long conversation with the *chef d'orchestre* of the Opera House. He showed great interest, and his remarks on the choice of music for our ballets and their interpretation were most flattering, and made one feel that minute attention to the musical side of ballet production was not waste of time.

Modern Choreography
III. Production: Theatrical Presentation [*Dancing Times*, March 1933, pp.668-670]

The production of ballet must be regarded by the choreographer in relation to the following:-
1. Music.
2. Theatrical Presentation.
3. Décor and costume.
4. The dancers.

Music I have already dealt with. I have put these principles in the above order, not because I wish to declaim which is of the greatest importance, but practical experience is inclined to force the issue to be generally evolved in the above train of thought.

A dance production is subjected to the same variations as painting, music, sculpture and the drama. It may be slowly, dramatically, and very deliberately evolved from a lengthy subject, or it may be expressive of a mood, thought, or symbolic action.

No ballet should be condemned for its lack of subject matter, or because it is over-burdened with the same. It is a question of treatment, whether in the former case the mood or symbolic meaning contains a mental stimulus of any value, or whether in the latter case the subject matter is an emotional one moving forward with sufficient force and clarity. It is for these reasons alone the choreographer of today must be a willing slave of the theatre. From the ballet room to the playhouse, from the scene dock to the switch-board, should his feeling and imagination take him. Interest and knowledge should he cultivate in these things, outside that already bestowed on his dancers' respective abilities.

It is wise, when discussing the merits or faults of a ballet, to make sure what species of theatre the work is best suited. The theatre is divided in a banal fashion, to what we are pleased to call commercial and non-commercial. If the work is for the former, efficiency and a recognised style of production are the chief factors. If the latter, a certain standard in accordance with the highest traditions of the past and a sympathy with the movements of the present must be forthcoming.

The non-commercial theatre for ballet production, whether big or small, is the hardest but most satisfactory taskmaster of all. Not that any theatre in a sense should be non-commercial. I speak of the theatre that is built for keeping art alive and for giving the best to the public at a modest price. This form of theatre works for artistes expressing a highly-qualified unity, and does not rely on the drawing powers of one individual personality. To such an institution comes the man in the street, who takes his theatre seriously and critically, but with even more enjoyment than he who wanders into a place of amusement to while away a couple of hours.

But one still remains mildly amused and slightly puzzled by the two titles. The first eleven years of my stage work was spent in the "commercial" theatre, the last nine in the so-called "non-commercial". Yet I have seen in the former by far the greatest displays of inefficiency and waste. Vast sums of money thrown away on single productions devoid of wit or intelligence; in fact more money lost in a few weeks on such enterprises than Diaghilev, or Lilian Baylis of the Old Vic and Sadler's Wells, ever lost in the course of many years, in spite of large companies employed for nine months out of the year. Then, by saying one should allow for surroundings, I am alluding only to the function of the critic or critical onlooker, whether professional or otherwise. I believe in dancers and choreographers ignoring the above rule and remaining true to their intuitive impulse, particularly in the case of those possessing any sort of creative ability. Success, anyway, is something one cannot hope to acquire except through anything but sincerity of purpose and a steady belief in giving the best. The mentality of the public is greatly misjudged both by artists and managers. "Give the public what they want" is a foolish slogan. They do not know what they want, and I cannot imagine why they should. But the commercial theatre still worships at the shrine of this idea – and complains year in and year out of a terrible theatre slump.

Constant study for production work is essential. Not just the knowledge of classical dancing and new technical class-room methods, but the study of getting things into perspective. Logic and a level head play a very big part in the economic theatre of today. The choreographer cannot escape it. He must make his ballet a living and sincere thing of the theatre, something to be enjoyed by the actor, the musician and the painter, in the way these people can make a dancer appreciate their work.

It is here, if I may say so, the success of *Job* may lie. Produced for an experimental ballet society, with no certainty of its possible success (and frankly a great deal of doubt on the part of the producer) it has lived and proved to be actually a box office draw. It is not by any means my favourite ballet. I find it is too big a work for one to produce really successfully in this country at present, and it has never had anything approaching a flawless performance. But it evidently gives something that appeals to the musical, dramatic and broad-minded dancing critic. I say "broad-minded" in the latter case, because I often hear it accused of not being a ballet. Let these dance critics try to cast it with anything but really skilled dancers. A production requiring such dancers *is* a ballet although it may not use one movement of an everyday class lesson. *Job* has never been perfectly cast. This statement is not made in a mind of ingratitude to those who have done so much for the work, it is not a slight on a dancer's abilities to say he is "miscast," on the contrary the performer who unselfishly allows himself to be so treated for the sake of a production is to my mind something of a hero. This has happened often in *Job*. Thirty performers for varied dramatic roles are hard to find at short notice, especially in a country with so few dancers experienced in repertory ballet. But we know how successful those rightly cast have been in this work. Anton Dolin's amazing and virile "Satan," and Stanley Judson's beautiful study of "Elihu" are the principal examples.

In the study of the theatrical presentation of a ballet, whether period or modern, the principal stage pictures, the pictorial mood of the opening and finish, together with the all-important central point, should be decided upon after a few days' familiarity with the music. Next a discussion of all these points with the artist who is to design the costumes and scenery. Then I think the choreographer is safe to embark on setting his dancers to study the choreography.

Lighting should always be in the mind of the producer. If his thoughts continually centre round this matter, it is easy to give an impression of harmony when he has to enlist the help of a lighting technician. Further, the importance of the join between dances, scenes, etc., and the length of certain light plots, are points to sit and visualise in solitude for many hours, and, if necessary, make copious experimental notes for reference at final rehearsals.

I call special rehearsals to study the harmony between dances – there must be an invisible link, if necessary one dance actually intruding on the music of another – and this can be done after the arrangement of the dances. It is the point where choreography has to meet production on an absolutely even footing. It is the rhythm of ballet production. A ballet which relies for a round of applause to break the atmosphere for the next movement (as in perfectly straight forward *divertissement*) is theatrically wrong. It is a mistake every choreographer makes from time to time, and I can attribute some personal failures to this very fault. Some may say this rule need only apply to the ballet with definite action – but it should apply to the two forms of ballet I allude to in the first part of this article, which can only be relaxed in real *divertissement*, where neither costume, dance or music bears any relation to the number before or after, a form of entertainment I find more disturbing than diverting.

The ballet production of today is inclined to follow the two rather sharply divided lines of the "pictorial" and "architectural". I think the great possibilities of the future (especially the complete harmony with the modern theatre) lies in the progress and development of the latter. I feel the greatest day in the history of ballet production will come when the sculptor is employed for the mounting of ballet as generally as the painter and theatre designer is today. The choreographer works in the same dimensions as the sculptor, therefore surely they should work together to achieve a real masterpiece.

Modern Choreography
IV. Décor and Costume [*Dancing Times*, April 1933, pp.9-10]

The modern designer for ballet, especially in England, is beginning to understand that a certain unity of outline is necessary in the dancers' costumes, an outline in sympathy with the pattern of the ballet as a whole.

Movement has in every period been greatly influenced by costume. The rigid formality of pattern, coupled with a certain roundness of movement, so prevalent in the early ballets, is a direct answer to the eighteenth-century costume. The freedom and certain angularity of our times is portrayed in the clothes of to-day, whether speaking of theatrical design or the fashion plate.

When discussing the mounting of a ballet with the scene and costume designer, it is wise to make him visualise the dancers as representing so many "tones". Quite unconsciously I think most choreographers form in their minds that certain groups and scenes are meant to convey a half or full tone. One's imagination sees some particular group sombre or bright, and the movements take on a similar form.

You will undoubtedly find by the time you are ready to go into practical detail with the designer, that your imagination has settled the following points about the ballet:-

1. Whether the deeper note should prevail in the costumes or the settings.
2. Whether the general effect should be pictorial or architectural.
3. Whether it is a production that can utilise both forms.

The Purcell Choral ballet lately produced at Sadler's Wells is an example of both. The chorus of forty singers had to be treated statically. They formed the abstract stylised framework to the picture, and before any design for a back-cloth was started, it was decided that two rostrums should be set on the stage, as a necessary architectural background for the chorus. The God Phoebus was to be the central figure, and to receive the same static treatment, making the frame complete for the ballet. The dancers were to be regarded as the pictorial element with costumes colourful and varied, the back-cloth a compromise between the two, extremely simple in design, and subordinate in tone to everything else on the stage. The result, carried out by John Armstrong, was a picture of real imagination.

I am entirely against settings and costumes being the work of two separate artists. They should be related, and appear incomplete when viewed apart. When working with the Russian Ballet, I well remember a lesson in abstaining from criticising costumes apart from their setting. It was during the production of *Zéphire et Flore* at Monte Carlo. One day in the rehearsal room we had a dress parade of the costumes. Diaghilev, and Braque, the designer were both present. The nine muses were very depressed, our costumes seemed dull and incomplete, and Diaghilev, overhearing our grumblings told us to "stop wondering whether the costumes suited us, but to consider instead whether we suited the costumes". He went on to tell us that the costumes had been designed to fit the ballet and the scene, and not, as we imagined, for each individual dancer. The next morning I went into the theatre to see the backcloth for the ballet. It was then I understood. In this simple cloth lay the key to everything that one could not find an explanation for in the costumes. My mind could put them together there and then, and I stood as entranced as if the whole ballet had been paraded for my special benefit.

I think it is wise to be sparing in enthusiasm over the ballet costume that is "modish" in design. It is permissible in a work for something so essentially topical as revue, but out of place in more serious ballet production. Real creative work cannot be truly fashionable, because it is something of all time and space.

In England there is a tendency, when designing on delicate, intimate lines, to strike a note of "pastiche" or "mode" of the fairy fashion.

Like all good things when they are gone we become particularly aware of their virtues. Sir Nigel Playfair in his many intimate Lyric Theatre productions, always steered clear of designers with this "pastiche" failing. One may not have liked some of their things, but there was always a feeling of a complete and positive work, and it is this I like so much about George Sheringham's setting and costumes for Frederick Ashton's ballet,

The Lord of Burleigh. The French Players in their staging of *Lucrèce*, gave a simple and elegant picture, modern in conception but strong and convincing in the homage it paid to the period it was treating. Perfect taste rarely becomes precious, it demands too great a technique. Yet in two play productions lately (showing the influence of the French Players, both in production and mounting), one felt the absence of effortless taste and deep creative instinct. The settings continually suggested an interior at Heal's, and the costumes an eccentric note in a current number of *Vogue*, which had borrowed its line from the very periods these plays were supposed to represent.

Great care should be taken not to exaggerate the modernising of the mountings in relation to the revival of the old classical ballets. They should not be completely isolated from the period or the nationality of the characters. In the revival that takes the original choreography as well as the music, it is only logical that the designer should make some concessions.

I think the designs by Edward Callagan for Sadler's Wells production of *Coppélia* will be interesting. They are gay, and modern in the sense that they portray the spirit of fantasy that runs through the story of *Coppélia*.

But the spirit of ballet is always artificial, it is too much of the theatre and too little of the world or reality not to permit at all times and in all places, the mark of the individual whether designer, choreographer or dancer. The artist may be concerned with the reconstruction of another age, but outside the necessary basic form and convention, he sees it through the progressive theatre of his own time, and to stifle his creative imagination, even on a work of reconstruction, is to choke the progress of ballet production.

Provided all is held within the bounds of good taste, dancers must realise they should allow the same liberties, in the staging of a Petipa ballet, that honest lovers of the play allow and indeed expect from all producers experimenting in the production of Shakespeare, the Restoration comedies, etc. In fact, the mounting of a ballet is subjected to all the rules of serious production, *i.e.*, taste, knowledge, imagination and the will to meet the choreographer on practical points at issue.

Next month my concluding article will deal with the part played by the dancers in a ballet. They are the part of the whole which I want to leave for my final essay.

   All the world's a stage /And [all the] men and women merely players...

So spoke one many years ago, one who knew that the life and mind of man runs its allotted span because it must, because it needs become a tragic or comic, successful or unsuccessful part of a whole. The whole is a presentation without end, breaking up into varied isolated patterns, and it is by these patterns, manifested in the arts and sciences, that the world keeps its sanity and its meaning.

Modern Choreography
V. The Classical Dancer of Today. [*Dancing Times*, May 1933, pp.122-125]

In England, through lack of opportunity, very few of our dancers know what it is to develop their powers in a really congenial atmosphere. Training is expensive, good work scarce, and lacking a traditional ballet of many years' standing there is a natural tendency to force an issue on the psychological side, as well as on the technical.

The dancer must go through three stages: (1) studentship, (2) apprenticeship, (3) specialisation.

The studentship contributes the many years that should be spent in the classroom. The apprenticeship, the first two to three years as a member of the ballet company. The third step is the development of the young dancer on more individual lines, an acknowledgement as well as a realisation of marked abilities in any special line or style.

Up to the present the danger in England has been the direct jump made from the first to the third stage. Most young dancers in this country consider themselves fortunate if they miss the middle stage, but how unfortunate they really are the writer of this article can tell them, who, half-way through a professional career, found it necessary to join unconditionally the *corps de ballet* of a famous ballet company to acquire certain essential knowledge which previous stage experience had not provided.

Early and forced development of individuality in young artists is a great mistake. It is a blunder as unpardonable as the failure of the teacher or director to realise their latent abilities. The first few years in the theatre should be devoted to the whole, and not the part. It is well to stumble through every conceivable role in relation to the highest form of ballet production, to be often miscast and never to be likened to a known star.

The mediocre mastering of roles unsuited to the performer's natural abilities is a valuable mental stimulus, and is known to strengthen the side of their work that will eventually help them to specialise.

This system is naturally most successful in a repertory ballet company where appreciation of standard can be felt by the dancer in any ballet, however different in mood or style. I am averse to forcing highly-trained young dancers into the uncongenial atmosphere of musical comedy work; the gap is too big, and it leads to disappointment of the loss of all ideals; it is a drastic step only to be taken when financial matters absolutely demand it.

Once the stage of apprenticeship is completed, a certain amount of self-analysis is necessary on the part of the dancer, and a sympathetic interest on the part of the director. The young dancer will have formed many half-truths as to future style and development, and must be assured that such views will receive every encouragement. Freedom to attack this new path with a mind quite unattached to the ways and achievements of others, freedom born of a disciplined period of theatrical adolescence that has given them a shrewd idea of where to seek both knowledge and success.

They should study under many masters. Experience has taught us the advantages of different schools and the influence of varied personalities.

One of the most impressive things about the Russian Ballet was the methodical outlook of state-trained dancers. They had two masters to serve – the ballet and themselves. The nine months' season would be devoted to the study and mastering of the roles required of them by the theatre, the daily class a means of obtaining the necessary physical discipline. But towards the end of the season, and for at least three-quarters of the ensuing three months' holiday, all concentrated on strenuous class-room studies under other professors than those appointed by the director. Practice was no longer just a method of keeping fit, but a means to an end in itself. This sudden self-centred application made progress a certainty, and checked the danger of too great an interest in the ballet itself acting as a check on technical development.

The psychological effect of anyone remaining a member of the *corps de ballet*, instead of progressing to the ranks of soloist, was also interesting. The *corps de ballet* was a complete world where all the members were regarded as artists of very great value to the standard of the Ballet. It is often some great physical advantage that gives a dancer an individual opportunity, and any choreographer knows that the loss of a disciplined highly-trained member of the *corps de ballet* is as serious as the loss of a good soloist, and can be a great deal harder to replace. They so often possess a wider and more varied knowledge than a soloist, and these two possessions lead to a third, namely a higher state of intelligence.

There should never be in any good company a line drawn between the

artists, or any feeling of superiority or inferiority. Culture and understanding should bar any such form of stupidity.

But this is not always a view that is taken over here; for in spite of the
good team-work English dancers are capable of giving, they are inclined
to develop an inferiority complex over this very point. Further, they have a
lack of self-preservation utterly unknown to their foreign contemporaries. You may find it necessary to tell foreign dancers to work hard, but you
never have to tell them to make the best of themselves. You seldom have
to ask good English dancers to work, but it needs a certain amount of
persuasion to convince them how necessary it is to make the best of their
physical appearance. One hears so much about unstudied charm; very
little real charm is unstudied – it is the outcome of an intelligent and
enlightened mind. In the theatre perfect artificiality comes before any
form of natural expression; as an example I have so often asked dancers to
paint their faces – not to make them up. It is the subtle difference between
the application of everyday cosmetics and the theatrical that counts behind the footlights. We have reached the enlightened stage in everyday
life which admits that a well-made-up face is preferable to one ruined by
indifferent natural colouring.

Lighting and make-up dispense with any need for a dancer to worry
over the demands made on their faces. In the theatre a face is a mask of
many moods and expressions, and the bolder your demands on its capabilities the better. But there is one issue a dancer must face more warily,
and that is the question of their general physical proportions. Happy is
the dancer who possesses perfect proportions, for more than half the battle is won. But it is so rare a thing to find, that from an early age one
should develop a sensitive reaction to the smallest shortcoming in this
direction. Submit yourself to severe personal criticism. What you find you
cannot cure, make every effort to hide, even if during the process your
dressmaker or wardrobe mistress becomes your deadliest enemy. I must
add that there is a strange lack of the slightest instinct among our dancers to hide any defect in their build until it is asked of them.

One must now consider the question of the "star," and here it is necessary to speak generally, sweeping all performers of the theatre into the
argument.

What is a star? That depends on your theatrical enterprise. In the commercial theatre the star is an individual of some great personal
magnetism, or possessed of some ability, not necessary far reaching but
of great personal significance.

In the non-commercial theatre (such as a repertory venture or state-aided Opera House) the star has a more awe-inspiring part to play. He or she is a being capable of setting a standard in a recognised art with many and varied recognised forms. This standard is confiscated for the good of the theatre and the progress of its work, just as the discovery by an individual in the medical or scientific world becomes the common property of humanity. Such people cannot withhold themselves or set a price on their own heads; they are, in a way, a part of the institution that made them, and they should pay their debt cheerfully and ungrudgingly.

A Melba night at the Opera used to fill the theatre, and financially her services were always properly rewarded. But Melba's name on the play-bills outside was the same size as the many other singers playing both big and small roles in the opera. How right this method is in theory, for it is well known the civilised can discriminate, and where everything is good everything is of unequal standard.

The playbill one knows of in the average theatre with its varied types is a vulgarism that circumstances make inevitable. But one thing is certain – it is not worth any serious discussion or comment.

Ballet today offers in every country a far greater chance to youth than ever before. All grooves harbour waste and stagnation, and what one occasionally sees proves that there are countries suffering more from these troubles than we are.

My readers may say that a lot of the foregoing remarks breed a philosophy rather than definite action. But perhaps it is a philosophy our English dancers may need. Empire flags may well be folded up, or opened out without comment until we have submitted ourselves with good grace and a little humour to some sort of five-year plan, even it if takes ten in the end, as so many five-year plans do.

It is the irony of life that the work laid out by a good brain can never make either the noise or money of a quick wit. Not that it matters, for all good things are in time accepted as a matter of course, and only their removal causes a hubbub.

Madam and the Betrayed Girls: The Dancers' Perspective

An Introduction by Nicola Katrak to the DVD recording.

This thirty-minute presentation consists of filmed and live interviews, as well as a semi-staged extract from the final scene of Ninette de Valois' 1935 ballet, *The Rake's Progress*. The aim was to illuminate from the inside the role of the faithful young heroine, drawing her out of the shadows often cast by the work's exceptionally strong male characters.

The contributors represented several Royal Ballet generations as well as both Companies. Julia Farron first performed the Betrayed Girl in 1944, teaching the role to Elizabeth Anderton in 1961. Watching her was Alfreda Thorogood, who first danced the part in 1966. Margaret Barbieri and Marion Tait appeared as the Betrayed Girl many times throughout the 1970s, and learning from these ballerinas was Nicola Katrak, who performed the role until the 1980s. Belinda Hatley danced in revivals in the late 1990s and the early twenty-first century.

The presentation evolved from lengthy interviews filmed in January 2010 with Anderton, Hatley, Tait and Thorogood under the expert guidance of experienced dance film-maker, Lynne Wake. A wide range of questions without a fixed agenda was pursued, resulting in an extremely rich resource of personal memories and attitudes to the role, the work and its choreographer. This material was then tightly edited into five short themed sections. These extraordinarily articulate women showed themselves to be true descendants of de Valois: cutting their fascinating thoughts into soundbites was not easy. However the original tapes have now become a valuable addition to The Royal Ballet School Collections.

This controlled filmed material was enhanced by the spontaneity of live contributions from Farron, who vividly evoked the early days of *Rake*, and Barbieri who, among other excellent insights, also added an American perspective of the work.

The resulting unforgettable atmosphere of close connections between all parts of The Royal Ballet family was extended yet further during the closing demonstration of a section from the Bedlam Scene. The Betrayed Girl was danced by an Upper School 2nd Year student, alongside an unplanned, hugely generous appearance by former Principal dancer, David Wall, as the insensible Rake. Further support was given by a student as a Lady of the Town and by pianist, Andrew West, as well as atmospheric lighting by Marius Arnold-Clarke.

Little rehearsal had been possible for this staging due to time-con-straints and, in an ideal world, more of the past interpreters of the Betrayed Girl might have been involved in coaching the student in addi-tion to Katrak. However, the young dancer showed mature sensitivity towards a role that Anderton calls a "privilege ...phenomenal even to cover", in a work that, as Thorogood notes, "says Madam all over it. It is stamped with Madam."[1]

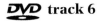 **track 6**

Coaching Roles in *Orpheus and Eurydice and Promenade: An Introduction*

Anna Meadmore

These two short films (each about seven minutes long) represent the edited highlights of two days' filming, which took place at The Royal Ballet School in Covent Garden. Prompted by the wish to create a record of some of de Valois' lesser known ("lost") ballets for The Royal Ballet School Collections, and bolstered by the support of the Linbury Trust, it was possible to secure this marvellous footage of original cast members coaching young dancers in their former roles.

Filmed in July 2003, on a blisteringly hot day, Pamela May (1917 – 2005) coached students of The Royal Ballet School in Eurydice's solo from Ninette de Valois' *Orpheus and Eurydice* (1941), which tells of Orpheus' attempt to recover his beloved Eurydice from the Underworld. The two-act work was based on a libretto of 1762 by Calzabigi, and set to music by Gluck with designs by Sophie Fedorovitch. The original cast included Fonteyn as Love, May as Eurydice, and Helpmann as Orpheus. For the reconstruction, Gillian Revie of The Royal Ballet was able to assist Pamela May, from whom she had learned Eurydice's solo for a gala at The Barbican, held in 1998 to celebrate de Valois' hundredth birthday.

The next recording was made in June 2005. Pauline Clayden (b. 1922) is seen coaching students of The Royal Ballet School in the "Promenade" girl's dance from Ninette de Valois' *Promenade* (1943). This plotless one-act ballet, set in a sunny park, had music by Haydn, arranged by Edwin Evans, and designs by Hugh Stevenson. The "Promenade" solo interacts with several other members of the cast, so we also catch glimpses of a Lepidopterist, a Schoolmistress and a group of Schoolgirls. Leo Kersley, who had inherited the role of the Lepidopterist from Gordon Hamilton, was present for part of the filming, and noted that Pauline Clayden's quality of movement reminded him very much of de Valois' own as a dancer. As Kathrine Sorley Walker wrote:

> The role that at one time de Valois would have danced was the Promenade solo, with its speed, sharpness and vivacity. There were parallels in construction between the Promenade girl and Papillon ...in [Fokine's] *Carnaval*.[1]

It should be noted that – as it was a purely archival exercise – the budget for filming was modest, a fact which is reflected in the quality of the recording. However, the standard of the material itself is superb: the dancers from The Royal Ballet School (2nd Year Upper School) gave their all, and received expert support from Guy Attew on the piano. It goes without saying that Pamela May and Pauline Clayden themselves were extraordinary; their energy and commitment a testament to the high regard in which they held de Valois and her work.

Both dances were meticulously recorded during rehearsals by Kendra Johnson of the Institute for Benesh Movement Notation. Kendra is visible in some of the shots, as are Dr Geraldine Morris and Anya Linden, Lady Sainsbury, who sat in on some of the rehearsals.

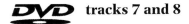 **tracks 7 and 8**

Crafting a Collaboration of "Talents"

Susie Crow and Jennifer Jackson

Soon after her death, we were commissioned to write an article reflecting on de Valois' legacy. Our research drew attention to shifts over time in practice and thinking. In *Come Dance With Me* de Valois herself had reflected on "a sobering truth: I am convinced that we shape no event as forcibly as events shape us".[1] As she was shaped by her experience, so her choices have shaped our growth as artists. For us, as members of that tiny demographic of women ballet choreographers, de Valois is a figure towering in her achievement but controversial in her impact. Ten years ago she was a part of the present, today she feels part of our history. But who and what constructs that history? What became of her dancerly and choreographic gifts as a woman? To what extent are we shaped to this day by her creative light – and shadow?

This essay is provoked by the dedication on the memorial plaque laid at Westminster Abbey on 17 November 2009 and inherent contradictions in de Valois' life – and the way in which these play out beyond her person. American Dance Historian, Jennifer Homans, talks of the rise "as if from nowhere" of The Royal Ballet as an "undisputed world leader in dance" in the mid-twentieth century.[2] At the memorial event four key players, Ashton, Fonteyn, Lambert and de Valois, were awarded full posthumous honours as the founders of the Company. Seen thus, the emergence of a British world class ballet is framed as the result of a highly successful collaboration of talents, an example of what contemporary Creativity Studies theorist, Keith Sawyer, calls "group genius".[3]

Yet arguably, The Royal Ballet as an institution is de Valois' "great work", for which she sacrificed the recognition as dancer and choreographer that her "co-founders" Fonteyn and Ashton enjoy. The lonely path of her early years as a jobbing dance artist, generated not only a bold personal vision for the future of ballet in Britain but also a do-it-yourself attitude to developing an educational and artistic institution she never had the benefit of herself. Arguably her sense of service to building a tradition led to her own self sacrifice as an artist. Looking at her from today's perspective with the work of women choreographers in eclipse (as suggested by the 2009 debate at the Queen Elizabeth Hall *Where are the women?*) and films such as *Black Swan* making victims of women in ballet– can de Valois be read as the archetypal example of the self-sabotaging female artist?

Research on creativity and collaboration across both industry and academia highlights the inter-relational nature of the workplace and the social character of art-making. Vera John-Steiner draws on psychologist Lev Vygotsky's idea that "thinking is not confined to the individual" but knowledge is co-constructed and arises from its cultural and historical setting. Expert in corporate creativity, Charles Handy, comments that – "organisations are micro-societies, not objects".[4]

De Valois' career reveals that she was well able to collaborate with fellow creatives, the movers and shakers in politics and theatre – Lilian Baylis, Maynard Keynes, Terence Gray, William Butler Yeats, Constant Lambert, Arthur Bliss, Philip Richardson, Frederick Ashton. Yet the relationship of "Madam" with her dancers could not be described as collaborative. Even near-contemporary and long-term colleague, Leslie Edwards, refers to her as "Miss de Valois"; actors in Cambridge nick-named her "the games mistress" for her bracingly disciplined rehearsal style;[5] and dancers over the generations recall her appearances in the studio with terror. In interview, Moira Shearer remarked on de Valois as "a ruthless dictator", but also:

> ... a choreographer of immense talent and perception [with] a complete vision of taking the work of various painters and magically translating this into stage movement. Rehearsals with her were hell. But performing these ballets was a delight.[6]

Her choreographic working method did not involve the dancers in the process of creating movement material in the manner evolved by Ashton and MacMillan (and so much an accepted element of today's choreographic practice). Instead she valued clear boundaries between dancers and choreographer and even appears critical of other approaches. Of Balanchine she writes: "His facility was astounding; but he was very influenced by the personalities of his dancers and quite obviously exploited them in preference to his own ego."[7] Choreography is the most exposing of creative processes. Seen in the light of John Berger's critique of the social construction of Western art, vulnerability in the female artist would be perceived through her gender rather than her artistry. Men survey women before treating them. Consequently how a woman appears to a man can determine how she will be treated.[8] Where male choreographers might work through their uncertainties in the studio, de Valois' methods masked hers.

But the notion of collaboration can be seen not simply in terms of outward-facing collaborations with others. Sawyer claims that "the mind itself is filled with a kind of internal collaboration, that insights that emerge when you are completely alone can be traced back to previous collaborations".[9] In a similar way de Valois' different talents – as dancer, choreographer, teacher, director, pedagogue, thinker and poet – collaborate in forming her vision and facilitating the "magical" translation of ideas to reality.

The period of her intense artistic development in the 1930s, when these roles were in creative balance, followed formative experiences in the 1920s: her dancing with the *Ballets Russes*, work for Lilian Baylis, involvement with experimental theatre in Cambridge with Terence Gray and in Dublin with William Butler Yeats. Frances Harris suggests that it was awareness of the "inadequacies in her education" and need for the "tools to get on with the job" that led her to Diaghilev and then – having sharpened those tools – to setting up her aspirational Academy.[10] De Valois the analyst would have benefited not only from her observations of other artists' work but also from her participation in and embodiment of choreographic and class material. The exercise of transmitting her learning to her budding School and Company further honed her practice-based knowledge. Leo Kersley evokes the spirit of creative endeavour at this time: "De Valois had a wonderful company where Fred [Ashton] did the romantic ballets and she did the serious ones".[11] A prolific flowering of dancing and dance-making in challenging but artistically stimulating circumstances enabled her creation of a handful of major works.

De Valois' collaboration with Yeats invites us to consider the *integration* of dancerly and choreographic talents in her artistic development. Richard Cave highlights the somatic dimension of de Valois' dance in her work with Yeats – her embodiment of (female) power through the choreographic structures that she invented and performed.[12] Being considerably older than her, Yeats was also de Valois' mentor and champion and their working process mobilised her gifts for performing and choreographing. They shared a belief in rigour, mastery and the interdisciplinarity between literary and theatrical "texts". However, in sharp contrast with many of her other artistic relationships, de Valois' combined talents were being employed to realise *his* theatrical project.

Yeats' methods resembled a kind of "performance-based research" –

where personal and disciplinary knowledge is reintegrated into embodied form. Cave's descriptions of *The King of the Great Clock Tower* (1934) point to strong aesthetic and thematic relations with *Checkmate* (1937): in the architectural geometry of the staging and the contest between male and female symbols of power in the interplay between the personal and the public in the characters of the King and Queen. This ballet, which David Bintley says was her favourite, [13] combines classical dancing (which remains technically challenging) and choreographic invention. She manages to resolve in the *form* of the work the aesthetic (and philosophical) tensions that she perceived between modern expressionist and traditional ballet and about which she writes in 1937. When discussing "The Choreographer" in *Invitation to the Ballet*, de Valois sees "a lack of true theatrical education, and complete confusion as to the meaning of the synthesis of the arts", which theatrical production demands.[14] She describes the struggle facing the young choreographer and dancer between "the function of the medium and the exploitation of his own ego":

> [...] when confronted with the necessity of discipline and adjustment; and the amount of sheer technique and knowledge the theatre demands of him to achieve his end... It seems the true 'choreographic' theatre is the classroom, quite complete in itself as far as this art is capable of being self-sufficient.[15]

De Valois proved her own ability to bring the parts to harmonic whole. But her choreographic output withers during the 1940s with her last major production, *Don Quixote* of 1950, drawing a mixed reaction.

The move to Covent Garden in 1946 seems a defining moment.[16] Having reached the BIG House – she had to fill it with certain kinds of ballets and dancers, whose bodily architecture would *read* in that context. She recognised the backbone of the Imperial Ballet schooling in the success of the *Ballets Russes* and wanted a British ballet institution strong enough to challenge the Russians. Seeing that Petipa's choreography would underpin the development of dancer's 'classical' fitness, she imported key works that, as Beth Genné eloquently identifies, have come to represent a 'classical canon' in the repertory worldwide.[17] The strategic employment of these works during the war underpinned her Company's graceful move to the Opera House. De Valois understood embodiment of the dancer – you are what you dance – well-structured classical material nurtures the dancer's instrument.

But is there a perceptible shift towards preparing for already existing rather than unknown works? In the push towards home grown "classics" in the 1950s, did she *direct* her interests away from her modernist principles of choreographic exploration towards production on old models? Did she lose touch with the embodied practice of dancing? De Valois' rehearsal style prevented her from drawing on the creativity of dancers to invigorate her language and ideas. Her meticulous preparation in advance of rehearsal might suggest doubt as to her own powers of invention in the moment, but her ability to move between roles and circumstances belies this. In his research into collaboration Sawyer discusses the role of improvisation as generating the highest form of creativity.[18] Much of de Valois' own work was made under pressure with little time or money, her qualities of practicality and pragmatism ideally suited to making good. Her ability to respond to volatile circumstances, to negotiate opportunities and improvise with available resources is convincingly exemplified by the extraordinary growth of popularity of the Sadler's Wells Ballet during the war.

But increasingly from 1940 her ballets can be seen as being made not to forward her own choreographic vision and artistic impulses but more and more as providing *pièces d'occasion,* making work for others, for establishment or didactic purposes, for special events, to fit in productions of other ballets, or nationalistic work for the Turkish. David Bintley, who revived *The Prospect Before Us* for her hundredth birthday, remarks that, while Ashton was making the sombre *Dante Sonata,* she would have thought: "Better do something cheery", a revealing reversal of roles.[19] Even *Don Quixote* she took on when Helpmann could not do it, because of another commitment. It was on a large scale with a distinguished score and designs by respected artists.[20] Press reviews of the work, however, suggest an uneasy balance between narrative expressionist and classical principles, as theorised in her writings and which she had successfully bridged earlier in *Checkmate* and *The Rake's Progress.*[21]

The work was austere. Richard Buckle (1950) criticised a lack of dance and dancing, and A.V. Coton (1950) was also unconvinced: "Characters are conceived largely in two-dimensional shapes and rarely expand into live men and women."[22] But Sorley Walker as a female critic found much to admire in the work:

…its slow and dignified movement, the half comic touches, the refined inflections of mime and reflections of the score, and the way effects were built up by sparse and economic means, using snatches of dance and movement, brief pas de deux, uncompleted gestures, to contrive a wonderfully moving whole.[23]

De Valois herself thought that it might have worked better on the smaller stage at Sadler's Wells. In her drive to establish the national Company, had she successfully developed a context and an audience that was not interested in the sort of creative work that she herself could do? Buckle's criticism can be seen in the light of his championing Balanchine's work; an early salvo in an ongoing ideological conflict in ballet between a European expressionist aesthetic with close links to theatre and American formalism. The negative response of the American public when the piece was performed on the 1950 US tour reinforces this and, as Sorley Walker states, "sealed its fate".[24]

Paradoxically, at the same time, Martha Graham's embodied exploration of theatre dance expressionism was becoming the pillar of modern dance. De Valois was suspicious of the "singular" artistic vision of artists such as Graham and Wigman – regarding "their creation as based on a destruction *of* rather than an evolution *from* what has gone before".[25] She saw her work as springing from and feeding a collective body of knowledge – more in common with Richard Sennet's craftsman than a lone genius.[26]

Decades later in her magisterial but contestable history of ballet Jennifer Homans names as the two pillars in the Vic-Wells repertoire: "Ashton's ballets (along with de Valois') and the Russian Imperial classics of Marius Petipa".[27] Homans' perspective is clearly shaped by her experience as an American who danced for Balanchine; and, though she writes dancers and choreographers into her account, none of de Valois' ballets are cited. In her discussion of The Royal Ballet's rise – and "fall" – she claims that "Ashton's ballets and Fonteyn's dancing seemed to hold a mirror to some of the best qualities of British National character".[28] But, writing in *The National Ballet: A History and a Manifesto*, Arnold Haskell, pointed to qualities of interdependence that Homans misses:

Three groups of people, working independently and at the same time co-operating in a spirit that is only possible with the much abused British temperament, formed the beginnings of British ballet proper. ...[He then devotes sections to Rambert; Markova and Dolin]...The third and most important force in the founding of the National Ballet was Ninette de Valois.[29]

Educational psychologist, Howard Gardner, identifies four types of extraordinary minds as models of creative achievement: the Master whose mastery of a domain of accomplishment enables innovation within the form, the Maker who creates a new domain of achievement, the Introspector who explores and illuminates the interior life of persons, and the Influencer who changes the thinking of others.[30] Ashton and Balanchine might be seen as Masters within ballet. De Valois, however, can be seen as both a Maker and an Influencer: she built a ballet establishment; her best work resolves questions between modernist and classical principles and moves towards a new choreographic aesthetic; her dissemination of ideas about pedagogy underpin ballet attitudes to this day.

But her significance as a choreographer and her role in enabling the flowering of other artists are dangerously marginalised. She consistently downplayed her achievements as a dancer and choreographer in later life. Leslie Edwards writes of theatricals changing trains at Crewe on Sundays – the actresses in their heels and the dancers in their brogues, as demanded by de Valois.[31] The feminine qualities of discretion, modesty and service, which de Valois possessed and also expected of her female dancers, appear now to stand for her achievements in the histories as they are being written by scholars such as Homans. Her stated priority to establish a repertoire and institution would have left her with little energy for her own work. Her withdrawal from choreography appears inevitable; but at what cost, both personally and to the art form today? In a conversation with Peter Wilson in the last decade of her life, she revealed that giving up her choreographic career was "the greatest disappointment of my life".[32] Her housekeeping role is now played out in contemporary dance, where female administrators service the careers of male choreographers.[33] Her example of self sacrifice and thinking has arguably contributed to a dance culture that lacks confidence in female choreographic voices. Looking at de Valois' life we better understand the on-going debates and contradictions in ballet culture today and the gendered experience of women – the paradox of their numerous bodies and relatively few voices. Without her it is a given that *we* collectively would not have had the benefit of the learning and performance opportunities that she never had. That the Westminster plaque commemorates her collaboration and her self-effacement above her individual gifts or talents attests to the contradictions in her life and legacy.

Part Seven: Collaborations

Ninette de Valois, the Bloomsbury Group, and the role of visual culture in the formation of the early Royal Ballet[1]

Helena Hammond

Recalling a "brief, sharp picture of Gordon Square in the [nineteen-]thirties" Ninette de Valois remembered how:

> I am at No. 46; it is the drawing-room and *tableaux vivants* and theatrical playlets are in progress. The curtain parts: it reveals Lydia and Maynard but it is also "Victoria and her Albert". By this time Bloomsbury has discovered Lydia's undoubted resemblance. What an audience! In silhouette I can recognise the following heads: Lytton Strachey, G.B. Shaw, Clive Bell, Duncan Grant, Vanessa Bell, Roger Fry, Virginia Woolf – all Bloomsbury in force – to complete the picture of those years.[2]

This chapter focuses on the symbiotic and multi-faceted relationship between Ninette de Valois, ballet, and artistic culture. It pays special attention to the bonds that connected de Valois to the Bloomsbury Group, the early twentieth-century social and artistic network of painters, writers, and figures engaged in allied cultural fields, centered on the Bloomsbury area of central London, and on Gordon Square in particular. The powerful hold exerted on the Bloomsbury Group by dance in general, and by the Ballets Russes in particular, has begun to receive some attention and acknowledgement.[3] In comparison, the significant parts played by visual culture generally, and by painting especially, in determining de Valois' artistic formation have received far less recognition. It is this imbalance that this chapter seeks to address and correct, by demonstrating the formative influence of visual culture on de Valois.

Painting and art history not only shaped de Valois' thinking about the role of stage design and costume in ballet, they also informed her aim to establish, rapidly, a ballet repertory intrinsic to her project to equip Britain with a national ballet company. They even influenced her choreographic practice to the extent that de Valois can be seen to have brought an unusually pictorial eye to the act of making dances. To paraphrase Stravinsky, if watching Balanchine's choreography amounted to hearing the music with your eyes,[4] de Valois' choreography evidently inspired an equally forceful and deep-seated rapport with pictorial sources. According to dance critic, Arnold Haskell:

> With Hogarth as her inspiration Ninette de Valois has succeeded in *The Rake's Progress* not merely in creating compositions that if you know the vivid series of paintings you will readily recognise as coming from Hogarth, but in creating thousands of other pictures, each lasting for a fraction of a second, that Hogarth himself might have composed.[5]

And Haskell detected the same privileging of pictorial sources as the seedbed of de Valois' choreographic inventiveness in other of her key choreographies of the 1930s. In *The National Ballet: A History and a Manifesto*, he wrote of how in *Job*, "based on the drawings of William Blake with music by Vaughan Williams... she created a thousand pictures each one of which bore the unmistakable stamp of Blake. Later she repeated this *tour de force* with Rowlandson".[6] For Haskell, *Job*, created in 1931, marked a decisive crossroads in de Valois' development as a choreographer. The powerful impression made on Haskell by the ballet's danced dialogue with painting extended to informing the actual vocabularies of his writing about *Job*. In this ballet, de Valois

> pointed a totally new choreographic direction, one that was the exact opposite to that of Ashton. In terms of painting she was becoming a master of the *Conversation Piece* [italics are Haskell's]. Her point of departure was the most risky of all, literature, literature inspired by painting at that.

> De Valois' work can be divided in two groups, the first suggested by painting or by a literary conception – *Job*, *The Rake's Progress*, *The Prospect Before Us*, *Checkmate*, *The God's Go A-Begging* (Watteau); the second by the music or by a more conventional "ballet story", *Prometheus*, *The Haunted Ballroom*, *Les Douanes*, *Barabau*.[7]

"When de Valois chooses the right material," Haskell concluded, "Cruikshank and Callot, Goya and Greenaway await her, she produces something that will live."[8] Writing on *Job*, also at the time of the ballet's first performance in July 1931, critic Frank Howe was similarly alert to de Valois' same capacity to elucidate and extend pictorial meaning through dance:

What the dance does is to give movement to Blake's drawings, to add temporal rhythm to graphical design, to absorb and be absorbed by the music, which has itself the double inspiration of Blake and the Bible.[9]

Association with the artists and intellectuals drawn to Bloomsbury, especially to 46 Gordon Square, the home of economist John Maynard Keynes and his wife Lydia Lopokova, the former Ballets Russes dancer whom de Valois called "my greatest friend in the theatre", was to prove crucial for the early history of the Vic-Wells (later Sadler's Wells Ballet) Company.[10] As de Valois recalled:

Once we had headlines in an evening paper – "Bloomsbury Ballet for the Highbrows for 9*d.*" – an allusion to the current production – the Duncan Grant décor and costumes for Doone's *Tombeau de Couperin*, and our modest gallery price. My own production of *Création du Monde* (Milhaud) with décor and costumes by Edward Wolfe (inherited from the Camargo) appealed to the minority and enraged the majority: Miss Baylis, I fear, heavily on the side of the majority....Slowly our more severe critics decided that, with the assistance of the classics, the Bloomsbury set and our growing English repertoire of ballets, we were bearable between September and May – when there were no Russians to view at Covent Garden.[11]

Endorsement from members of the Bloomsbury Group would furnish ballet in Britain – and de Valois' fledgling Company in particular – with precious cultural kudos and capital at vital points in their early formation, as Beth Genné has begun to explore.[12] Familial connections between de Valois and Bloomsbury (Bloomsbury artist, Duncan Grant, was a distant cousin); the seminal role played by John Maynard Keynes in helping to obtain establishment recognition and some degree of financial security for de Valois' Company; as well as de Valois' work with Bloomsbury artists (Vanessa Bell in particular) through the Camargo Society ballets of the early 1930s, are all instances of the bonds of connection between de Valois and the Bloomsbury Group.

Having explored some of these critical early interconnections, this chapter moves to offer an assessment of the impact of Bloomsbury on de Valois in terms of the broader implications and legacy for the Company she founded, as it went on to secure cultural prestige and a surer footing through its incorporation as part of the British arts establishment and –

with the installation of the Sadler's Wells Ballet at the Royal Opera House in 1946 – recognition as part of the theatre that became the "jewel in the crown of the post-war arts firmament".[13] A particular preoccupation of this chapter is therefore with the way in which this formative interface between de Valois, literary and – especially – *visual* cultures helped shape the future direction of the Company that was to become The Royal Ballet. "Until I married in 1935 I lived within a few hundred yards of Gordon Square, and was a member of the Bloomsbury ballet contingent" de Valois would later recall. "Around me there gradually formed a Bloomsbury contingent of the ballet. Within two years Frederick Ashton was a near neighbour, Michael Somes eventually reached Lloyd Square, and Ursula Moreton lived in Mecklenburgh Square." De Valois was at pains to acknowledge the debt she owed to Bloomsbury: "46 Gordon Square, the home of the Keynes family, was for me and for other dancers a refuge from everyday life. Lydia and Maynard took on themselves, as it were, the care of the British Ballet."[14]

Ballet and Bloomsbury

This early twentieth-century dialogue between visual culture and dance, of an unprecedented intensity within a British context, was not one-sided. Writing to the poet Rupert Brooke, Edward Marsh, a civil servant and assistant to Winston Churchill, described Vaslav Nijinsky's *Jeux* as a "Post-Impressionist picture in motion...it has almost brought me round to Matisse's pictures!".[15] The role of the London seasons of the Ballets Russes, as danced interlocutions that mediated Post-Impressionist exoticism for Bloomsbury Group artists, hungry for news of the latest artistic developments in Paris, is just one example of ballet's impact on Bloomsbury. With the first of the London performances of the Ballets Russes, in April 1911, the Company's "compelling dance style was epitomised by a new emphasis on the sensuous presentation of the body which was a major influence on [Bloomsbury artists Vanessa] Bell and [Duncan] Grant".[16] Certainly the choreographers' own accounts of these ballets resonated with the same liberating terms, so redolent of relaxed codes of social and sexual discourse, to which the Bloomsbury artists subscribed. Describing her brother Vaslav's *Jeux*, Bronislava Nijinska wrote of how "everything in the choreography was new – free movements and positions of the body, applied to classical ballet technique".[17] Quick to identify the dancing body as a key driver of modernity, the Bloomsbury artists soon came to regard the Ballets Russes as a kindred project. For the

Bloomsbury group, "to respond to the Russian dancers was to emerge from ossified forms of Victorian and Edwardian artistic and cultural constraints into a new sensibility".[18] According to Leonard Woolf, writing in 1911:

> It looked for the moment as if militarism, imperialism, anti-Semitism were on the run... The revolution of the motor car and the aeroplane had begun; Freud and Rutherford and Einstein were at work beginning to revolutionise our knowledge of our minds and the universe... And to crown it all, night after night we flocked to Covent Garden, entranced by a new art, a revelation to us benighted British, the Russian Ballet in the greatest day of Diaghilev and Nijinsky.[19]

"Night after night," Woolf continued,

> one could go to Covent Garden and find all round one one's friends, the people whom one liked best in the world, moved and excited as one was oneself. In all my long life in London this is the only instance in which I can remember the intellectuals going night after night to a theatre.[20]

The Bloomsbury Group's excitement over the Ballets Russes may not necessarily have extended to enthusiasm for the dancers themselves – news of former Ballets Russes ballerina Lydia Lopokova's marriage to John Maynard Keynes, for instance, was met with a mixed reception by the artists drawn to Bloomsbury.[21] Yet it paved the way for the series of working relationships and alliances which members of the group, following the lead of Maynard Keynes, established with de Valois, who had herself danced with Diaghilev's Company in the 1920s. As de Valois' biographer, Kathrine Sorley Walker, has stressed, this experience left a lasting impression on the young de Valois:

> Many characteristics of the Diaghilev Ballet were absorbed to future advantage. The concept of unity, with composer, designer and choreographer each contributing vital elements to a production, appealed to her greatly and would govern not only her own ballets but her general policy in the Vic-Wells Ballet and its successors.[22]

And this point is also made by Beth Genné: "everything of value to do with the presentation of ballet, the study of choreography and the development of the artist" de Valois learned from "her apprenticeship with The

Russian Ballet".[23] De Valois' close identification with Diaghilev's precepts for ballet, with his advocacy of ballet as one-act, total art work, in particular, enabled the choreographies she created to register in terms readily recognisable to Bloomsbury artists. "We know that what she saw of the traditional repertory did not really excite her when she was in the Diaghilev Company in the early twenties," Genné emphasises. "The small company made up of her pupils at her first school, the Academy of Choregraphic [de Valois' spelling] Art, danced an exclusively modern repertory."[24]

And de Valois adhered closely to the maxim of ballet as *gesamtkunstwerk*, or total art work, that was so significant for the Ballets Russes. Ballets Russes designer, Alexandre Benois, defined the *gesamtkunstwerk* as a process of "collective mastery", whereby "the charm of each artist flowed together in the beauty of the ensemble".[25] This notion of ballet as unprecedented collaboration between choreographer, composer, designer and librettist, fusing dance, music, costume and design into an apparently seamless whole was championed by de Valois in her own writing on "Modern Choreography". "A dance production is subjected to the same variations as painting, music, sculpture and the drama" she urged in the *Dancing Times* in 1933. "The non-commercial theatre for ballet production, whether big or small, is the hardest but most satisfactory taskmaster of all. This form of theatre works for artistes expressing a highly qualified unity and does not rely on the drawing powers of one individual personality." Working in this theatrical setting, the choreographer "must make his ballet a living and sincere thing of the theatre, something to be enjoyed by the actor, the musician and the painter, in the way these people can make a dancer appreciate their work".[26]

The Camargo Society[27]

Founded – to quote from the preliminary announcement of the Camargo Society's Savoy Theatre 1932 summer season – "two years earlier", the society had been set up in "close relation [with the] Vic-Wells Ballet [which] under the direction of Ninette de Valois [was enjoying] such remarkable success", as well as in connection with Marie Rambert's Ballet Club. Chief among the "Objects of the Society" was "the aim of establishing Ballet as an indigenous and permanently based art in England" with, as another, related "prime objective", the provision of "training and opportunity to British dancers, composer and artists." Consequently, just as music was to be "mainly selected from new or unfamiliar pieces by English composers... the collaboration of artists such as John Banting, Vanessa Bell and Duncan Grant is expected" announced the Society in 1932. John Maynard Keynes was its treasurer, and de Valois and Lydia Lopokova members of its General Committee. Significant among the Society's patrons and guarantors was the industrialist, Samuel Courtauld, who was simultaneously assembling one of the world's most important collections of works by those same Post-Impressionist painters that had been so inspirational for the Bloomsbury artists. Artistic decisions were referred to Arnold Haskell, in his role as the Society's Art Director. Unsurprisingly, given both the composition of its guiding committee, and the purpose of its establishment as "the best means of fostering the art of Ballet – then recently bereaved of a valuable guiding influence in the lamented death of the late Serge Diaghilev", the Camargo Society was founded on Diaghilevian principles: "Ballet being a collaboration of the three arts of dancing, music and decorative design, the first step was to obtain the collaboration of those versed in them", the *Dancing Times* recorded in its March 1930 issue, covering "The [Inaugural] Camargo Dinner".[28]

Job and *The Origin of Design* were among the choreographies the Camargo Society commissioned from de Valois during its years of operation in the early 1930s. The second of these, "a pseudo-classical production" danced to Handel and featuring Lopokova in its cast, with décor by William Chappell conceived as "faithful renderings" of designs for a masque by Inigo Jones, was used by de Valois, as part of her blueprint for "Modern Choreography" as published in the *Dancing Times*, to exemplify ballet that is "pictorial both in construction and design".[29] The artistic aims and tastes of the Bloomsbury Group and de Valois especially aligned in the ballets she created under the patronage and funding of the Camargo Society, with its recruitment of artists drawn from Bloomsbury and the surrounding cultural milieu. Edward Wolfe, responsible for the designs for *La Création de Monde*, having exhibited with the Omega Workshops co-directed by Duncan Grant and Vanessa Bell, went on to join the London Artists' Association (LAA), for several members of which "the influence of [the Post-Impressionist] artist Matisse was decisive".[30] In existence from 1927-33, the LAA enjoyed the support of Keynes as guarantor. Artist Gwen Raverat, as the designer-interlocutor for *Job's* visual sources in William Blake was a member of the Neo-Pagans, a group closely allied to Bloomsbury and whose interest in ceremonial and processional art lent itself very well to adaptation as theatrical design.

But de Valois' strongly Bloomsbury-oriented artistic affiliations reverberated also in *Bar aux Folies-bergère*, the ballet she created in 1934 for Marie Rambert's company to a scenario by Ashley Dukes. Dukes "appealed to her [de Valois'] lasting appreciation of painting by linking the pictures of Manet and the Paris of Toulouse-Lautrec".[31] Manet's painting was to be interpreted and translated for the ballet in theatrical terms by the designer William Chappell. Promoting Manet in this way, de Valois' ballet joined the Bloomsbury artists, for whom Manet was a "tribal deity" in championing Post-Impressionist art at a time when its reception by the British cultural establishment, even in the London metropolis, was still shaky and by no means assured.[32] The National Gallery, Millbank (the present-day Tate Britain) had only acquired its first four paintings by Picasso the previous year.[33] At least one of these paintings, Picasso's very early still-life work, *Flowers*, painted in 1901, and so belonging to the artist's naturalist period, was highly unrepresentative of his later innovative avant-gardism. The often jingoist, nationalist, and conservative climate and rhetoric of national debates then circulating about visual culture and its public display are indicated in the publication, in a 1930 edition of *The Daily Telegraph*, of a letter calling for the removal of all foreign works from the Millbank museum.[34] And only a decade before de Valois' Post-Impressionist ballet, Courtauld needed to donate £50,000 as the Samuel Courtauld Fund to the National Gallery, Millbank. This was with the express intention of building up the Tate's holdings of foreign modern art, through purchases "confined to a specific list of French artists", as part of its collection.[35] Works by Cézanne, Matisse and Picasso were still being refused by the gallery's directors as recently as 1926.[36]

At the same time, it is important not to overlook de Valois' showcasing, through so many of her ballets, of a pantheon of *British* visual artists. Taken together, these ballets almost amounted to a danced gallery of artistic worthies, at a time when confidence in – and so the championing of – a history of indigenous, British visual culture, as an intrinsic part of the public sphere, was still a relatively new phenomena. It had only been with the establishment of the National Gallery of British Art at Tate Millbank in 1897 that "for the first time the British nation had a picture gallery in which works of national artistic talent could be viewed by a worthy and self-consciously national audience".[37] Describing *The Rake's Progress*, designed by Rex Whistler and made in 1935, just one year after *Bar aux Folies-bergère*, as "the first all-British ballet", Anton Dolin wrote of how de Valois' choreography for this later ballet "translated Hogarth's pictures into movement. She was not afraid of the painter's realism or the truths about the town life of the period as lived outside the fashionable houses. No attempt was made to refine the horrors...".[38] De Valois herself similarly described the "drop scene" curtain by Roger Furse for her wartime (1940) ballet *The Prospect Before Us* "in the style of Rowlandson's cartoons"[39] as depicting "[Thomas] Rowlandson's eighteenth-century theatre in flames, and the audience of that period in a state of moral panic... the bucolic and bawdy painting which spelt Rowlandson."[40] If the Ballets Russes mediated a modern re-conception of the body for the visual artists of Bloomsbury, de Valois' reciprocated the interest visual artists had shown in dance by offering an embodied and visceral choreographic commentary on the history of satire and British graphic visual culture. The emphasis Rowlandson and Hogarth had placed on a bodily sense of buffoonery and bawdiness lent itself very well to this sort of adaptation in dance. As Haskell commended in his endorsement of *The Rake's Progress* as part of a discussion of choreographers entitled "Sculptors of the Human Body": "Anyone who is creating a ballet that has been inspired by, let us say, El Greco can make a static picture in the Greco manner; what is important and difficult is to create every movement as if it were inspired by El Greco."[41]

In taking her cue from Keynes and simultaneously commissioning a *new* generation of British artists, de Valois simultaneously showed herself increasingly keen to engage with the *sculptural* as well as pictorial inheritors of British visual traditions. Writing in 1933, she observed:

> The ballet production of today is inclined to follow the two rather sharply divided lines of the "pictorial" and the "architectural". I think the great possibilities of the future lies [sic] in the progress and development of the latter. I feel the greatest day in the history of ballet production will come when the sculptor is employed for the mounting of ballet as generally as the painter and theatre designer is today.[42]

In nominating Henry Moore, Britain's foremost twentieth-century sculptor, as a possible future designer for ballet, Arnold Haskell was characteristically quick to endorse this call made by de Valois' for a new sculpturalism in British ballet:

> English painting has not yet had an opportunity of making use of the ballet medium, the fresco as Diaghileff once said, of the contemporary artist. I would like to see added to the list that contains Burra, Hurry, Piper, Sutherland, such names as Henry Moore, Frances Hodgkins,

Ivon Hitchins, to name but three artists each of whom has something to express through the medium of ballet.[43]

The impact of this visual acuity which de Valois brought to ballet has had a far-reaching effect on the Company she founded. One only has to think of this legacy in terms of the "fused" ballets, with their characteristic equal emphasis on choreographic, musical and design texts, that defined so much of the work of Frederick Ashton and Kenneth MacMillan as they followed in her footsteps as subsequent choreographer-directors of The Royal Ballet.

De Valois as Colleague and Collaborator
A Discussion led by Gerald Dowler[1]

Gerald Dowler (GD): This panel, comprising Dame Beryl Grey, Dame Antoinette Sibley, Sir Peter Wright and David Wall, is meeting to discuss the more personal side of de Valois as a collaborator and colleague. Sir Peter, from your experience as a Company Director, could you speak a little about de Valois's planning and also the rehearsing of revivals of her work?

Peter Wright (PW): My association with Madam goes back to 1942. Up and down, I've had good times and I've had terrible times. As a dancer not much of a relationship really, mostly because I kept hiving off and going to other companies; but she always had me back. I really got to know her and love her when I was her side of the fence, as it were. When it came to working on her productions, not rehearsing them but getting them on and getting them sorted out, she was very, very difficult. Part demon and part angel, I might say; and very changeable in her ideas about casting, about steps, and ideas about lighting. She also was quite crafty. What was amazing about Madam was that she always actually did come and rehearse. Though she could never spend very much time, she got incredible results but she used certain ploys, I discovered. There was one particular instance when we were reviving *The Rake's Progress*; we'd done it several times but she wanted to rehearse the Brothel scene; she was very anxious to get that moving, she said. Well, she came to a rehearsal, I wasn't taking it but John Hall, my wonderful assistant, was; and he'd rehearsed it absolutely marvellously; I have to say he got those girls really into 'whores'. Madam came in, settled herself down, and said, "Right, we'll go from the beginning."   Those girls started and they were fantastic. After thirty seconds she raised her hand [Sir Peter clapped his hands]; she said: "Stop. Might I remind you young ladies this is not *Le Lac des cygnes*." [General laughter] She said: "You're in a brothel; it is a whorehouse and you're out to get what you can." And then she went back and sat down: "We'll go through it again now." I said to her, "Madam, do you really think that they were like swans?" "Oh no, of course I don't. I always say this sort of thing: it gets them on their mettle and then you really might get a performance." She said: "Right, once again from the top." And I saw those girls [think]: "We'll show her." I tell you it was the most fantastic performance and it stuck: they were incredible and remained that way.

But the thing too with Madam was how she changed her mind about things. In *Checkmate*, there is an entrance at the very end: the Black Queen is carried around the stage prior to where she is going to murder the old King. She's carried round the stage and, as she gets to the back, so a light in the footlights shines out and makes the most amazing shadows on the back and you see the Black Queen with her sword ready to murder the King. Well, that was how it was when I first saw it. She [de Valois] came back again [to the rehearsals]; when the Black Queen came on, of course the light didn't come on. She said, "Where is the light?" We had a very difficult chief electrician in those days. He said, "It's later, Madam." She said, "No it's not. It should come on now, as she makes the entrance." I said, "Madam, I think you'll find in the score it's...." "I don't care what it says in the score, it comes on as she comes on." So John Hall had to change it and it was difficult to change. It's not just a matter of bringing the lights up early, because the other lights have to co-ordinate the change. We actually had hardly any time to get the production on. She'd insisted on it going on, because we were going into the fortieth anniversary performance, 1977. Anyway we changed it all and the light came on, the effect had gone actually but she stuck to her guns until the next time when we got to the same place and the light came on. "I do not like that light coming on there, it's the wrong place. Cut it out." So again we had to change the whole thing and got it back to its right place, and of course it looked marvellous. But you see John Hall had the audacity to say, "You're very inconsistent, Madam." "Well," she said, "Consistency clearly means a feeble mind."

GD: Dame Beryl, I saw you nodding at many, many points there. In terms of your experience of Dame Ninette de Valois: she was Director during all the time that you were there. Did you have a lot of things in common, a lot of points that you agreed with?

Beryl Grey: Oh, yes. I agree completely, I suppose one could just say that she was very Irish. There were many things, little things, that, I think, perhaps haven't been known about her. Have you mentioned her continual illnesses before the war? I first came under the influence of this great woman when I was nine. She auditioned me in 1937 and took me into the School. Then I trained with her; I had at least one class a week from her for four years. During the second year in 1939, she introduced the history of dance lessons. We all used to go up into the opera room and sit cross-legged and she would give an hour's talk about the history of dance, which was very unusual at that time. We all adored and enjoyed it tremendously. When I joined the Company in 1941, Julia Farron was there, who recalls dancing for the troops; and that's what we had to do six weeks of every year in the war. Madam wouldn't allow any of the men not to go into the forces; she was insistent that they all fought for the country; and so sometimes we had about six or seven boys in the Company; and that's why the Waltz in *The Sleeping Beauty* was done only with girls, because we didn't have boys. Then, of course, after the war we travelled across Europe, which must have been nerve-wracking for her. Then there was the re-opening of Covent Garden in 1946, and the next terrific strain I am sure and challenge for her must have been when we went to the Metropolitan Opera House in 1949. That, I believe I am right in saying, was when the Sadler's Wells now The Royal Ballet was first internationally acclaimed and respected. Madam had really achieved this enormous goal from having started with six dancers in 1931 at Sadler's Wells. I'd always been in awe of Madam from the very first time I met her; but, terrifying and authoritative as she could be, she could also be very kind and caring. Several instances spring to mind from when I was in the School: her insistence that my teeth be improved and the outcome was two teeth removed from the top and lots of wire to re-arrange it. The next thing was she sent me to a physiotherapist called Celia Sparger, who was to check my back, which she was worried about, and my feet. Celia Sparger instructed me to put little match sticks under the two last toes, bound with cotton wool and cotton, in order to straighten them out. Madam had noticed that, because I'd been put on *pointe* for the Intermediate Examination at the age of nine, my toes had curled under. Madam wanted them straightened out, and of course I was given special exercises for my back. She was a very observant and a very caring person and she was always looking ahead. To me she was the woman who always was planning ahead, looking ahead. I stayed in the Company until 1957 and I came back regularly as a guest artist up to the time she left. Later, obviously, we always kept together. I used to come and see her, and she used to come when I was running Festival Ballet and her comments were always so helpful and so constructive. What amazes me about her is the time she had for everybody and everything. When we were in London in the Blitz, we came back to the New Theatre. She was nervous when we had all the bombing; she wanted me to go back home with her to Sunningdale. I was actually more frightened of her than the bombs.

GD: Dame Antoinette, as a young dancer did you have that terror, that awe? How would you describe your professional relationship with Madam? Did she prepare you for roles, was she nurturing in that respect?

Antoinette Sibley (AS): How did she go about maturing talent? Well, she did it, because she just had the most wonderful teachers imaginable. For instance, when I started (I was again nine), I had the most fantastic teachers: Winfred Edwards was my main teacher and she was for perfection and line and was very, very precise about everything. All my generation went back to classes with her, when we were in the Company. I did classes literally until she had to stop doing them. She'd come in privately and do them for us or we'd go over to West Kensington where she had a church hall and we'd do them there. Then there was Ailne Phillips who was terribly difficult: I mean the hardest classes I ever had to do; fantastic for you but really hard. Pamela May, of course, was all arms and shoulders and long red finger nails; and then there was Harold Turner, who was just a right charmer, like him [gestures to David Wall]; and Errol Addison who just made you believe you could do whatever he asked you to do, which of course you normally couldn't at all. He would say, "But I know you can do this, you just go like this and you do four *pirouettes*", and you went: "No I can't do four *pirouettes* to the left." So he said: "Yes you can, *pointe tendu*, boom and one, two, three, four." And you did it. When he left the room, of course, you could never do it again. He was very down to earth.

And then Madam herself. My goodness! I went right the way through the School doing the Summer Schools, so I was in the littlest class then the next class and so on. The main basic thing about all her work was that, after the *pliés*, you had to do things very, very quickly. When you came to do *tendus* instead of just *en devant*, you went [demonstrates with the supporting leg changing direction on each *tendu*]. This leg [the supporting leg] never stood still, that leg had to change direction all the time that you were doing it; you were changing the direction of your poor standing leg and so you had to be on balance all the time to do this. Every step was the same when it came to *rond de jambe*: it was movement, movement, movement and the speed of light of course, because she always moved at the speed of light so she thought we ought to. After we all went to Russia, we were doing that with having to lean back like [demonstrates *cambré*] this.

About the maturing: when one got older, when I got in the Company, this maturing business stopped. You came out quite a good dancer from just your teachers. Then you were in the big Company and she'd suddenly go to you. "Oh, right". She was watching a rehearsal of Fred Ashton's *Birthday Offering* and I was doing Rowena [Jackson]'s jumping solo [AS clarifies with Grey: the Spring variation] and de Valois was up in the paint shop. She shouldn't have been taking any notice of this at all: Fred was taking the rehearsal out front; she had nothing at all to do with this. She came on stage after the ballet had ended and she got me and she got another girl, who was doing [Elaine] Fifield's solo and she said, "You've got to change places. Change places. No, no, it's absolutely impossible, Sybil [Sybil was what she called me]. Sybil, it's absolutely impossible; you can't do that jumpy thing; you must do the first one, all those turns and things like that." I didn't know what I was going to do. The performance was that night; she was manic like that. I cannot remember what happened in the end. I think I did suddenly have to change and learn the other one. It upset us all: our positioning was different throughout, because you had a different coloured costume. I was once called into her room. "I want you to do Swanilda in *Coppélia*," she said, "for the first ever school performance." I said, "It's absolutely wonderful Madam." (I was actually in the Company at this point, but the School was doing the rest of the ballet.) She said, "You can do it with Graham Usher"; and I said, "That's wonderful". So, she then came in and we started rehearsing, and she said, "This is in nine days time." Graham and I went, "Nine days time! We have to learn the whole three acts?" And she said: "Yes, it's in nine days time and I've got to tell the School that as well." And then a much worse thing happened: she called me to her room: "Yes, I want you to do *Swan Lake*," and I went: "Oh my goodness! that's absolutely amazing"; and she added, "In ten days time". I said: "It's absolutely impossible. I won't be able to bring anything to it. I won't even have learnt it." "Oh, you must have learnt it from being in the *corps de ballet?*" "No, no, I never learn roles above me, I'm only learning roles that I'm doing at the same time." So she said: "Well anyway I realise that's difficult, so I've got Michael Somes to rehearse you every day and he will do the performance with you." I went, "Michael Somes!" I'd never said 'boo' to him (it was long before we were married obviously). I said, "I can't possibly do that, it is absolutely not on." And Madam said: "Yes you can and yes you must."

GD: We've heard how Madam liked the boys in the Company. Is that true in your experience [directed to David Wall]?

David Wall (DW):   The awesome figure of Dame Ninette de Valois, I think, was more so for the girls than the boys. She used to love rehearsing the boys and spent hours and hours with them in the rehearsal stage and went completely haywire. I was very fortunate to rehearse with her in *The Rake* [*The Rake's Progress*], Satan in *Job* and her last production of *The Sleeping Beauty* in 1977. It was great to be in a studio with her; she had an air of being awesome about her but once you started to move and she started to move, and she started to talk, there was a great feeling of camaraderie. She didn't like to be bored, however, and she always wanted something more out of the steps than just perfect technique and precision. With her roles you really didn't have to put a lot more into them than she had actually given you choreographically, therefore one sometimes felt that one wasn't performing. I did *The Rake's Progress* when I was eighteen. I was really really frightened of doing it, because she'd had these wonderful names like Walter Gore, Bobby Helpmann, Alexander Grant, Brian Shaw; and I, as an eighteen-year-old confronted with this role, was really frightened. In fact probably as frightened as I was when I was a nine-year-old, when I was in front of her at an audition in little black trunks. But the steps that she produced, a lot like her poetry, made you look inside yourself, and you didn't actually have to put anything on top of them. They were wonderfully constructed. With The Rake particularly you went through every form of emotion: bawdiness, humour, drama: it was all there in that wonderful ballet. It was the first anti-hero I managed to portray. After that, I think, because she influenced so many other choreographers especially Kenneth MacMillan, and through the steps and through presenting a different form of performing to a young dancer, she certainly changed my whole idea of what a dancer should be. Prior to working on The Rake I wanted to be Rudolf Nureyev who'd just defected from Russia, and I wanted to be a classical dancer. I'm very glad that she gave me the opportunity to dance *The Rake's Progress*, because otherwise my career would have been quite different.

PW: I asked Madam about The Rake and I said who did she like best. Who did she really feel was the best for that role? She came out straight away: Walter Gore, David Wall and David Poole. I said, "Oh, what about Bobby Helpmann?" "No," she said, "he was very dramatic, far too elegant. Because those three I mentioned were all intelligent enough to make it [the role of the Rake] into a young man up from the country who had no training or anything; and that makes the ballet work." She was absolutely specific about that: Walter Gore, David Wall and David Poole.

Ashton and De Valois

Alastair Macaulay

The Royal Ballet today names Ninette de Valois as its founding artistic director and Frederick Ashton as its founder choreographer. There is a minor inaccuracy here: Ashton did not join the then Vic-Wells Ballet until after its foundation. Other problems should be addressed. How did these two collaborate to turn this Company into what became the most prestigious ballet company of the Western world? I start with two contrasting images from my own experience; each is taken from around the times of their respective eightieth birthdays.

In summer 1978, The Royal Ballet at Covent Garden gave a gala in honour of de Valois' eightieth birthday. It performed her production of *The Sleeping Beauty*, new that season. At the end, de Valois, with her gift for selflessness, came onto the stage to join her dancers and colleagues and to thank the audience. She said: "I stood on this stage in 1949 when the Company came home from New York, and I said to the audience 'It takes more than one to make a ballet company.' I say it to you again now." Ashton and Kenneth MacMillan were onstage with her: it was clear she included them in her point.

In summer 1984, I conducted an interview with Ashton to mark his own forthcoming eightieth birthday. I put to him that all the other great classical ballet companies had each been shaped by a single ballet master who both taught and choreographed: August Bournonville in Copenhagen, Marius Petipa in St Petersburg, George Balanchine in New York. "But The Royal Ballet came out of de Valois and you: she ran the classical teaching of the Company while choreographing in a style that tended to be either expressionistic or *demi-charactère*, whereas you, who choreographed intensely classical ballets, did not teach." When I asked Ashton if that was a fair description, he acquiesced, but in a low key. Then, after a long pause, he suddenly said, "Of course, we were cat and dog the entire time."

How do we reconcile these two views? Here follow some basic facts about their work together. She and he became aware of each other in the 1920s. In 1926, she congratulated him on his first ballet, *A Tragedy of Fashion*; he took some classes at the Academy of Choreographic Art, which she founded that same year; both of them danced for the Royal

Opera in the 1920s, she as its lead ballerina. From 1931, they encountered each other in many ways: they both contributed – as dancers and as choreographers – to the Ballet Club or Ballet Rambert (which was Ashton's main dance home between 1926 and 1935), to the Vic-Wells Ballet (which de Valois founded in 1931), and to the Camargo Society. As early as 1932, a year after she had founded the Vic-Wells Company, she imported ballets that he had made for the Camargo (starting with *The Lord of Burleigh*). They created roles in each other's ballets.[1]

In 1935, she brought him into her Vic-Wells fold, hiring him as resident choreographer to the Company. He remained in that capacity until 1963 – twenty-eight years. The Vic-Wells, he said, "gave me security. It gave me a regular salary, which I hadn't had before, and I was immensely appreciative of the luxury of using proper dancers at last and having proper facilities."[2] He was always, however, more than a choreographer there, and the connections between him and de Valois were complex. They continued to use each other as dancers in new ballets.[3] She supervised the Company's stagings of *The Sleeping Beauty*, *Swan Lake*, *Giselle* and other classics, but, after the Company moved to Covent Garden in 1946, she brought him in to stage supplementary dances for all three of those ballets; he also staged a version of *Casse-Noisette* for Sadler's Wells Theatre Ballet in 1951, keeping the Ivanov grand *pas de deux*.[4]

He succeeded de Valois in 1963 as artistic director of what was now The Royal Ballet, remarking, "I feel rather like James I succeeding Queen Elizabeth."[5] She had retired at the age of sixty-five; he in due course retired at precisely the same age in 1970. Ashton in semi-retirement was a recurrent figure in the artistic lives of both Royal Ballet Companies right up to his death in 1988; de Valois' involvement with those Companies was at times more intense, at others more intermittent, but certainly the Companies and the School remained part of her life up to her death in 2001.

But the same history may be told other ways. I contend that, without Ashton and Constant Lambert, The Royal Ballet might not even have been seriously theatrical. Before they came to the Wells in 1935 (Lambert as musical director), the Vic-Wells repertory looked, in the words of Marie Rambert, painfully dowdy.[6] Belinda Quirey, who had watched the Diaghilev Ballet in the 1920s, always related the difference: Rambert's Ballet Club in the 1930s, despite its poverty, continued the elegance, theatricality, lighting and adult atmosphere of Diaghilev, whereas the Vic-Wells reeked of the classroom.[7] Agnes de Mille in 1951 recalled that the Vic-Wells company in 1933 had been "merely a troupe of students located way out to hell, and gone, herded and driven by the implacable Ninette de Valois", whereas she could already see how inspiring the climate was at Rambert's Ballet Club.[8] Ashton long recalled how Lydia Lopokova called de Valois' dancers "the ugly ducklings", whereas Rambert's dancers, he said, "were beautiful".[9] Only when Ashton and Lambert came to the Vic-Wells did this change. By 1938, however, both men were chafing. Lambert felt free to write to Ashton that year: "I quite realise that the schoolroom atmosphere must irritate you even more than it does me." This atmosphere was made by de Valois, who elsewhere had been nicknamed "the games mistress".[10]

Ashton was a classicist, whereas de Valois favoured academicism. What does this distinction imply? Academicism, essentially negative, is about correctness. Classicism, essentially positive, is about philosophical connection with form and tradition. What were the signature works of The Royal Ballet? I would name five classical peaks: *The Sleeping Beauty*, *Symphonic Variations*, *La Fille mal gardée*, the Nureyev staging of the Shades scene of *La Bayadère*, and *Monotones* (both pas de trois, not just the "white" one). In those works, it set world standards that other companies have been trying to match ever since. Three of them were choreographed by Ashton; and the two others were partly shaped by Ashton.

It should therefore be said that, without Ashton, the Vic-Wells/Sadler's Wells/Royal Ballet might have been a strong, vivid academic Company with a strong *demi-caractère* quality. It would certainly have danced *The Sleeping Beauty* and *Swan Lake*, but very differently: their classicism came from Ashton. Without Ashton, the Sadler's Wells Ballet would not have projected into the depths and heights of Covent Garden, let alone the Metropolitan Opera House in New York. Without de Valois' Vic-Wells Company, however, Ashton surely would not have made the breakthrough into classicism. This happened for him when he made his second ballet for the Vic-Wells, *Les Rendezvous*. De Valois gave him dancers with technique he could play with (she herself was one of them); in that technique he found inspiration.

The Second World War and its aftermath elicited further tensions between the two. Ashton felt that it was he, not she, who kept the Company going when the war began. With the financial backing of his friends, he organised a tour, with Constant Lambert and Hilda Gaunt at the two pianos and with dancers including Margot Fonteyn, June Brae, Pamela May, Julia Farron, Robert Helpmann, and Michael Somes. De Valois' subsequent comment was merely, "It was like a little concert party; I let them do it on their own, there was no point in me going." Ashton bitterly insisted that "Ninette – *wonderful* Ninette – said that a woman's place is the home and she went away and disappeared. She absolutely abandoned us. But that's never written about. When Ninette saw it was going to work, she came back and took the whole thing in her hands again."[11]

When the war ended, it was Ashton, not de Valois, who felt the Company should move to Covent Garden. She was not convinced her Company could re-illumine the old Opera House. He simply said: "If you won't, I will." One friend later said: "He didn't want to supplant Ninette, but he felt that, if he did not, the Russians would be back and English ballet would be on the fringe forever."[12] And when it came to the crucial stylistic matter of coaching the dancers how to project into the depths and heights of Covent Garden, it was again Ashton, not de Valois, who led the way.

This really is at the heart of any history of The Royal Ballet. His accounts of how in particular he coached Margot Fonteyn's dancing in *The Sleeping Beauty* to register and fill the theatre are well known.[13] Where Fonteyn led the way, others followed – with Ashton helping them, because he had made new supplementary dances in Acts One and Three that challenged them to project.[14]

De Valois had realised as early as 1933 that Ashton had what it takes to make a great coach of a ballerina role. Pamela May, herself a distinguished Aurora in the Company's first years at Covent Garden, related how much she had learnt at Sadler's Wells from watching him coach the Act III "Aurora" *pas de deux*, when both Alicia Markova and Pearl Argyle danced it.[15] Ashton was a mime of genius, and he had excellent recall of the characteristics of the great dancers he had seen. Fonteyn describes how he would tell them every day of such dancers as Anna Pavlova, Tamara Karsavina, Olga Spessivtseva, and Lydia Lopokova, recreating them both in physical imitation and in words, challenging them to learn from his evocations.[16] Later Auroras he also coached in the complete role included Lynn Seymour in the 1960s and Lesley Collier in the 1970s.[17]

May remembered how, in the *pas de deux*, he taught Aurora in 1933 to walk slowly around the stage, using her weight as she walked. He himself especially recalled coaching Fonteyn in 1946 in the supported *pirouette* that ends in first *arabesque*. In 1984, he showed me, with his fingers, how bland supported *pirouettes* into first *arabesque* can be; then he showed how the point was suddenly to explode from the *pirouettes* into an immediate and perfect *arabesque*. He said he told Fonteyn: "It's like you've been shot in the *back*!"

Because ballet is about big spatial projection, it can marry music to dance in space to phenomenal effect: ballet's musicality becomes an expression of the time-space equation in physics. *Symphonic Variations* is an object-lesson in this. It was the first new ballet Ashton made for Covent Garden, also in 1946, a little later than his new dances for *The Sleeping Beauty*. When *Symphonic Variations* is well performed, it becomes the perfect work for the dimensions of that theatre. It makes you feel music in space; and that, in ballet, becomes one of the hallmarks of classicism. An immediate success, it was not, however, a one-off at that period of his career. The years 1946-53 proved the greatest period of Ashton's classicism so far, establishing him, in Britain, and his contemporary Balanchine, in the United States, as the master-classicists of international ballet, a position in which they remain unequalled by any successor. Ashton in these years made supplementary dances for *The Sleeping Beauty* and *Swan Lake*; he made *Valses nobles et sentimentales*, *Scènes de ballet*, *Cinderella*, *Daphnis and Chloë*, and *Sylvia*; he applied his thought to developing classicism in pure-dance terms and in narrative contexts; and he, usually so fond of minor nineteenth-century music, turned to scores by Ravel, Stravinsky, Prokofiev, Gluck and others.

De Valois, however, felt otherwise. After watching a rehearsal of *Scènes de ballet* (the ballet in which he took greatest pride throughout his life), she wrote in 14 January 1948 to her colleague, Joy Newton: "It is choreographically elegant, sincere, and in perfect taste even if it is, as usual, for the chosen few & slightly repetitive. We still await a giant in this country."[18] This explains why now, when he was entering his prime as a choreographer, she chose to bring Léonide Massine to Covent Garden and Sadler's Wells to stage ballets, old and new. The late 1940s were not a vintage time for the Russian choreographer. De Valois told Julie Kavanagh, Ashton's biographer, that to bring Massine into her Company was "necessary":

> I did it for the men who were madly weak after the war. It wasn't as if I'd brought in some little Englishman; I brought in a distinguished choreographer from the last generation. Fred wasn't interested in the men, he never was. He was principally a woman's choreographer.[19]

It is baffling to think that the founder director of The Royal Ballet thought that the choreographer of *Façade*, *Les Rendezvous*, *Les Patineurs*, *A Wedding Bouquet*, *Harlequin in the Street*, and *Symphonic Variations* was not interested in choreographing for men. It is more baffling that she said so decades later, when he had choreographed *La Fille mal gardée*, *The Dream* and many other ballets that extended the male repertory very considerably.

In 1980, de Valois went so far as to tell Massine's former assistant, Mary Anne de Vlieg, that Massine had been "the greatest choreographer of the century".[20] Her taste, after all, was for character ballets. She never thought *Symphonic Variations* a masterpiece: "People scream at me, but it has never been my idea of an Ashton work. It doesn't stress his individuality."[21] Actually, Ashton's individuality was no more the point of *Symphonic Variations* than Petipa's individuality is of *The Sleeping Beauty* or Balanchine's is of *Serenade*. But then Balanchine's work in America raised her strongest objections. To Joy Newton she wrote that the 1952 Covent Garden season by his New York City Ballet had been "a painful experience. To understand, you must picture Fred in his immediate post-war egotistical mood in complete control (both privately and publicly) to know what mischief Balanchine is doing to his own fine beginnings."[22] It was his plotless ballets she despised; her letter pours scorn on a ballet she does not name but sounds entirely like *Serenade*.

Ashton's choreographic methods involved using the dancers improvising to help him find the movement. De Valois had no respect for that. "Laziness, nothing but laziness," she called it later: "Real old pros wouldn't attempt anything like that. Balanchine didn't and Nijinska didn't – I worked with them both. You did what you were told."[23] Actually, many of Ashton's long-term dancers came to understand that he usually knew very well what he was driving at: he knew the construction of a piece before he came to rehearsals, when people made exits and entrances, who would dance to what music, where the climax should occur, what kind of images he was seeking. De Valois chose not to appreciate this.

Nobody, however, could contradict herself or himself better than she. She dedicated her 1959 book *Come Dance With Me* to Fonteyn and Ashton; in it she describes *Symphonic Variations* as "one of our major successes" and "a study in neo-classicism of the highest quality".[24] In her 1977 book *Step by Step*, she recalls the scandal created by the critic Richard Buckle about Ashton's 1951 ballet *Tiresias*, when Buckle blasted de Valois, Ashton, and Lambert as "three blind mice". De Valois' response, wittily picking up the Tiresias myth, is magnificent: "When I am struck blind again, may it be in such equally worthy company."[25] She goes on to say: "The Ashton scene is kaleidoscopic. I do not search among the dignified accepted classics of his that have received the accolade of the entire world of ballet. I search for my own special loves." She dwells on *Birthday*

Offering and *Ondine*; and she recalls dances from *Apparitions*, *Nocturne*, *Cinderella*, and his supplementary dances for the Petipa classics.[26]

Ashton and de Valois had plenty in common (not least a vital sense of humour). He as a choreographer loved brilliant footwork: her dancing exemplified precisely that. Fonteyn writes of de Valois: "Her movements were quick, like her temper.... I can remember her on stage doing *brisés* that seemed faster than the speed of light, and faster than any conductor could catch or musicians play."[27] The critic Arlene Croce has called the *pas de trois* in *Les Rendezvous* "the ultimate instep dance": "its leitmotif is *pas de cheval* done around and around the stage, alternating with hop in *arabesque* and small beaten steps. It is all set in a single rapid tempo, and it must be the most difficult-to-sustain number in the ballet."[28] The woman in that *pas de trois* was Ninette de Valois. In her teaching, she proceeded to make neat, fast, brilliant footwork the hallmark of the British style. She often voiced her theory that a company takes its style from the local folk dance idiom: the Russians dance big with imprecise footwork like the Cossacks, but the British travel less but with much more intricate footwork. Nonetheless teachers at The Royal Ballet School told Mary Clarke in the 1960s that, in the 1950s, their students had only reluctantly learnt the British folk "Dances of Four Nations". Then, however, Ashton made *La Fille mal gardée*, with its wealth of folk-related dances, and the penny dropped. Henceforth they danced those folk dances with real motivation.[29] This is a perfect example of how repertory and school can feed each other – and of how de Valois needed Ashton, to give new meaning to the syllabus in which she believed.

They even shared features as choreographers. (Both learnt from Massine and Bronislava Nijinska.) The more dancing characters of de Valois' *The Rake's Progress* are not far from the Dancing Master in Ashton's *Cinderella*, for example. Ashton had a lifelong genius for sublimating the acting qualities that de Valois and others felt were core characteristics of the British or English style in ballet.[30] The main differences between them are that de Valois never knew how to transcend character and to achieve pure classicism, while Ashton seldom if ever had her strong penchant for expressionistic use of gesture. Even his most expressionistic work, *Dante Sonata* (1940), is carried by a pure-dance lyricism that is miles from any de Valois ballet.

A major difference between de Valois and Ashton concerns *épaulement*. De Valois may have choreographed it, but it played virtually no part in her early teaching. Julia Farron has said: "When I think back to how Madam used to teach us, it was all beneath the waist – really, all beneath the knee."[31] To Anderson, Farron called de Valois' teaching "straight up and down... It was all so fast, you couldn't really bend."[32] After Ashton's first leading role for Fonteyn, Tamara Karsavina praised Fonteyn's line and musicality to him, but said, "She has no conception of *épaulement.*" Ashton replied, "From tomorrow I will ensure that she does."[33] Everything they learnt about matters of *épaulement*, Farron has said, "We learnt from Fred."[34] By the 1960s, precise and vivid *épaulement* had become a characteristic of The Royal Ballet and The Royal Ballet School. What had changed? De Valois had gradually adjusted the syllabus to accommodate the style that Ashton was demanding of his dancers onstage – not least because dancers valued by Ashton had now become teachers at The Royal Ballet School. He particularly mentioned this in 1984: "Some of the dancers who worked with me a lot over the years have gone on to become teachers, like Pamela May and Julia Farron; they know what I like to see in dancers."[35] May and Farron, important teachers at both The Royal Ballet School and the Royal Academy of Dancing, have spoken about just how Ashton affected their teaching: *épaulement*, for example, but also bending, presenting the body on angles, and how to present the hands.[36]

After de Valois retired from the directorship and Ashton took over, he went on developing a Royal Ballet style with renewed vigour. In the *pas de quatre* and final act he added to *Swan Lake* in 1963; in every role he made in *The Dream* (1964); in both halves of *Monotones* (1965 and 1966); in the pure-dance allegro and adagio of *Sinfonietta* (1967); in the prince's solo and Awakening *pas de deux* and solo for the Fairy of Joy that he added to *The Sleeping Beauty* in 1968; in the meeting of character and classicism that he made in *Enigma Variations* (also 1968), he was refining his style and the Company's style in multiple new directions – upper body and lower, adagio and allegro, phrasing and line. In particular, the roles that he made on Anthony Dowell had no stylistic precedent. Because of Ashton, male style changed in those years. Across the world to this day, male dancers are still working hard to keep up to the standards he set them. The Royal Ballet School kept up; most of those ballets have been danced by its students in subsequent years.

How did de Valois react? The answer is dismaying. Although officially retired, she energetically involved herself in terminating his career as artistic director and in having him replaced by Kenneth MacMillan. The startling details of her machinations are given in Kavanagh's biography of Ashton and Zoë Anderson's history, *The Royal Ballet* (2005); the witnesses include John Tooley, later the general director of the Royal Opera House.[37]

In consequence, de Valois herself curtailed the classical peak of the Company she had founded. Apart from his own work, Ashton had added to the repertory such works as the Shades scene from *La Bayadère*, Nijinska's *Les Noces* and *Les Biches*, Balanchine's *Apollo* and *Serenade*, Antony Tudor's *Jardin aux Lilas*, MacMillan's *Concerto* and *Song of the Earth*. He commissioned the *premières* of MacMillan's *Romeo and Juliet* and Tudor's *Shadowplay*. Under him, the Company commanded yet greater triumphs in America than ever before. The *Bayadère* Shades Scene and *Monotones* became two of the Company's signature works for the next fifteen years. The new generation of principals – notably Antoinette Sibley and Anthony Dowell, but others too – was epoch-making. *Les Biches* and *Les Noces* still occupy valued places in the repertory. *The Dream* and *Monotones*, which have moved on into international repertory, are generally accepted as being among his greatest works.

Why did de Valois seek to depose him? Probably she thought he would be more prolific in retirement. Not for the first time, however, she misjudged her man. Deeply hurt, Ashton sulked for years. From then on, he made far fewer ballets. She also misjudged his successor. Under MacMillan, complaints grew about the decline of Royal Ballet classical style.

How fascinating, then, that this gloriously inconsistent woman next decided that The Royal Ballet needed not only herself but Ashton too. In 1977, she and The Royal Ballet Board decided that she should stage a new production of *The Sleeping Beauty*. (This directly forced the resignation of MacMillan; he had directed the Company's 1973 staging of that classic.[38]) She could have returned to her legendarily successful 1946 production with its designs by Oliver Messel; and she did revert to parts of it (the Garland Dance and Florestan *pas de trois* that Ashton had added in 1946 and the solo for the Vision of Aurora that he had added in 1952). Yet she chose also to include three dances Ashton had added in 1968: the adagio solo made for Dowell, the Awakening *pas de deux* made for Sibley and Dowell, and the 5/4 Sapphire solo made for Georgina Parkinson as the Fairy of Joy. This de Valois production lasted for fifteen years at Covent Garden and has not been equalled since. Today, when it is danced by the Boston Ballet, it remains the finest *The Sleeping Beauty* production in the world.

This 1977 staging, with its inclusion of Ashton's brilliant and diverse later additions, showed de Valois now embracing ways in which Royal

Ballet style had moved on since her day. You could call this British compromise. I call it outstandingly far-sighted and large-minded vision. She was a famously self-contradictory woman in all respects; but in no area did she continue to contradict herself more than regarding Frederick Ashton. On one point, however, she never contradicted herself: "It takes more than one to make a ballet company."

Ninette de Valois and Kenneth MacMillan

Jann Parry

Kenneth MacMillan was the first home-grown choreographer whom Ninette de Valois believed she could mould and mentor. She had known him since he was a boy of fifteen, when he auditioned for her School during the Second World War. At seventeen, he joined the newly-formed junior Company, the Sadler's Wells Opera Ballet (soon to become the Sadler's Wells Theatre Ballet). He graduated into the Covent Garden Company in 1948, in time for the historic tour to America, but needed leave of absence four years later because he was suffering from crippling stage fright. He joined John Cranko's pick-up Company, performing in the little Kenton Theatre in Henley-on-Thames, and came back to the Theatre Ballet a choreographer – encouraged by Cranko. His early ballets were for the experimental Choreographic Group until his first commission, in 1955, which was *Danses Concertantes*.

De Valois was, of course, taking a keen interest; she monitored closely what the second Company was up to under its artistic director, Peggy van Praagh. De Valois had instructed MacMillan to use "proper" music, not jazz, and she had vetoed his first choice of Stravinsky's *Le Baiser de la Fée* because it required too big and expensive an orchestra. She took MacMillan to the Slade School of Art to choose a designer for *Danses Concertants*, after he'd rejected her suggestion of Andrée Howard. The artist he chose was Nicholas Georgiadis – the first of their many collaborations.

MacMillan, at twenty-six, was capable of standing up to de Valois, which is probably why she liked him. John Lanchbery[1] told me how impressed he and Theatre Ballet members had been when they overheard MacMillan daring to argue with her in the Sadler's Wells canteen. He insisted on stopping dancing now that he was recognised as a choreographer after *Danses Concertantes*. She said the Company couldn't afford to lose a useful dancer but she gave in and docked his weekly pay by a pound.

Danses Concertantes was soon taken into the Covent Garden repertoire, by which time de Valois had commissioned *Noctambule*s for the senior Company in 1956. She told him to draw up a scenario and discuss it with her before consulting the Company's musical adviser, Humphrey Searle, about suitable music. Sir Peter Wright tells me that he, too, had to show his scenarios for ballets to de Valois when he started choreographing, before she would let him go ahead.

I do not know whether she did this with every choreographer she commissioned or just the relatively inexperienced ones. She had been criticised by P.W. Manchester, in her 1942 book about the early years of the Vic-Wells Ballet for "a marked lack of encouragement to potential choreographers".[2] Most of the pre-war repertoire had been by her and Ashton. Post-war, she had been damned by Richard Buckle in *The Observer* in 1951 for being too preoccupied with administrative duties, lecturing and 'propagandising abroad' to oversee the ballets she had commissioned. His initial broadside had been headed "Three Blind Mice". He went on: "Did you ever see such a thing in your life? Sadler's Wells has three artistic directors. See how they run. Ninette de Valois is too busy to supervise every detail of production; Frederick Ashton is too easily reconciled to compromise; Constant Lambert, one imagines, looks in occasionally with a musical suggestion."[3]

That caused a lot of trouble (and a letter from Lambert's solicitor). The ballets at the start of the 1950s that Buckle must have had in mind were Ashton's *Tiresias* (1951), Massine's *Donald of the Burthens* (1951) and Roland Petit's *Ballabile* (1950), all regarded as unworthy of a national ballet. So I suspect that de Valois, who would not have interfered with those three established choreographers, had become very diligent by the mid-1950s with the younger choreographers within her own Companies, trying to ensure that she knew in advance what they were intending to do.

She may not have had much luck with John Cranko, who knew his own mind by the time she commissioned his *Prince of the Pagodas* in 1956 (postponed till 1957) as a three-act ballet. Neither he nor she managed to revise it and make it a success. Cranko, in any case, had become fed up with his low pay (£15 a week) after ten years as resident choreographer of the Touring Company and was taking his talent elsewhere, including La Scala, and directing his own revue shows. Alfred Rodrigues, too, was choreographing for La Scala and other places. Like Cranko, he had created a number of ballets for the Touring Company under Peggy van Praagh and a few for the resident one. There were already such limited opportunities in the 1950s within the Covent Garden repertoire for new works, other than Ashton's, that Rodrigues and Cranko found other outlets. In fact, Cranko obliged John Tooley (then assistant to David Webster, General Administrator) to sort out a standard contract for Company choreographers who then wanted to mount their ballets elsewhere.

MacMillan may have seemed more biddable, though de Valois was keeping a keen eye on him to make sure he did not get away. She gave him leave of absence to make a work for American Ballet Theatre in 1956-7, at the request of Lucia Chase. MacMillan travelled with ABT on tour to Lisbon, where his ballet for Nora Kaye, *Winter's Eve*, had its première and then went with them to New York. He was so taken with America (and Nora Kaye, with whom he had an affair) that he stayed on to create a ballet, *Journey*, for the Company's choreographic workshop season, defying de Valois' demands that he return at once. He was probably contemplating remaining in America with ABT until de Valois' threats had their intended effect (and the American dancers warned him how precarious the Company's finances were).

I found a great range of correspondence from de Valois in MacMillan's effects: he had kept all her letters, cables and telegrams from that 1957 period. There is a charming two page letter from her, (dated 21 February 1957) soon after the American performances of *Winter's Eve* went on tour, when it received some less than favourable reviews. She consoles him over his first experience of a bad press, telling him: "You are only suffering the disappointments of all at your stage, and that applies to composers, writers, etc. You must expect to do a certain amount of good work that is not fully realised; it will be like this until your choreography is suddenly harnessed to a ballet that is, in its essence, really worth while."[4] (I suspect she's thinking here of *Noctambules*, which had its flaws in spite of her supervising its scenario).

Then she gets tough, not ruthless, tough. She wants him back to create a ballet for her Company's next tour of America in September 1957, so she will not prolong his leave of absence until May 6, 1957.

I cannot contemplate you putting a ballet into rehearsal round about May 10th and expecting to be fully dress rehearsed by about June 10th... You *must* come back next week – I think you need every bit of this time to decide on music, costumes and décor, and to work out something both of us will feel a satisfactory idea... I am sure that you will see that my attitude is not unreasonable.

Then she adds:

My attitude is slightly influenced by the fact that I understand your next production is not for a season of the ballet, but in some form of "workshop". I do not feel this is necessary for *our* choreographers. After all, we have always shown ourselves willing to give you opportunities. Of course, this rumour may be quite incorrect. I think I saw it in some dance magazine a short while ago.[5]

As an earlier letter from her on 4 January had made clear, he had not asked her permission to stay on.

He will not budge but she does not want to alienate him. Her next letter, dated 6 March, is handwritten and marked "Confidential", "Please do not discuss the contents of this letter with anyone." Since he is going to stay on in New York, "a pity, but nothing to be done," she warns him to watch what he says while he is with ABT.[6] It seems that "La Chase" [Lucia Chase, one of the founders of ABT] had been tactless in her press campaign about him, irritating the American press and failing to mention that he was a staff member of The Royal Ballet, "this very naturally displeased us".[7] She had not told him this before because she thought he was coming back: "I think now that you should know about these balletic blunderings! Just work and keep out of things."[8] She ends with comments about *Winter's Eve*, which she had not seen, "I imagine your scenario was really too sinister for your choice of music" [Benjamin Britten's *Variations on a Theme of Frank Bridge*] and signs off, "Love and good to luck to you, Madam".[9]

Then she and Webster inform him by cable and letter that The Royal Ballet is going to include *Solitaire* on the next American tour, as well as *Noctambules*.[10] She asks for his views on casting but makes her own opinion clear. "As the ballet is so light, I think that the figure in the centre should not be in any sense statuesque – it gives the wrong twist to the humour – or for that matter, any moment of pathos."[11] That is an implied criticism of the dancer he made it on, Margaret Hill, who was tall and long-legged. Madam would prefer "little Park" [Merle Park] who has "a note of hopeful vivacity about her and great charm". Taller Anya Linden, she thought, could do the secondary role.[12]

MacMillan was not going to give in. If he could not have Margaret Hill, he wanted Anya as the *Solitaire* girl. Madam agreed in her next letter dated 15 April 1957, and in the event, Margaret Hill was taken on the tour to alternate with Anya Linden in her created role. De Valois assured him in a cable from New York during the autumn tour that his ballets had had an excellent reception and favourable press, and that Margaret was doing well.

He had finally returned to London in May 1957, after five months away. His next ballet, *The Burrow*, was to be for the touring group. There is a letter from de Valois mentioning composers he might use, which he ignored.[13] The Swiss composer, Frank Martin, whom he had used before for *Laiderette*, was his own choice. De Valois would not let him go ahead until she had approved his ideas for *The Burrow*, scheduled for a triple bill of new works in December. (The other two ballets were by Cranko and Wright.) Because she was busy with the American tour, *The Burrow* had to be postponed until January 1958, which meant it was reviewed on its own. "Glad that you have swapped dates with John [Cranko]", she wrote in a chatty letter from Washington. "You will at least feel that there is no one on your heels." She adds: "I have some amusing stories for you" [about the American tour] and signs off affectionately, "love, Madam".[14] So she had forgiven him for disobeying her.

De Valois was now backing MacMillan as the standard-bearer for a new generation. She offered to "defer" her own next ballet, which was going to be *The Lady of Shalott* in 1959, in favour of a work by him. (She never did do *The Lady of Shalott*). She was prepared to support the choice of music for which he was eager to choreograph: Mahler's *Song of the Earth*. She told the Ballet Sub-Committee that he had worked out a synopsis and that it could be done simply against a plain cyclorama in practice clothes. It could prove a "considerable artistic event", she promised; she was planning to schedule it six times in late 1959 and mid-1960.[15]

The proposal was put to the Board, whose members objected.[16] Ballet should not be done to great music not written for the purpose, some of them decreed and said so again in 1965, when he finally created *Das Lied von der Erde* for Stuttgart Ballet, six years later.[17] De Valois had no such qualms: she had been in Diaghilev's Company and she knew, as the Board evidently did not, that Massine had choreographed to classical music for the later Ballets Russes companies. But she could not overrule the Board and the musical adviser, Sir Adrian Boult, who had vetoed the Mahler.[18]

Instead, she managed to secure a budget for MacMillan to create *Le Baiser de la Fée* in 1960 to Stravinsky's music, the score he had wanted to use before *Danses Concertantes*. De Valois sent him notes after watching rehearsals, advising him to adapt lifts for Svetlana Beriosova as the Fairy of the title. De Valois was not keen on tall dancers, as noted above, and she thought Beriosova risked looking ungainly. She ended her letter by congratulating him on "a very beautiful work, musical, refined and clearly stated".[19]

The next correspondence with de Valois is an angry letter from MacMillan to her about the way *Le Baiser de la Fée* had been presented at the Edinburgh Festival later that year. There had been too little time for

music rehearsals and part of the scenery fell down during the first performance. MacMillan told de Valois that it was the most amateur show he
had ever seen on any stage. He berated her for the fact that not one member of the administrative staff had been present. And just as bad, Lynn
Seymour's name, as the Bride in the ballet, had been left off the list of
Company members. "As far as the audience was concerned, she could
have been from anywhere." He concluded his stroppy letter with a threat
to resign: "My list of grievances is so long that I feel I must sever my
connections with The Royal Ballet... after my next production."[20]

Shy, taciturn MacMillan was always prepared to stand up for his ballets
and to stand up to de Valois. She described him in *Step by Step*: "On the
surface, I do not know a more reserved, unspectacular and sensitive person, nor do I know a more sincere, granite-like character underneath."[21]
I was assured, however, that he would never have dared try to mislead or
deceive her. So I am still flabbergasted by my discovery of two very different scenarios for his next production, *The Invitation* (1960). They are in
the manuscript file of Matyas Seiber's score for *The Invitation* in the British
Library. De Valois had urged MacMillan to use a commissioned score for
the first time, and he had worked very closely with Seiber, as the typed
scenarios attest, heavily annotated in Seiber's hand.

In the first scenario, there is no rape. In the ballet as it was subsequently performed, however, two young people have their first sexual
experiences during a rather strange house-party in a tropical country.
The boy is seduced by a married woman, which is not too distressing. The
girl has an encounter with the married man, which is a shattering experience, the violation of innocence. But in the first scenario, the sexual
encounter is described as a love scene and the girl as enraptured. At the
end, the girl and boy leave together happily, while the married couple
remain apart on either side of the stage. It is only in the second scenario
that the minutage prescribes four minutes of violent music, *"brutale"*, for
the rape. At the end, the girl, traumatised, rejects the boy and is left alone
as the curtain falls to face an embittered future.

It certainly does not look as though the first version, with all its annotations, was a dummy copy to hoodwink de Valois. Maybe MacMillan
changed his view of what the ballet was all about. De Valois does not seem
to have known about the graphic rape scene in advance. She first saw *The
Invitation's* final rehearsal on tour in Oxford, and suggested the girl's so-
called "seduction" should take place off stage. When MacMillan objected,
saying that some minor character would then have to come and mime
what he had seen, she gave way, saying "It's your ballet".

De Valois retired as artistic director in 1963, handing over to Ashton. She had seen MacMillan through three more ballets for the Covent Garden Company, including his *Rite of Spring* (1962), which she admired. His *Romeo and Juliet* in 1965 was Ashton's responsibility, as was the decision to let MacMillan go to West Berlin in 1966 to direct the Deutsche Oper Ballet. De Valois certainly lobbied behind the scenes for him to succeed Ashton as artistic director of The Royal Ballet in 1970, as Richard Glasstone overheard in Turkey, when she was there with him, overseeing the Turkish State Ballet. She kept in touch with MacMillan in Berlin, as letters from her testify, but she was too busy with her work in Turkey to visit him in Germany, as she had done with Cranko in Stuttgart.

When MacMillan took over The Royal Ballet as the first director from within its ranks, de Valois monitored his progress with Sir John Tooley, the General Director of the Opera House, through regular meetings at her house in Barnes. She supported him in public, whatever she might have thought or said privately. As she wrote in *Step by Step* in 1977: "Better to live through controversy than to exist in an atmosphere of apathy... To stand still, however skilfully, would be to court disaster."[22] She always sent MacMillan telegrams of good luck before his premières. One telegram, after *Triad* in January 1972, when he was feeling very low, assures him: "For me your finest work. I loved every minute of it, perfectly danced... much love, Madam".[23]

Actually, I believe his *Song of the Earth* was her favourite: it was the only ballet about which she wrote a poem.[24] However, she must have known that he was in a bad way at the time of *Triad*, having had what was in effect a breakdown after the hostile reception of his three-act *Anastasia* in 1971. In her letter, she encouraged him to keep going: "Please embark on at least a 2 act one as soon as possible. I wish you could find a composer to write for you."[25]

Even though she was long retired from The Royal Ballet, she would sit in on rehearsals of MacMillan's ballets during the 1970s and give notes to Wright, his assistant director, to pass on to MacMillan, such as: "Tell him her entrance is all wrong...", which MacMillan usually ignored. Wright says she would change her mind the next day, anyway, so he kept his role as go-between to a minimum. MacMillan asked him not to let her near *Manon* (in 1974), whose final stages she was very keen to see.

Deborah MacMillan tells how de Valois came up to her at the first night party after *Manon* and said: "I know he's not talking to me, but there's something for him at the stage door." It was a painting by Sydney Nolan, who had designed MacMillan's *Rite of Spring* in 1962. De Valois had written on the back: "I think this belongs to you." She had recently been awarded the Erasmus Prize by a Dutch foundation in 1974, and had spent some of the prize money on a present she knew MacMillan would value, a generous and thoughtful gift. Though MacMillan resisted her interventions in his choreography, Deborah MacMillan says he was very fond of her and they got on well, apart from the rumpus in 1985 when de Valois gave a talk to the London Ballet Circle. She laid into certain unspecified modern choreographers, who she felt muddled classical ballet and contemporary dance, to the detriment of ballet.

She had asked the chairman, Michael Broderick, to invite the dance critics, which was unusual, to hear what she had to say. Her remarks appeared in *The Stage* newspaper, which mentioned MacMillan as a notable offender.[26] Her perceived attack on him soon reached his ears while he was away in New York. He was deeply hurt by what he took to be her public disapproval of his work in front of the critics who had damned his recent ballets. He was spending more time with American Ballet Theatre in the mid-1980s than with The Royal Ballet, who, he believed, no longer valued him or his ballets. De Valois had always represented a kind of mother-figure to him, and here she was rejecting him, ejecting him from The Royal Ballet aesthetic she had established.

De Valois hurried off a four-page letter to him, protesting that she had not meant him at all and had never mentioned his name. She was referring to "young choreographers of the present moment .... who live in a world of confusion between contemporary and classical – and no one could accuse *you* of that". But she *had* deplored the use of music by two different composers, which seemed a direct dig at MacMillan, whose *Different Drummer* (1984) had just been revived with music by Berg and Schoenberg. She denied that he was the only choreographer in her thoughts, though he had been at one time "because I wanted to see you get to where you have got to". [27]

They forgave each other with MacMillan pointing out in his letter to her that she had said to him privately some of the critical remarks that had appeared in *The Stage*, which were now on record. It is evident that she still regarded herself as his mentor, even if he was not prepared to take her advice. She outlived him, as she had Ashton. In her tribute to MacMillan at the Westminster Abbey Memorial Service in 1993, she made a point of reclaiming him as central to "our national ballet's achievement". "His is now a great international name ", she wrote. "We are all filled with memories of intense pride and admiration for what he achieved .... I hope that in future his ballets will remain in the English repertoire as classics of the English scene." He was Scottish, but then she was Irish, and for her, English meant national to the British Isles. MacMillan, like Ashton, had become an essential element of the heritage she left to future generations.

Re-creating the King of the Great Clock Tower

Richard Allen Cave

DVD track 9

Readers are recommended to watch the performance before reading the following essay. All credits concerning the production are to be found on the recording.

The King of the Great Clock Tower was the last collaboration between Yeats and Ninette de Valois: it marked the end of a creative relationship that had lasted some seven years. Staged at the Abbey Theatre in Dublin in 1934, it was the fourth in a series of productions of Yeats's plays for dancers to be choreographed by de Valois and the third in which she performed the central, danced role.[1] The first three productions had been part of the agreement de Valois had entered into with Yeats after they met at Cambridge in 1927: that she would come to Dublin to help him stage his dance plays and to found a school of ballet at the Abbey.[2] By 1934 de Valois' workload in fulfilling her ambition for a ballet company meant that she began to shed other work in the theatre that she had been under-taking since the mid-1920s, first her involvement with Terence Gray at the Festival Theatre in Cambridge and subsequently that with Yeats in Dublin. For Yeats it was the end of an era, though he understood de Valois' commitment to her personal vision and respected her determina-tion to realise it. The new play that he devised for their final collaboration was to honour a special occasion: a thank-offering, which would show not only how much he had come to appreciate de Valois' creativity as a choreographer but also her remarkable versatility as a performer. All Yeats's dance plays make considerable demands on everyone involved in a performance, chiefly because of their unusual and eclectic mix of styles: they fuse a performance mode inspired by the Japanese Noh play with themes and narratives deriving from his engagement with Irish myth. From Noh, Yeats took the power of sustained silence to create and aug-ment dramatic tension (and silence has a crucial, indeed centrally determining function in *The King of the Great Clock Tower*), the use of masks for the major figures, of hieratic song and ritual, of a climactic dance to resolve narrative and theme and, above all, the rigorous aes-thetic discipline that eliminated all but the absolute essentials for clarity of expression. As choreographer and performer, de Valois had willingly to embrace that discipline yet find a freedom to work expansively within such seeming restrictions and match her powers of physical invention with Yeats's, if a true collaboration were to be achieved.[3] As a dancer, she had too to work with an eclectic mix of performers and practitioners: two trained singers, two actors with developed expertise in movement, a mask-maker, composer-conductor and small orchestra.

Since there has been no sustained effort to create a centralised national archive, detailed records of Irish dance from the 1930s are generally sparse.[4] This is not, however, the case with the 1934 Abbey Theatre staging of *The King of the Great Clock Tower*, though the details, now being widely scattered, have to be searched out. Assembled together, those details amount to a performance text (as distinct from a printed text) of the original production and it was that performance text that was the basis for a re-creation attempted in April, 2011.[5] I must at this stage abandon conventional academic detachment for a more personal engagement with the subject, since the quest for available records of the Abbey staging and the devising of a possible performance text and scenario from the evidence they afforded were mine; and I directed the re-creation.[6] So: what were our sources?

I had long had an interest in this particular play, fostered in part by conversations with Ninette de Valois in the late 1970s. (At that date I was pursuing research into the Cambridge Festival Theatre and Terence Gray's productions there, for which de Valois had often been what we nowadays would call the movement director.) That interest deepened when I was invited to edit the manuscripts of both versions of *The King of the Great Clock Tower* and of a related dance-drama, *A Full Moon in March*.[7] The various manuscripts abounded in revisions, marginalia and a number of inserted documents, which sent me off to investigate further likely possibilities: contemporary reviews, references to the production in correspondence (published or in archives), sketches, photographs, publishers' proofs (clean and revised). Editing required me to scan the texts as they changed through revision prior to publication and to ponder what might have motivated subtle changes to dialogue, songs and stage directions. Alterations made to the proofs for the Cuala edition, which appeared to bring the text into line with what had actually occurred in the Abbey production, suggested that the final text printed by Cuala closely reflected what audiences heard (with a few notable exceptions) and some of what they had seen in 1934.[8] It is worth exploring this point in relation to each of the constituent elements of the production in turn.

Two of six typescripts of the play are extant which were clearly intended for the use of actors and the director, Lennox Robinson.[9] One of these, presumably Robinson's, which is to be found in the Abbey collections in the National Library of Ireland, contains an inserted sheet of graph paper on which is sketched a floor plan of the setting; it is to scale for the known dimensions of the Abbey stage. (See plate 16) The sketch is annotated in what appears to be Robinson's hand, detailing what coloured hangings were to be used from the Theatre's stock to edge the playing space and to create two sets of curtains across the proscenium, one a few feet behind the other; the shape and dimensions of a set-piece of scenery; and the disposition of four thrones within that scenic structure. Each of the thrones is labelled to show how they were to be used by the actors at various points in the performance.[10] An earlier extant manuscript reveals that Yeats had himself evolved two of the three major elements of the setting (the sets of curtains and the thrones) virtually from the start of the process of composition; revisions on the typescript next prepared from this manuscript show that he had appreciated a need for some sort of backing for the thrones and proposed either a further curtain "hung in a semi circle or a semi circle of one-foot Craig screens so painted that the blue is darker below than above". It was in the many revisions Yeats made to this typescript that he first began working out a potential colour-scheme for the costumes and setting, prescribing a bold use of primary hues.[11] What Yeats's revisions do not include is any suggestion of the castle-like formation in which the screens were grouped for the production (a wide apse, culminating on either side in a narrow tower-like structure); the shape is, however, clearly visible in the floor plan and was presumably the invention of Dorothy Travers Smith, the designer, or possibly Robinson. A floor plan and brief indications in the stage directions about the colouring of the set nonetheless fell short of what the audience actually saw in three dimensional terms. That information together with the measurements of the Abbey stage fed into a computer programme devised for stage designers and architects rapidly produced a realisation of the setting, both as it might be viewed end-on and in an isometric format.[12] Here was information that might be handed to stage carpenter and painter. The one uncertain feature was the precise shade of blue that was to graduate from light to dark down the length of the screens (in building the set for the re-creation, a primary shade was chosen, following Yeats's other prescriptions for colour in his stage directions). Time-constraints necessitated that bands of colour were deployed rather than the steadily graduated changes that Yeats seems to have envisaged, but the resulting impact when the set was first viewed under full stage lighting was highly dramatic, accentuating details in costuming and masks with remarkable clarity. Yeats had studied painting early in his career and he was the son of a brilliant portrait painter, who chose to show his sitters against a simple but often radiantly coloured, if indeterminate background. When Yeats and his fellow directors were preparing to take over the Abbey Theatre as their future home, he had written at some length about reforms he would wish to see implemented in the new theatre. Of scenery, he wrote:

> As a rule the background should be but a single colour, so that the persons in the play wherever they stand, may harmonise with it, and preoccupy our attention. In other words it should be thought out not as one thinks out a landscape, but as if it were the background of a portrait, and this is especially necessary on a small stage...[13]

The re-staging showed how assured Yeats was of its appropriateness, seeing that it persisted in his staging practice and in the visual dimensions of his dramaturgy from 1903 (the date of his essay) to 1934. And how right he was too in believing that such a design technique would bring a concentrated focus and a rapt attentiveness to the audience's awareness of the performers.

Yeats describes his chief characters, a King and Queen, as "seated" when the audience first sees them: she, still and impassive; he, intently gazing at her. From the point in the play's gestation where he began to visualise characters and setting, introducing directions for colour in costumes and background, Yeats specified that the seats or thrones should take the simple form of "cubes". These details were introduced through the many revisions made by Yeats on the earliest extant typescript.[14] An unusual feature of this document is that on the verso of the final page there are four small sketches in ink, clearly made by Yeats, in which he worked out his idea for the thrones, steadily refining his initial conception till the simplest of shapes, a cube, emerged. Initially (perhaps influenced by talk with de Valois about design-work for Diaghilev's productions), he drew a double throne in an orientalist style, such as Bakst might have conceived, with an ornately decorated, high-arched back and draped bench-like seat. It would be perfect for the King and Queen in the final act of *The Sleeping Beauty*, but far from ideal for the less openly affectionate pair in *The King of the Great Clock Tower*. Yeats's King and Queen need to sit apart to define their emotional division, and some raised level was also required on which to rest the Stroller's mask, as representing his severed head before which the Queen eventually dances. Yeats next thought of stools and drew two designs for conventional four-legged structures; the second of these, open at the front but with solid sides and back, emphasises an overall cuboid shape; the fourth design offers an exact cube, as prescribed in his stage directions. (See plate 17) The geometrical precision of the setting, its dimensions and positioning within the known space of the Abbey stage made its recreation for the revival by Marius Arnold-Clarke relatively easy.[15] Steady-state lighting, designed to flood the playing space evenly, provided a startling contrast to the calculated obscurity of the opening of the play, where two black-clad Musicians sing against darkened curtains, their white-painted faces and hands having a strange luminosity in the prevailing gloom. The brilliance of the stage-picture, once the Musicians opened the curtains, seemed to grip our audience's attention immediately and sustain it throughout the long-held silence with which the main action begins.

Costumes and masks posed far more difficulties. The evidence for how the three main characters appeared is far sparser than for the setting and less precise: it comprises Yeats's descriptions in his stage directions of the colour schemes to be followed and the general look of the two masks, and a single black-and-white photograph, which shows the initial performers of those roles in costume. (See plate 18) De Valois as Queen is flanked by Dennis O'Dea (Stroller) to the left, and to the right, by F.J. McCormick (King); they are standing near a stage-setting that shows the rear of a conventional scenic flat and what appear to be three of Craig's hinged screens; de Valois and O'Dea wear the masks designed for them by George Atkinson. What the materials were from which the costumes were made is not known, though their construction is largely apparent from the photograph. De Valois herself in interviews with me and also on a different occasion with Professor Sam McCready had discussed how Yeats's prescriptions for the costumes in terms of their colour-relations were carried out.[16] When realised by Tessa Balls for our recreation, the degree of similarity between the two male costumes in black and red was striking, one appearing a reverse image of the other: only the mask worn by the Stroller and the King's frilled cuffs distinguished between them: it was as if the Stroller were an earthier, inner persona of the King. Though Yeats described the Queen's costume as predominantly orange, de Valois insisted the finished effect was of a pale gold with red detailing at waist and neckline complementing the red in the men's costumes. What is not clear in the photograph is how the sleeves of de Valois' dress were formed:

close-fitting sleeves are apparent but these are backed by soft drapes of material. Were these hanging loose from the shoulders to either side or were they parts of one continuous piece of material forming a cape? The practical demands of the role, including the sustained lifting of the head (mask), suggested the former rather than the latter construction was preferable; a cloak might prove too constricting. No precise record remains of what the Attendants wore for this production, but an extant newspaper photograph of Lennox Robinson playing a Musician in a revival of Yeats's *The Only Jealousy of Emer* (1926) shows him wearing a black kimono and a black Japanese-style hat with black bands around his jaw-line, rendering his white-painted face like a mask, an effect augmented by the highlights of dark make-up accentuating cheek-bones, nose and lips. A full- cast photograph of the revival of *Fighting the Waves* (1929) shows the Musicians identically clad and made-up like Robinson. From this evidence that the Abbey redeployed the costuming over several productions, we felt confident in recreating that design for the Attendants in this play.[17]

Yeats's directions specify only that the Queen should wear "a beautiful impassive mask" while the Stroller's should appear "wild half-savage" with a "red beard" covering his lower face. It is immediately apparent that de Valois' mask is modelled on a traditional Noh mask (the inspiration may be the conventional representation for an innocent, young girl or the *Deigan* mask representing a ghostly, beautiful woman whose destiny remains unfulfilled).[18] A difficult task confronted Vicki Hallam, our mask-maker, since the Queen's "face" is the constant focus of the audience's gaze for a long period of stage time. "Impassive", given the way the play develops, must not indicate vacancy but rather a depth of withheld emotion: this Queen is self-possessed and self-communing but acutely perceptive of what is happening around her. It is a complex face, full of potential that should leave the audience like the King tantalised by her refusal to communicate directly and tense with expectation that such marmoreal stillness *has* to move; and, in moving, will define that potential. A mask evocative of this complexity is essential to assist the dancer in sustaining immediacy, credibility and audience scrutiny throughout the long-held silences at the start of the play: a mask that was too easily read would dissipate the intensity that the opening must establish and then augment. The mask for the Stroller is more a constructional challenge: the actor's lower jaw is to be concealed by the red beard, which must be attached to the main mask in a way that allows the actor comfortably to articulate with full use of his jaws; yet the beard must stay in position, when later the mask is removed to represent a severed head, when it comes to suggest the (stylised) flow of blood. Initially the red beard must define the Stroller's identity; but later, when it depicts his fate, it must appear suitably gruesome without being nauseating: it must assist the dancer to define and communicate the ambivalence of her response, which Yeats described as shifting between "horror and fascination".[19]

The music composed for the Abbey production by Arthur Duff survives in two forms: in Duff's own manuscript within the Macmillan archives and in xeroxes of the personal script owned by Robert Irwin, one of the original Attendants in 1934, and copied by him for Professor McCready.[20] Both of these sources give the accompaniments for the songs in redaction for piano rather than as orchestrated for the Abbey staging. Musical resources at the theatre were rarely on a large scale, and this influenced Craig Fortnam's choice to re-work the score for this production with a chamber group, comprising piano, percussion and individual selected strings. Studying the play decided him on starting with just a piano accompaniment for the opening song and then gradually adding in other instruments as the dance approached, subliminally building audience expectation of an imminent dramatic climax.

The real crux facing anyone attempting a recreation of *The King of the Great Clock Tower* is the dance. Duff's score at the appropriate position baldly states: "Here the dance"; but no music follows. All that Ninette de Valois would impart to me in conversation in the late 1970s about the choreography was that it was not on *pointe*, but danced barefoot or in pumps, like much of her own work at the time and in the style she termed, "abstract expressionism". How could one recreate what is the central sequence of the dance drama in performance seemingly from nothing? Millicent Hodson and Kenneth Archer write, when defining their guiding principles in recreating works by Nijinsky, of the importance of *traces*, which handled scrupulously can prove helpfully revealing.[21] A chance comment of de Valois' that the two halves of the play were of equal length in their original staging gave some useful indication of the duration of the danced sequence. The manuscripts through which Yeats worked to achieve the version that the Abbey staged and the first publication of the play by the Cuala Press offer a wealth of information about Yeats's possible intentions with a performance, particularly in respect of the changes he effected to his stage directions and most notably for the dance. Yeats's letters, especially to Olivia Shakespear, and the few reviews of the production are highly revealing, when viewed with a recreation in mind. Yeats is concerned with details, specific highlights, points of emphasis; and the focus of his account is almost entirely on the dance. Reviewers are more preoccupied, once they have outlined the plot, with describing their emotional responses and with analysing what in the dance appeared to elicit these reactions.[22] Taken together, such shards of evidence offer two main insights into the dance: that its length is determined by the need for the choreography to shape a narrative that shows the Queen undergoing an emotional and spiritual journey (the physical has to be sensed as emblematic of the psychological); and secondly, that in terms of tone the dance should alternate between states of awe and loathing, between revulsion (at the horror of the reality of the severed head) and attraction (a developing fascination and love for the Stroller, because he has so fearlessly accepted his fate, confidently dying to prove his truth to self and to her), but that this conflict of feelings in her should eventually resolve and find union in acceptance.

With all this in mind, I created the following scenario for Will Tuckett, as choreographer, and Craig Fortnam, as composer. Yeats's stage directions are given in square brackets with the content printed in italics; my suggestions as to how these should be interpreted in relation to the surviving evidence of its original staging are given in rounded brackets with the content printed in bold.

The King of the Great Clock Tower: the dance sequence – a scenario.

[*The King goes out right and returns with the head of the Stroller, and lays it upon the cubical throne to right, nearest audience.*]
THE KING: Now I shall know if those lips can sing. [*He sits on the other cubical throne to right.*] You have our attention. Sing Stroller and fool.

(The Queen is by now standing and looking towards the King and the Stroller's head. She approaches the head and bows before it (reverence) before lifting it in her hands.)

[*The Queen begins to dance.*] **(Whenever the head is in her hands, the dance should become like a *pas de deux* in which she mimes the weight of the head but lifts, turns and generally moves it in the manner that a male partner would normally support a woman. She in a sense should animate the mask. Her movements generally should suggest elegance, civility and grace. The dance should**

steadily move throughout the available space and bring the Queen to the centre of the stage where no one yet has been positioned. This should be achieved before the next line of text and the ensuing stage direction.)

That is a good thought. Dance! Turn him into mockery with a dance. O, a good thought.

[*He laughs. The Queen lays the head on the ground at the centre of the stage, stands motionless looking at the head.*] **(Again, this a moment of awe and stillness with the focus not on the head now, but on the Queen contemplating it.)**

Dance! Dance! If you are nothing to him but an image, a body in his head, he is nothing to you but a head without a body. What is the good of a lover without a body? Dance! He thought you were not so fine as the image in his head, nor so tall, nor so red nor so white. Dance! Display your beauty!

[*The Queen dances.* **(Yeats described the dance as long and loving and as moving between horror and fascination. This suggests two contrasting musical themes and tempi.)** *Then stands in the centre of the stage, facing audience, the head upon her shoulder.*]

The lips are opening. The eyes are moving.

FIRST ATTENDANT [singing as head in a low voice] **(How much interaction there is between head and dancing Queen at this point is for us to decide. Clearly she is brought to capitulate to the Stroller's ordering of events and her fascination is to bring her eventually to kiss the head, but too much movement would distract from the song)**:

> Images ride, I heard a man say,
> Out of Benbulben and Knocknareagh,
> *What says the Clock in the Great Clock Tower?*
> Out of the grave. Saddle and ride
> But turn from Rosses' crawling tide,
> The meet's upon the mountain side.
> *A slow low note and an iron bell.*

What made them mount and what made them come,
Cuchulain that fought night long with the foam;
What says the Clock in the Great Clock Tower?
Niam that rode on it; lad and lass
That sat so still and played at the chess?
What but heroic wantonness.
A slow low note and an iron bell.

Aleel, his Countess; Hanrahan
That seemed but a wild wenching man;
What says the Clock in the Great Clock Tower?
And all alone comes riding there
The King that could make his people stare,
Because he had feathers instead of hair.
A slow low note and an iron bell.

[*When the song has finished, the dance begins again, the Clock strikes. The strokes are represented by blows on a gong struck by second attendant. The Queen dances to the sound, and at the last stroke presses her lips to the lips of the head.* **(The dance is reaching its mystical climax now and should logically move towards the kiss as inevitable. Much will depend here on how rapidly the blows to the gong are struck. Yeats liked really slow beats full of resonance as in the Japanese theatre. The dance could move through a series of held poses or alternate movement with poses but always the focus should be on the two heads of dancer and mask, which must be moving into closer and closer conjunction. The kiss should be sustained before the next sequence of movement commences.)** *The King has risen and drawn his sword. The Queen lays the head upon her breast, and fixes her eyes upon him. He appears about to strike, but kneels, laying the sword at her feet. The two Attendants rise singing, and slowly close the inner curtain.*]

(Overall I think the dance should move by contrasting stages representing horror (rapid movement) and fascination (moving steadily towards stillness) into a kind of hieratic ritual once the terms of the "contract" with the Stroller (dance, then song, then kiss in gratitude) take possession of the Queen. The logical place for the ritual to begin is with the song.)

The alternating emotional states offered Fortnam potential for two contrasting themes and tempi, while their recurrence (the Queen's is not a straight psychological progress) invited variations and developmental potential. An inspiration for him was the music Duff composed for the Queen's song, which is in a different, elaborate but highly controlled idiom from the rhythmic "Irish folk" quality of the remaining songs. The recurrent motif of the three rising chords draws on material from Duff's setting of the Song for the Severed Head.

Tuckett consciously decided to avoid any hint of pastiche of extant de Valois choreography (though there are scattered traces, hints of favoured de Valois steps). The idea of horror changing to fascination afforded him opportunities to create floor patterns that extended and contracted within the geography of the playing space but always in ways that carried psychological resonances. The result is dance but always mindful of the full theatrical demands of its performance. Note how once she rises from her throne, the Queen stays oblivious of the King's presence; Tuckett's choreography takes her first to the head, which she is compelled to take in her hands, and then increasingly to the centre of the stage, which till now throughout the action of the play has remained unoccupied. At first the dance shows how she senses that the centre is the rightful place for the Stroller's head, but increasingly she is drawn to join it there. Once the dance brings her to the centre, she takes full command of the space and of the events that ensue, culminating in the mimed emasculation of the King. She achieves a different stillness now: she no longer broods inwardly as at first but faces the audience to become, as the focal point in the final tableau, a figure of absolute, public authority. Tuckett's invention in its discipline, subtlety and attention to detail serves the narrative trajectory scrupulously, but with no loss of emotional intensity.

The King of the Great Clock Tower might have been a sad occasion in 1934 for Yeats: his hopes of an ongoing dance school at the Abbey had been dashed the previous year, when the Theatre's directors were reluctantly forced to close the School for want of adequate funding to continue its activities. De Valois had moved on in her career, the Vic-Wells Ballet Company requiring all her attention and stamina. Yeats composed the dance play specifically for her and she chose to return to Dublin for its performance.[23] How could she not have returned, when the play is such a celebration of her gifts as a choreographer, mime-artist and dancer? Attempting to re-create that production of 1934 makes one appreciate just what extraordinary demands Yeats made on her and appreciate too the absolute confidence he had in her powers of invention that she could meet them. His play is an act of homage to de Valois as an artist of rare ability and a collaborator for whom he had the profoundest respect. It is as an act of homage that this re-creation was staged and as a collaboration between the present and the past with the aim of retrieving what might otherwise be a forgotten but remarkable achievement in the history of performance and in de Valois' early career.

Part Eight: Herself

De Valois: filmed interview

Anna Meadmore

David Drew (b. 1938) joined the Sadler's Wells Ballet after graduating from the School in 1955. Promoted to Soloist in 1961 and Principal in 1974, his long career with The Royal Ballet has been influential: as a notable Character Artist; teacher of *pas de deux;* choreographic mentor to generations of students (as Norman Morrice's assistant on the School's Choreographic Course), but also as an active observer of The Royal Ballet during the last half century. This film, which is a fourteen-minute edit of around one and a half hours of footage, was made in 1989, entirely as a result of David Drew's determination and enthusiasm. Filmed with basic equipment, the sound and visual quality is imperfect – but in terms of content, it is archival gold! The full recording, now digitised, has kindly been given by David Drew to the Royal Opera House Collections, and to White Lodge Museum's Ballet Resource Centre, along with other historic film interviews he recorded during his career with The Royal Ballet Company and School.

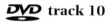 **track 10**

Part Nine: Appendices

Invitation to the Ballet: Ninette de Valois and the story of The Royal Ballet

Cristina Franchi

Introduction (incorporated from the texts accompanying the displays in the exhibition referred to in the opening sentence)

A major retrospective exhibition, *Invitation to the Ballet, Ninette de Valois and the story of The Royal Ballet*, was mounted by Royal Opera House Collections at The Lowry in Salford in October 2010 as part of Royal Opera House On the Road. Part of the exhibition transferred to the Royal Opera House in March 2011 to celebrate Ninette de Valois' legacy ten years after her death. The exhibition tells the story of The Royal Ballet from its foundations in the late 1920s and early 1930s until the present day, beginnng with the struggles of de Valois herself as a young dancer trying to find training in England, where there was no national English ballet school or company unlike the situation in Russia, France, Italy and Denmark where ballet had been an established art form for many years. The exhibition follows de Valois and her collaborators as she founds a school, works with Lilian Baylis, attaches the School to the Old Vic and Sadler's Wells Theatres, establishes a company, recruits collaborators, develops dancers and choreographers and builds a repertory. Treasures on display from Royal Opera House Collections included costumes, designs, photographs, letters, music and choreographic scores, film and sound. De Valois' own words, as well as some of her writings read by Jeanetta Laurence, Associate Director of The Royal Ballet, provided the sound-track for four segments of specially commissioned archive film, directed by Lynne Wake, which explores aspects of de Valois' journey and legacy throughout nearly one hundred years of ballet in England.

Ninette de Valois

Ninette de Valois' early childhood was spent in her beloved Ireland, where she discovered a love of the written word and of country dancing, which were to remain with her throughout her life; and here she was taken to the theatre for the first time: "The clear cut joy of my first theatre visit. This was to the Gaiety Theatre in Dublin. Prophetically it was the pantomime of *The Sleeping Beauty*." The family relocated to England where de Valois began dance classes before becoming a professional dancer in London at age 16. The years of World War I and the early 1920s see de Valois dancing in pantomime, music halls and revues. Friendship with Russian Dancers leads to two years working with Serge Diaghilev's *Ballets Russes* in France. Gradually she realises that what is needed in England is a national school and a company. She returned to London where she was one of a small group of pioneers working for an English ballet. De Valois took her school to Lilian Baylis at the Old Vic and in 1931 the Vic-Wells Ballet, the forerunner of today's Royal Ballet, took its first steps.

An Irish Jig

Ninette de Valois was born Edris Stannus on 6 June 1898 at Baltiboys, the family home near Blessington, County Wicklow, Ireland. De Valois' mother was a formidable woman who ran her own Grayston glass factory and who could trace her family back to the Irish Kings. She later chose de Valois' stage name, as she believed the family to have links to the French Royal house. De Valois' father was a professional soldier, who fought gallantly in World War I, before being killed on the Somme in 1917. His bravery was recognised in the awards of both the Distinguished Services Order and the *Chevalier Legion d'Honneur*. De Valois was the second of four children; her younger brother, Gordon, was also to pursue a career in the theatre as the celebrated photographer, Gordon Anthony. De Valois loved the Irish countryside, as well as losing herself in books. The estate farmer's wife taught her an authentic Irish Jig and de Valois discovered that she liked to perform her jig along with a piano accompaniment.

'Come Dance with Me'

De Valois' family moved to England when she was seven years old, living first with her grandmother in Walmer, Kent, and then moving to London. She and her sister Thelma were sent to "fancy dancing" classes for young ladies at Mrs Wordsworth's school. When she was not dancing, de Valois amused her siblings by compiling a magazine of her own short stories and by mounting plays using figures cut out of magazines. De Valois' mother decided she should be trained as a professional dancer at the Lila Field Academy; by the age of 14, de Valois was appearing with the Lila Field Wonder Children, at seaside pier theatres. "I think that I can boast of having danced on every old pier theatre in England!" De Valois danced

Anna Pavlova's *The Dying Swan*, a role she had learnt by taking notes from the balcony at Pavlova's weekly Wednesday matinées at the Palace Theatre. The 1914 tour was cut short by the outbreak of World War I and de Valois returned to London where she secured her first professional engagement, in the Lyceum pantomime. By now de Valois had become aware of the inadequacies of her training and she began to attend ballet classes first with Edouard Espinosa and then with Enrico Cecchetti. She met Lydia Lopokova and other Russian dancers who worked for Serge Diaghilev, the impresario of the Ballets Russes. De Valois danced for the first time at the Royal Opera House, Covent Garden, in 1919 as *première danseuse* in Sir Thomas Beecham's season of International Opera.

Serge Diaghilev (1872-1929)
The great Russian impresario, Serge Diaghilev, first brought his Ballets Russes to London for seasons at the Royal Opera House in 1911 and 1913. For de Valois, the impact of seeing dancers such as Vaslav Nijinsky and Tamara Karsavina and works such as *The Firebird* was huge. Diaghilev believed that ballet had to have the best choreographers, composers and designers, so he gathered around him the most extraordinary artists of the day. He presented the classics with amazing new designs as well as commissioning pioneering new works. De Valois' friendships with Russian dancers led to her being asked to join the Diaghilev Company in Paris in 1923. De Valois claimed to have learnt everything she needed to know about running a ballet company from the two years she spent observing Diaghilev and the *Ballets Russes*.

Constant Lambert (1905-51)
Constant Lambert was a talented young composer and conductor, who had composed *Romeo and Juliet* for Diaghilev. He was at the heart of intellectual and aesthetic life in London in the 1920s and 1930s and a key member and conductor of the Camargo Society, founded in 1930 by Philip Richardson, Arnold Haskell and Edwin Evans to promote evenings of ballet. Its committee included Maynard Keynes, Lydia Lopokova, Marie Rambert and Ninette de Valois. In 1931 de Valois asked him to be Conductor and shortly after Music Director of the Vic-Wells Ballet. He was to exercise a profound influence on the young Company. He suggested and orchestrated music for ballets, composed scores for new works, and worked closely with de Valois and Frederick Ashton.

'Step by Step'

De Valois realised an English ballet company would need a school from which dancers could in time be drawn to form a company. In 1926, she opened her Academy of Choreographic Art. She then approached Lilian Baylis who owned the leases of both the Old Vic and Sadler's Wells theatres, about her plans for founding a company. Baylis engaged her to teach movement to the actors and drama students, to arrange choreography and to appear with her students at the Old Vic. Baylis planned to restore the bomb-damaged Sadler's Wells Theatre as a home for the School and future Company. On 5 May 1931, de Valois' company, the Vic-Wells Ballet, gave its first complete evening of ballet entirely choreographed by de Valois.

Her Early Ballets

In the early years of the Company, de Valois herself was a regular performer, dancing roles such as Swanilda in *Coppélia*, the Foreign Visitor in *Regatta* (Frederick Ashton's first ballet for the Company), and the Tight-Rope Dancer in her own ballet, *Douanes*. She was also director, teacher and choreographer. She created twenty works for the Company between 1931 and 1935, including *Job*, *The Haunted Ballroom* and *The Rake's Progress*. The choreography for her ballets was carefully worked out in advance with drawings of stick figures and in the case of *Job*, beautiful drawings inspired by William Blake. De Valois believed that if she was to have a successful English ballet company then she needed to develop English ballets. She drew inspiration from British themes, commissioned British composers and designers, and had a particular love of the eighteenth century.

Coppélia

In 1933, de Valois invited Nicholas Sergeyev to stage *Coppélia* for the Company, their first classical work. Sergeyev had worked as *régisseur* at the Mariinsky Theatre in Leningrad and had left Russia in 1918, with a trunk full of his notation notebooks. He had staged *The Sleeping Princess* for Diaghilev in London in 1921, a work which was to influence profoundly both de Valois and Ashton, and which he staged for the Vic-Wells Ballet in 1939. De Valois always had a soft spot for *Coppélia* and appeared in the production herself, alternating the role of Swanilda with the Russian ballerina, Lydia Lopokova.

Alicia Markova (1910–2004)

The English dancer Alicia Markova joined Diaghilev's *Ballets Russes* as a "baby ballerina" aged 14, where she first met de Valois. She was well known to audiences when she joined the Vic-Wells Ballet at the beginning of 1932 and became the Company's first ballerina. Markova appeared to great acclaim in her first *Giselle*, partnered by Anton Dolin, the leading British male dancer. She also assisted de Valois with the staging of ballets such as Mikhail Fokine's *Les Sylphides*. De Valois was keen to give her and the young Company their first opportunities to dance *Le Lac des Cygnes* and *Casse-noisette*, and engaged Nicolas Sergeyev to stage them.

Frederick Ashton (1904–88)

Frederick Ashton was born in Ecuador and brought up in Peru. In 1917 Anna Pavlova toured to Lima, and Ashton knew from the moment he saw her dance that he wanted to be a dancer. In London, he was a founder member of Marie Rambert's Ballet Club and she encouraged him to try choreography in 1926. He then spent a highly influential year working with Bronislava Nijinska in France. Returning to London, he created works for Ballet Club and the Camargo Society and from 1931 for the Vic-Wells Ballet. De Valois persuaded him to join the Vic-Wells Ballet as resident choreographer in 1935.

The Rake's Progress (1935)

De Valois was fond of narrative ballets. Her one-act work, *The Rake's Progress*, was influenced by William Hogarth's series of paintings. The ballet like the paintings shows the gradual decline of the Rake character in eighteenth-century London. De Valois followed Diaghilev's precepts about working with the best collaborators: the music was composed by Gavin Gordon, while Rex Whistler designed the sets and costumes, based on Hogarth. *The Rake's Progress* is very much an example of an English ballet and continues to be performed regularly.

The Vic-Wells Ballet 1935-39

In the autumn of 1935, de Valois had succeeded in recruiting the team which would take the Vic-Wells Ballet forward over the next twenty years: she shared the artistic direction and development of the Company with Constant Lambert and Frederick Ashton. Lambert was the nearest the Company had to their own Diaghilev: a man of great aesthetic taste and sensibilities, he had an encyclopaedic knowledge of music and the arts and proposed suitable subjects and collaborators for new works. In addition, he was a fine composer, orchestrated and arranged music for ballets, and was a conductor of genius. Ashton, recently installed as resident choreographer, began to create a stream of new ballets. It quickly became clear that he was a choreographer of huge range, equally at home creating dramatic, romantic ballets as he was creating broad comedies. Ashton shared de Valois' conviction that a foundation of the classics was essential for the development of their young dancers. He assisted her in staging these, including the landmark production of *The Sleeping Princess* in 1939.

Checkmate (1937)

In the 1930s it became clear that Europe once more stood on the brink of war; de Valois worried about what the future might hold for her young dancers. She and Lambert were only too aware that their great friend and supporter the economist, Maynard Keynes, was engaged in frantic diplomacy behind the scenes. Against this background, de Valois created *Checkmate*: the relentless and merciless progress of the Black Queen and her pieces against the Red King and his Knights echoes the growth of fascism across Europe. The ballet is played out on a stylised chessboard in stunning, fractured designs by Edward McKnight Kauffer. For the music de Valois commissioned an equally dramatic score from the English composer, Arthur Bliss. The ballet had its première at the Théâtre du Champs Elysées with the Company representing Great Britain at the Paris International Exhibition.

Margot Fonteyn

Frederick Ashton was initially ambivalent towards the charms of the dancer who was to prove his greatest muse. Both de Valois and Lambert had spotted the rare quality of the young Peggy Hookham, later renamed by de Valois as Margot Fonteyn. De Valois persuaded Ashton to use Fonteyn for his first ballet as resident choreographer, *Le Baiser de la fée*. She was partnered by the Manchester-born dancer, Harold Turner. By all accounts, rehearsals were somewhat of a battle until one day Fonteyn burst into tears and flung her arms around Ashton's neck. This broke the stalemate and a great creative partnership developed. Alicia Markova decided to leave the Vic-Wells Ballet in 1936 to start her own company with her partner, Anton Dolin. De Valois could have looked for another established ballerina but she decided to develop the seventeen-year-old Fonteyn as the Vic-Wells first home-grown ballerina. Her partner was to be the Australian dancer-actor, Robert Helpmann, who had a magnetic stage personality. Ashton created a series of ballets for Helpmann and Fonteyn over the next few years, establishing them as one of the great ballet partnerships.

The War Years 1939-45

Britain entered World War II on 3 September 1939 and immediately all theatres were closed. It looked as if this would be the end of the Vic-Wells Ballet. However, the Home Office soon realised that entertainment was going to be essential for keeping up public morale. Frederick Ashton and Constant Lambert were able to lobby successfully for the Company to go on a three-month UK tour, and in late September 1939, the Vic-Wells Ballet set off from Paddington Station for Cardiff, where they rehearsed and prepared for their first wartime tour. Initially they were not allowed to have an orchestra, so Lambert and rehearsal pianist, Hilda Gaunt, ac-companied performances on two pianos. The Company, now known as the Sadler's Wells Ballet, became part of the war effort: they did valuable work in keeping up the morale of both service personnel and the general public, touring tirelessly around the country and winning a new audi-ence for ballet in the process. De Valois spent the war years juggling running the Company and School with supporting her GP husband, Dr Arthur Connell, standing in as receptionist when she was able to. She recognised the importance of continuing to give her audience new work and of providing a respite from everyday cares. She choreographed a number of new ballets including the comic ballet, *The Prospect Before Us*, which is set in an eighteenth-century theatre, and she created the role of the drunken stage door keeper, Mr O'Reilly, to give full rein to the comic balletic genius of Robert Helpmann.

Frederick Ashton's 1940 ballet, *Dante Sonata*, was a response to the outbreak of war. Inspired by Dante's *Inferno*, it explored the conflict be-tween Children of Light, led by Margot Fonteyn and the young Michael Somes, and Children of Darkness, led by Helpmann, and June Brae. Nei-ther group triumphs; and twice there is a double crucifixion. The Company performed it on a propaganda tour to Holland in 1940. Ger-many invaded and the Sadler's Wells Ballet made a dramatic escape across the North Sea, locked in the hold of a cargo boat. Ashton was called up in 1941 but continued to choreograph when he could, collabo-rating with such war artists as Graham Sutherland and John Piper.

Australian Robert Helpmann was exempt from call up and played a crucial role in keeping the Company together. In Ashton's absence, he joined de Valois as choreographer. His most successful ballets were the powerful dance drama, *Hamlet*, and *Miracle in the Gorbals*, set in the Glasgow slums.

In early 1945, the Company led by de Valois, Fonteyn and Helpmann, embarked on an ENSA tour to Belgium and Paris to perform for Allied troops on 48-hour leave. ENSA, the Entertainments National Service Association, was set up to provide entertainment for British armed forces personnel. Sadler's Wells Ballet was the largest company to be sent on tour by ENSA and the first British company to entertain European civilians since the war started. Only one performance had to be cancelled due to preparations for the Battle of the Rhine and the tour was a great success.

1946-56 A new home for Sadler's Wells Ballet

By the end of the war, the Sadler's Wells Ballet had become the national company in all but name. In 1945, de Valois was asked to bring the Sadler's Wells Ballet to make their home at the Royal Opera House and to reopen the theatre as a lyric theatre after its World War II service as a Mecca dance hall.

De Valois thought it was the right time for both the Company and for its young ballerina, Margot Fonteyn, to have a full-length version of *The Sleeping Beauty*. Sergeyev agreed to stage the work and both de Valois and Frederick Ashton contributed choreography. Oliver Messel designed magical sets and costumes, no mean feat at a time when rationing was still in full force. *The Sleeping Beauty* has since become the signature work of The Royal Ballet. The first performance was on 20 February 1946, and for everyone there it felt like a new beginning. The Royal Family attended in force and went backstage to meet the cast after the performance.

The next ten years were to be a busy time for de Valois as she established the Sadler's Wells Ballet at the Royal Opera House, started a second Company at Sadler's Wells Theatre, and the Ballet School continued to grow. This period also saw the Company's triumphant first tour to North America. De Valois was concerned to secure the long-term future of all three organisations, independent of their parent theatres or buildings; and she began to lobby behind the scenes; her efforts were rewarded when in 1956, the year of the Company's 25th birthday, a Royal Charter was granted to The Royal Ballet, The Royal Ballet Touring Company and The Royal Ballet School.

Establishing a repertory at the Royal Opera House

Ninette de Valois found herself facing new challenges at the Royal Opera House. The Company and their repertory had to be adapted to the larger stage. Initially there was no opera company to share the theatre, so Sadler's Wells Ballet began the season with seventy performances of *The Sleeping Beauty*. The Covent Garden Opera Company shared its first performance in December 1946 with Sadler's Wells Ballet in a production of *The Fairy Queen*. De Valois provided dancers and choreographers for the opera ballets rather as she had done for Lilian Baylis. She supervised the staging of her own ballets as well as commissioning new works.

De Valois continued to invite colleagues from her Ballets Russes days to come and work with her dancers. In 1947 Léonide Massine staged three of his ballets *Le Tricorne* (The Three Cornered Hat), *Boutique fantasque* and *Mam'zelle Angot*. George Balanchine staged *Ballet Impérial* in 1950, and in 1954 the Company acquired Mikhail Fokine's ballet, *The Firebird*.

Frederick Ashton's first new ballet at the Royal Opera House was the plotless *Symphonic Variations*. Working with his great friend the artist Sophie Fedorovitch, he created a pure classical work of great beauty. *Scènes de ballet* had Ashton pouring over Euclid's geometry to create a work that overturned perceptions about how space could be used in the ballet.

In 1948 Ashton became the first British choreographer to create a three-act ballet. In *Cinderella* he wove together elements of fairytale as well as Victorian music hall and pantomime in the characters of the Stepsisters, memorably brought to life by Ashton and Robert Helpmann. The 1950s saw an outpouring of new ballets including *Daphnis and Chloë*, *Sylvia* and *Ondine*. *Homage to the Queen* in 1953 was created to mark the coronation of Her Majesty Queen Elizabeth II.

De Valois' last work for the Company was *Don Quixote* in 1950, with music by Roberto Gerhard and stunning designs by Edward Burra. Another narrative ballet, it was a thoughtful and serious portrayal of the story with Robert Helpmann in the title role. De Valois believed that the making of new ballets was safe in the hands of Frederick Ashton and therefore decided to concentrate her energies on the Directorship as well as overseeing the second Company and the School.

Sadler's Wells Theatre Ballet

De Valois wanted to keep faith with the wider ballet audience, who had supported the Company during the war years, and she decided to establish a second company at Sadler's Wells. Sadler's Wells Theatre Ballet was to continue the tradition of touring, to maintain some of the works from the early repertory, which were not suited to the Covent Garden stage, and to produce new work, giving opportunities to young choreographers. This last aim was spectacularly successful with the emergence from the Company's own ranks of three great choreographers: John Cranko, Kenneth MacMillan and, more recently, David Bintley. Their first director was Ursula Moreton, who had been with de Valois since the beginning. She was assisted by Peggy Van Praagh as Ballet Mistress, who took over as Director in 1952 when Moreton took over the Directorship of Sadler's Wells Ballet School from de Valois.

Kenneth MacMillan was the first British choreographer to be produced entirely by Sadler's Wells Ballet. He was a pupil of Sadler's Wells Ballet School and a dancer with both Sadler's Wells Theatre Ballet and Sadler's Wells Ballet. MacMillan choreographed his first ballet, *Somnambulism*, in 1953 for the inaugural evening of ballet presented by Sadler's Wells Theatre Ballet Choreographic Group and it was clear that here was a promising new talent. In 1955 Ninette de Valois gave him his first commission to create a ballet, *Danses Concertantes*, for Sadler's Wells Theatre Ballet. This was also his first collaboration with designer Nicholas Georgiadis. It proved hugely successful and de Valois offered MacMillan the post of Resident Choreographer.

Securing the future

De Valois had been concerned for some time that the grants made to the Royal Opera House and Sadler's Wells Theatre were for the staging of ballet and opera and not for any specific company. She wanted to secure the future of the two Companies and the School. In 1954 she drafted a Memorandum setting out the position and arguing that the time had come to "establish this threefold institution as a separate entity under a name which recognises the fundamental unity of the two Companies and the School". One of the names she suggested was The Royal Ballet.

In 1956 Ashton paid tribute to de Valois on the occasion of Sadler's Wells Ballet's 25th birthday by creating *Birthday Offering* as a showcase for the Company's seven ballerinas and their partners. Later in the birthday year came the news that the Royal Charter had been granted. The Royal Ballet was constituted "to promote and advance the art of the ballet and in association therewith the literary, musical and graphical arts and to foster public knowledge and appreciation of the same". The organisations were to be known as The Royal Ballet, The Royal Ballet Touring Company and The Royal Ballet School.

The Touring Company had temporarily lost its links with Sadler's Wells Theatre in 1955 and made its home too at Covent Garden, but it continued to tour and produce new works under the directorship of John Field.

Sadler's Wells Ballet School had moved to Colet Gardens, Baron's Court, in 1947 where it continued to expand. It was joined in the early 1950s by the Company, which established ballet studios and offices in Talgarth Road. In 1955 the School was offered the use of White Lodge in Richmond Park, a former Royal hunting lodge. The Lower School, of children aged 11–16, relocated to White Lodge where it remains to this day.

De Valois found herself acting as midwife to the establishments of ballet schools and companies around the world. Her first foray had been a ballet school attached to the Abbey Theatre in Dublin from 1927 to 1933. In 1948 de Valois visited Turkey and established a ballet school under the direction of Joy Newton; a ballet company followed in 1957. In 1949 she was asked about the establishment of a Canadian Company and recommended dancer and choreographer, Celia Franca. The National Ballet of Canada was founded in 1951 and its school in 1959. Asked in 1959 to recommend a successor to Edouard Borovansky in Australia, she recommended Peggy van Praagh. Van Praagh directed Borovansky Ballet for its final season before establishing the Australian Ballet in 1960. Robert Helpmann worked closely with Australian Ballet and became Co-Director in 1965.

Ninette de Valois: the legacy

Ninette de Valois retired as Director of The Royal Ballet in 1963. Her last public appearance as Director was on 19 May 1963 at the Metropolitan Opera House, New York. It was the last night of the Company's tour and appropriately it was after a performance of *The Sleeping Beauty* with Margot Fonteyn as Aurora. With typical modesty she did not want a fuss, but Frederick Ashton was determined to celebrate her achievements. He organised a retirement Gala, which took place a year later on 7 May 1964. The highlight of the Gala was a *grand défilé*, which began with the youngest pupils of The Royal Ballet School coming onto the stage at the Royal Opera House. By the end of the *grand defilé*, the pupils of The Royal Ballet School had been joined by all the dancers from The Royal Ballet and The Royal Ballet Touring Company and the ballet staff of all three establishments. Lastly de Valois herself came down the steps in the centre of the stage to a tumultuous reception.

De Valois retired safe in the knowledge that The Royal Ballet was now in the hands of Frederick Ashton, her Founder Choreographer and collaborator since 1935. Ashton's Assistant Directors, John Field, John Hart and Michael Somes, had all grown up with the Company, as had Kenneth MacMillan, who succeeded Ashton as Director in 1970. The years between 1963 and 1977 saw these two great choreographers continuing de Valois' legacy. The repertory included the steady acquisition of works from great choreographers of the twentieth century, including those who traced their roots back to Diaghilev, as well as new productions of the great classic ballets; and both choreographers created new works for the Company as well as encouraging the development of young dancers and choreographers. De Valois' legacy was secure.

Ninette de Valois in Royal Opera House Collections

Francesca Franchi

The Royal Opera House Collections provides a rich treasure trove of materials about Dame Ninette. We are fortunate indeed in having so much material that documents her achievements, both directly and by association. The Royal Opera House Collections holds the collection for The Royal Ballet, which aims to cover the history of the Vic-Wells Ballet from its earliest endeavours in the late 1920s and the first full evening of ballet at Sadler's Wells Theatre on 5 May 1931. Donations and loans from the Royal Ballet Benevolent Fund have provided programmes, press cuttings, designs and some administrative details from those early years before the Company moved to the Royal Opera House. Further donations from former dancers and audience members have swelled these records, as have commissioned interviews with members of the Company.

From 1946, when the Sadler's Wells Ballet moved to Covent Garden and the Sadler's Wells Opera/Theatre Ballet was founded, the administrative, production, technical and performance records provide a detailed record of de Valois's two Royal Ballet Companies, and her role as choreographer and director. This includes material on Birmingham Royal Ballet from 1945 – 1997. The material for both Companies include board minutes, press and other administrative files, press cuttings, production photographs, biographies and photographs of artists, contracts, synopsi of ballets, scores, choreographic scores, designs, lighting and hanging plots, stage technical drawings, model sets, costumes, accessories, shoes and props, recordings of interviews and educational events and dress rehearsal footage.

De Valois' early career as Founder Director and dancer is covered in the programmes, press cuttings and photographs in The Royal Ballet Benevolent Fund Collection, and the main Royal Opera House Collections record her appearances as a dancer in the opera seasons from 1919 -1928, and with Léonide Massine in the revue *You'd be Surprised* in 1928.

De Valois herself bequeathed her awards and honours to the Royal Opera House, and full details of these can be found on our website, at http://www.rohcollections.org.uk/CollectionPersDeValois.aspx. A further collection, of mainly personal correspondence dating from 1977-2000, has been donated by her family.

Material relating to de Valois can be found in other Special Collections, including photographs in the Frank Sharman and Roger Wood Collections, correspondence in the Frederick Ashton Collection, her ballet shoe worn in *Douanes*, a book she gave to Margot Fonteyn on her first appearance as Giselle at the Royal Opera House, and correspondence in the Margot Fonteyn Collection, and photographs in the Leslie Edwards Collection.

We continue to add material relating to Ninette de Valois to the Collections, mostly through donations. We recently received an audio recording of a Radio Ankara programme broadcast in 1959, which examines the establishment and development of the ballet company in Turkey. The recording includes interviews with de Valois, Travis Kemp and Valerie Taylor. A recent donation of programmes included several for the Vic-Wells/Sadler's Wells Ballet in the 1930s, and we were fortunate to acquire a collection of correspondence related to the Company's early years at Sadler's Wells which included the letter from Alicia Markova to de Valois that featured in the exhibition, *Invitation to the Ballet, Ninette de Valois and the Story of The Royal Ballet.*

For the exhibition ROH Collections commissioned independent film director Lynne Wake to create the film *Come Dance With Me.*

Researchers interested in viewing any of the above material relating to de Valois can apply to visit Royal Opera House Collections, details on our website: www.rohcollections.org.uk

Ninette de Valois Materials in The Royal Ballet School Collections

Edward Small

The archival Collections of The Royal Ballet School are a primary source of information about its Founder's life and work. Resources relating to de Valois derive from four areas of provenance:
• personal records accumulated by de Valois and the Stannus family, now on loan to the School;
• personal records accumulated by de Valois and given to the School by her or her colleagues during and after her lifetime;
• School administrative, teaching and performance/event records;
• other collections referencing de Valois' activities.

The Stannus Family Collection

The Royal Ballet School is privileged to hold the Stannus Family Collection on loan. This material, compiled by de Valois' descendants, covers the entire duration of her life and includes photographs, correspondence, memorabilia, appointment diaries, programmes, press cuttings, and literary papers (including her poetry, short stories and plays). Particularly charming are the many photographs portraying de Valois' childhood in Ireland. The Collection also contains much material relating to her brother, the theatre photographer Gordon Anthony, including many of his own photographic prints.

Personal records

The Ninette de Valois Collection includes personal portraits by photographers such as Gordon Anthony, Anthony Crickmay, and Lord Snowdon; also manuscript material comprising the draft of her book *Invitation to the Ballet*, annotated copies of sheet music for her ballet, *The Haunted Ballroom* (1943), and choreographic notebooks referring to her ballets *Job* (1931) and *Orpheus and Eurydice* (1941). Other unique items include the "big red book", a photograph album presented to de Valois following her television appearance on *This is Your Life* in 1964; as well as several annotated photograph albums presented to her at occasions marking various Company anniversaries. The Joy Newton Collection, held on restricted access, includes a series of letters from de Valois to her friend and confidante, Joy Newton, written between 1947 and 1990. The correspondence began when Newton was teaching in Turkey, prior to the founding by de Valois of the Turkish National Ballet Academy in 1948.

School records

De Valois' close association with the School continued well into the 1990s, and she features regularly in the School's administrative records, from the foundation of the School in 1926 to arrangements for her one hundredth birthday celebrations in 1998. The photographic records of the School, including some audiovisual material (recently digitised, but not yet fully catalogued), show de Valois conducting classes, or giving talks to the students. Photographs record a studio performance of *The Muses* made for students of the School by de Valois in 1962. De Valois is also invariably pictured at special events such as royal visits and award presentations. Records of de Valois' pedagogy exist in her own handwritten notebooks, and in the working notes of staff teachers such as Ursula Moreton, Audrey Harman, and Joan Lawson, as well as some class-notes made by students while at the School.

Other collections

Many of the School Collections are connected in some way with de Valois. Amongst these are the Camargo Society Collection, which includes programmes, administrative records and photographs which feature her; the design collection, which contains a costume design by Sophie Fedorovitch for de Valois' ballet *Douanes* (1935 revival); also the Ursula Moreton Collection, which includes a series of scrapbooks compiled from 1929 to 1950 during which the activities of de Valois and her Company were followed closely in the press. Scrapbooks belonging to Winifred Edwards and Wyn and Ivy Reeves also contain much information about de Valois.

Among the School's several Collections of ballet photographs are images of de Valois as a dancer. She is pictured, for example, in pantomime at the Lyceum (1915), as the *première danseuse* in *Aïda* at Covent Garden (autographed, 1919), in the dance-dramas of W. B. Yeats at the Cambridge Festival Theatre, and performing in many roles at the Old Vic and Sadler's Wells Theatres.

Finally, the Collections contain some original flyers and programmes for de Valois' performances with the Royal Opera at Covent Garden, Diaghilev's Ballets Russes and later the Camargo Society.

For further information and contact details, go to www.royalballetschool.co.uk/wl_museum

Part Ten: Notes

From Bad Fairy to Gramophone Girl: Ninette de Valois' early career in English popular theatre. Jane Pritchard

1 Programmes and material in the core collection of the Theatre & Performance Collections of the Victoria and Albert Museum and in Private Collections provide the source for much of this chapter.

2 Between June 1878, when Virginia Zucchi had danced in a *divertissement* by Joseph Hansen, and June 1909, when Olga Preobrajenska and Georgei Kyashst were seen in a divertissement following the operas, only one independent ballet had been presented. In June 1906, dancers from the Theatre Royale de la Monnaie, Brussels had performed *Les Deux Pigeons* (*The Two Pigeons*) choreographed by François Ambrosiny.

3 *Oh! Julie!* opened at the Shaftesbury Theatre on 22 June 1920 transferring to the Princes on 27 September. Ninette de Valois performed speciality dances with Fred A Leslie which, as Sorley Walker points out, had to be modified to prevent them from upstaging the star Ethel Levey who appeared as Julie (known as "La Soroska" the Russian Dancer). Although Sorley Walker notes that *Oh! Julie!* "failed to 'take' ", it did receive 142 performances. Kathrine Sorley Walker, *Ninette de Valois: Idealist Without Illusions* (London: Hamish Hamilton, 1987), p. 22.

4 In the programme for the Royal Court Theatre 29-30 June 1911 the groups of good and bad fairies are designated by the colours they wear. Curiously the range of blue, yellow, rose, green and mauve is the same for both the good and the bad. See programme in Royal Court Theatre collection, core collection Theatre & Performance, V&A.

5 For Lila Field's matinée at the Ambassador's Theatre on 14 July 1914 in *Cupid & Co. in Pierrot-Land* de Valois is listed as playing "The Great Pavlova".

6 David Dimbleby, "Dame Ninette de Valois: a lifetime in ballet" (From *Person to Person* BBC 1), *The Listener*, 26 July 1979, p.110.

7 Ninette de Valois, "The Wonder Children", *The Spectator*, 24 January 1964 reprinted in *Step by Step* (London: Allen, 1977), pp. 1–4.

8 Only in *Cinderella* does the cast list give her a role other than dancer. Here she was "Sunray" to Alex Goudin's "Moonbeam".

9 Philip Richardson, "Dancing in the Christmas Plays", *The Dancing Times*, January, 1917, pp.139-141.

10 "Ninette de Valois", *Era*, 23 December 1914, p. 11.

11 "Robert Roberti [sic] A Clever Dancer", *Era*, 7 July 1915, p. 14.

12 The Memorial Service for Dame Marie Rambert took place at St Paul's Church, Covent Garden on 30 September 1982.

13 Sorley Walker in *Ninette de Valois: Idealist Without Illusions*, pp. 25, 340, lists this tour's opening and the premières of de Valois' creations as 26 October, which was the day before reviews appeared in *The Stage* (27 October) and not the opening night which was the Monday. We also disagree on the allocation of composers for *An Idyll* and *The Letter*. I have based my reading on the slip for the divertissement at Holborn Empire rather than the slightly muddled review in *The Stage*.

14 These included charity performances at the Vaudeville Theatre on 4 January and the Criterion on 7 June, as well as at the recital by Lady Constance Stewart Richardson at the Royal Court on 2 June.

15 Sorley Walker quotes *Jan Caryll: a Dancer's Memories* 1981/82 in *Ninette de Valois*, p.25.

16 The "company" at the Royal Opera House consisted of Errol Addison, Alise Allanova, Marguerite Astafieva, Dorothy Coxon, Lydia Lopokova, Léonide Massine, Ursula Moreton, Jean Ochimovski, Vera Savina, Thadée Slavinsky, Lydia Sokolova, Ninette de Valois, Léon Woizikovsky, Rita Zalmani, Jean Zalmujinski.
17 Ninette de Valois, "Lydia Lopokova and English Ballet" in Milo Keynes (ed.), *Lydia Lopokova* (London: Weidenfeld and Nicolson, 1983), pp.106-115.
18 "Stravinsky's 'Ragtime'. Russian Dancers at Covent Garden", *The Times* 4 April 1922 p.12.

Ninette de Valois and Diaghilev. Clement Crisp

1 An edited version of this film is included on the DVD as track 10.
2 Ninette de Valois, *Come Dance With Me* (London: Hamish Hamilton, 1957), p.60.
3 Ibid.
4 Ibid, p.58.
5 Ibid. p.72.
6 Ibid, p.72.
7 Ninette de Valois, *Invitation to the Ballet* (London: The Bodley Head, 1937), p.24.
8 Ibid, p.29.
9 Ibid, p.30.
10 An anecdote (from the 1980s, I think): I was at the Royal Opera House, watching a performance, and also there with me were Alicia Markova and Alexandra Danilova and Dame Ninette. We met and were talking away blithely, when Dame Ninette pulled me to one side and said: "I don't understand! When I was with Diaghilev, Choura (Danilova) was older than I was, now she's seven years younger! What's happened?" (And then a burst of laughter.)

Evolution not Revolution: Ninette de Valois's Philosophy of Dance. Beth Genné

1 The form "choregraphy" was widespread at the time (it was used consistently, for example, by P.J.S. Richardson, the editor of *The Dancing Times*), although by 1937 de Valois had adopted the form in use now. Texts of these essays are to be found in this volume, pp. 149-168.
2 Ninette de Valois, *Come Dance with Me* (London: Hamish Hamilton, 1957), p.30.
3 Ibid.
4 Ibid. p.38. This may be the reason why de Valois later established a small library in the premises of the Abbey School of Ballet (see pp.59 and 61).
5 Ibid. p.32.
6 Elizabeth Stannus, the daughter of de Valois' brother, Trevor Stannus, in interview with Beth Genné, April, 2011. Her understanding was that de Valois' mother Lily (whom de Valois called Lillith) had grown estranged from her husband, a career army officer. His estates in Ireland were already failing at the time of their marriage, but eventually de Valois' mother's estate Baltiboys, where the family lived, fell on hard times as well. De Valois was sent to live with her paternal grandmother in Deal, while her mother went on to establish herself in London, eventually sending for her daughter. Though her mother and father lived separately, they did not divorce. De Valois' father, who had attained the rank of Lieutenant-Colonel, was killed in action in World War 1. Unusually, his death was announced in the *Dancing Times*, accompanied by a photograph.
7 De Valois' mother's relationship to PJS Richardson is evidenced from the number of

times she and her husband are mentioned in the Sitter Out section of the *Dancing Times* – including notification of one of her daughter's earliest recitals, which took place in her home, and the publication of photos from Mrs. Stannus's china figurine collection as well as a photograph of de Valois father after he died from wounds received in 1917.

8 De Valois in interview with Beth Genné, 5 December 1981.

9 This was said most famously at the celebration of her retirement as artistic director of The Royal Ballet; she also repeated the sentiment to me in more than one of our interviews (de Valois in interview with Beth Genné, Barnes, 5 December 1981 and 6 April 1985).

10 De Valois in interview with Beth Genné, Barnes, 6 April 1985. We had been talking about her bringing back into the repertory Diaghilev ballets like *The Firebird* and her commissioning of Massine's *Mam'zelle Angot*, and I think she was talking about her ballets in comparison to them.

11 See Jane Robinson, *Bluestockings: The First Women to Fight for an Education* (London: Penguin, 2010), p.210. See also the British Library's Timeline of Women's Suffrage, retrievable from: http://www.bl.uk/learning/histcitizen/21cc/struggle/suffrage/background/suffragettesbackground.html"

12 However much her actions belie her own beliefs, de Valois felt that women's capabilities, while very strong in some aspects, were limited in others: "Women are splendid pioneer workers. Pioneering gives full play to their sense of dedication, detail, intuition and fanaticism. The picture, though, is bound to change. Dedication has to develop objectivity of outlook, detail submitted to a fair balance between the part and the whole, intuition turn into logical reasonings and fanaticism give way to the acceptance of reality. It is essential that we realise that the real history of ballet – and by this I mean its creative work, its organisation, its pedagogy – has been a history of great male choreographers, directors and teachers." See Ninette de Valois, *Step by Step* (London: W. H. Allen, 1977), p.188.

13 Elizabeth Stannus in interview with Beth Genné, April 2011.

14 Niece Elizabeth recalls her Aunt Edris proudly showing off her impressively large book collection, when Elizabeth came to live with and work for her during World War II. "You can't consider yourself educated unless you have read all these books, as I have," she advised her niece, who was then all of nineteen years old. (Ibid.)

15 De Valois in interview with Beth Genné, Barnes, 1981.

16 P.R. Clance and S. Ament, "The Impostor Phenomenon Among High Achieving Women: Dynamics and Therapeutic Intervention" in *Psychotherapy Theory, Research and Practice*, Volume 15, #3, Fall 1978, pp.241–247.

17 The article was published in the *Dancing Times*, February 1926, pp.589-593. See in this volume, pp. 149-152.

18 *Come Dance With Me*, p.66.

19 For a more detailed account of what de Valois learned from Diaghilev, see Chapter 2 in Beth Genné, *The Making of a Choreographer*, Studies in Dance History, No. 12 (Madison, Wisconsin: Society of Dance History Scholars, 1996); and the essay by Clement Crisp in this volume, pp.13-17.

20 See the *Dancing Times*, 1926, p.238.

21 "The Future of the Ballet", p.589. See in this volume, pp.150-151.

22 Ibid. See in this volume, p.152.

23 Ibid. See in this volume, pp.149 and 150.

24 "The Future of the Ballet", pp.591 and 593. See in this volume, p.151.

25 Ibid., p.593. See in this volume, p.152.

26 Ibid. See in this volume, p.150.

27 Ninette de Valois in interview with Beth Genné, Barnes, 1985.

28 Ninette de Valois, *Invitation to the Ballet* (London: John Lane at the Bodley Head, 1937), p.178.

29 *Invitation to the Ballet*, pp.125-126. The notion of a national school was something that was very much part of the zeitgeist of de Valois' times. In part it was a by-product of the development of nation states in the nineteenth century, which, sometimes artificially, tried to identify and develop art forms that would reflect a distinctive national identity. The notion was certainly behind the fashion of investigating in music, for example, the folk songs and dances and themes of the natives of regions by composers like Vaughan Williams and Butterworth in England, Bartok in Hungary, Grieg in Norway, Copland in America. Her experiences with the Ballets Russes and its specifically "Russian" repertory were the immediate dance impetus for Dame Ninette to think in terms of an English school and repertory, and to express it in her own works.

30 Like Diaghilev, Dame Ninette inserted the "Three Ivans" *divertissements* in what is now the coda of *Sleeping Princess* (this has long since been replaced by a more traditional coda) and allowed Ashton to choreograph (in Petipa style) the opening divertissement for the Wedding in *The Sleeping Beauty* and the *pas de quatre* at the start of the party scene of *Swan Lake*.

31 *Invitation to the Ballet*, p.243.

32 George Balanchine in an essay written for George Platt Lynes, *Ballet*, (New York: Twelve Trees Press, 1956), quoted in Beth Genné, "Creating a Canon, Creating the Classics in Twentieth Century British Ballet", *Dance Research* (London), Winter 2000, pp.132–162.

33 See the essays on Notation in this volume, pp.117-134.

34 I would like to thank Darwin biographer, Janet Browne, Aramount Professor of the History of Science at Harvard University, for discussing these ideas with me and the intellectual climate in relation to theories of evolution during de Valois' time. All mistakes of course are my own. See Janet E. Browne, *Charles Darwin: vol. 1 Voyaging* (London: Jonathan Cape, 1995); Janet E. Browne, *Charles Darwin: Voyaging* (Princeton, New Jersey: Princeton University Press, 1996); Janet E. Browne, "Darwin in Caricature: A Study in the Popularization and Disseminaton of Evolution", *Proceedings of the American Philosophical Society*, 145 (4), December 2001, pp.496-509; and Janet E. Browne, *Charles Darwin: vol. 2 The Power of Place* (London: Jonathan Cape, 2002).

35 "Creating a Canon, Creating the Classics in Twentieth Century British Ballet".

36 De Valois' perspective on the value of training in the *danse d'école* has also slowly but surely entered the consciousness of the post-modern dance world outside England, and altered it. In America the once-reviled technique of ballet is increasingly a required part of the arsenal of skills expected by many post-modern choreographers from Cunningham to Tharp to Morris.

37 The folk music and dance revival of the early twentieth century, espoused in England by Cecil Sharp and composers like Ralph Vaughan Williams, had a strong effect on de Valois, see below pp.105-116 and the DVD, track 3.

38 New York City Ballet followed suit much later in the century with their establishment of classes in folk dance forms of North America.

Ninette de Valois, A Woman of the Theatre: A Discussion

1 The transcription was made by Elizabeth Marshall and edited by Libby Worth.

Developing a Training Style: Ninette de Valois and the cultural inheritance of the early twentieth century. Geraldine Morris

1 Brian Friel, *Making History* (London: Faber & Faber, 1989), p.15.
2 Ivor Guest, *Ballet in Leicester Square: The Alhambra and The Empire 1860-1915* (London: Dance Books, 1992).
3 Theresa Buckland, "Crompton's Campaign: The Professionalisation of Dance Pedagogy in Late Victorian England", *Dance Research*, 25, no. 1, 2007, p.22.
4 Alexandra Carter, "London 1908: A Synchronic View of Dance History", *Dance Research*, 23, no. 1, 2005, pp.36-51.
5 Richard Buckle, *Diaghilev* (London: Hamish Hamilton, 1984), p.202.
6 Dawn Horowitz, "A Ballet Class with Michael Fokine", *Dance Chronicle*, 3, no. 1, 1979, pp. 36-45.
7 All the material in this paragraph comes from John Singleton (ed.), *100 Years of Dancing: A History of the ISTD Examinations Board* (London: ISTD Examinations Board, 2004), p. 21.
8 Ibid. p.26.
9 Edouard Espinosa, "An Encyclopaedia of The Ballet', *Dancing Times*, August to January, nos. 443- 448. This quotation from January 1948, p.113.
10 Ibid. p.118.
11 Mark Konecny, "Dance and Movement in the Cabaret", *A Journal of Russian Culture*, 10, 2004, pp.133-146.
12 Olive Ripman, (1974) "Wordy", *Dancing Times*, LXIV, no. 766, July 1974, p.581.
13 Leslie Edwards, *In Good Company: Sixty Years with The Royal Ballet* (Alton and London: Dance Books, 2003).
14 Further discussion of these issues and the research that underpins it is beyond the scope of this chapter. It will be published in my forthcoming book, *Dancing for Joy: An Approach to Frederick Ashton's Choreographic Style*, (working title), to be published early 2013 by Dance Books.

De Valois as a Teacher: A Discussion led by Anna Meadmore

1 Transcript of panel discussion by Anna Fineman, edited by Anna Meadmore, who wrote the introductory paragraph about the speakers.

The Abbey Theatre School of Ballet. Victoria O'Brien

1 Cited in Liam Miller, *The Noble Drama of W.B. Yeats* (Dublin: Dolmen Press, 1977), pp.267-268.
2 Jill Gregory in interview with Victoria O'Brien (2002).
3 Ibid.
4 Sara Payne was known during this period in Ireland as Sara Patrick.
5 An Abbey School of Ballet programme, dated 10 April 1932.
6 This organisation is now known as the Royal Academy of Dance.
7 Significantly, research into the two methods of ballet training undertaken at the Abbey School, the Cecchetti system and the Royal Academy of Dance, has not revealed any data pertaining to either of these methods in Ireland prior to the foundation of the Abbey School. It is feasible then to claim that the Abbey Theatre School of Ballet was amongst the first, if not in fact *the* first dance school in Ireland to implement the two methods of ballet training and evaluation.

8 It is of note that the students were also paid for their performances: "We were paid the large amount of 30 shillings for a week's performance. At the age of 14 to get 30 shillings into your hand was huge" (Doreen Cuthbert reminiscing about being in training at the Abbey School, quoted in Deirdre Mulrooney, *Irish Moves* (Dublin: The Liffey Press, 2006), p.77. Thirty shillings in 1930 would be the equivalent of £50 in today's currency.

9 Students from the Abbey School appeared in three of Yeats's dance dramas choreographed by de Valois: *Fighting The Waves* in 1929, followed by *The Dreaming of the Bones* in 1931 and *At The Hawk's Well* in 1933.

10 Doreen Cuthbert, cited in *Irish Moves*, p.79.

11 Ibid. p.80

12 Ibid. p.79.

13 It is of significance to note here the value of the exams from the Association of Operatic Dancing of Great Britain, which were taught at the Abbey School, as Doreen Cuthbert, Thelma Murphy, Cepta Cullen, Muriel Kelly and Arthur Hamilton all became RAD teachers. In addition, Jill Gregory believed that her transition from the Abbey to Sadler's Wells Opera Ballet was made easier by the Elementary and Intermediate Examinations she had taken at the Abbey Theatre School of Ballet. Gregory feels that these examinations helped her adapt to the style and standard of ballet in England at the time. (Jill Gregory in conversation with Victoria O'Brien in 2001).

14 Ninette de Valois interviewed for the *Irish Independent*, 9 September 1938.

15 Arnold Haskell, *Ballet* (Harmondsworth, Middlesex: Penguin, 1938), p.131.

De Valois' invitation to Léonide Massine to teach Dance Composition. Kate Flatt

1 The Craftsman's Course had been set up by de Valois in 1964 and aimed to develop knowledge and understanding beyond that of the training of the classical dancer. This was well before any university courses in dance existed in the UK. De Valois had identified a gap in learning provision. She could see the need to develop not only dance teachers but also potential choreographers, with informed understanding of related studies such as dance history, anatomy and child psychology. Included in the course, was the study of a range of European dance forms: character dance, Spanish dance and the work of Joan Lawson on traditional dances from European Countries. Students as intending teachers were able to watch de Valois herself teach and attend her seminars on aspects of training, where she shared her knowledge. In the seminars she encouraged questions from students in order to stimulate a culture of enquiry.

2 Léonide Massine, *Massine on Choreography: Theory and Exercises in Composition* (London: Faber, 1976).

3 Léonide Massine, *My Life in Ballet* (London: Macmillan, 1968), p. 278.

4 Massine taught these courses in three week intensive periods each term from spring, 1968 to 1970 at The Royal Ballet Upper School, Talgarth Road. I was one of a handful of students who completed Massine's course in Theory of Composition. De Valois ensured that those who finished the course were awarded a diploma of completion. The core group named in his text are: Duygu Aykal, Margarite Banos, Susi Della Pietra, Kate Flatt, Audrey Harman, Lorna Mossford and Deidre Watts.

5 Ninette de Valois, *Come Dance with Me* (London: Hamish Hamilton, 1959), p. 64.

6 Rehearsals with Ninette de Valois in "Madam: the story of *A Rake's Progress*" featuring performance by Sadler's Wells Royal Ballet, Channel 4, 26 December 1982.

7 V. I. Stepanov, *Alphabet of Movements of the Human Body* (Cambridge: Golden Head Press, 1958). Stepanov's system had been used to record ballets at the Mariinsky, more as an *aide memoire* it seems, than as an accurate documentation of the ballets and de Valois

would have encountered it when Nicholas Sergeyev was reviving the choreography of Petipa's ballets.

8 Paul Hindemith, *Elementary Training for Musicians* (London: Schott and Co., 1974).

9 Examples among many include The Chinese Conjuror from *Parade* (1917), The Farucca from *Le Tricorne* (1919), The Can Can dancer from *La Boutique Fantasque* (1919).

10 *My Life in Ballet*, p. 68.

11 These statements and observations relating to Massine's teaching are drawn from my recollections of having been present in the classes in 1968 – 70.

12 I recall seeing de Valois show fervent interest and for instance, staying whole days to watch when she attended sessions, which was quite often.

13 Léonide Massine's class teaching with Royal Ballet School students on his "Theory of Composition Course" were filmed in 1969-70. Digital Copy of this film is part of The Royal Ballet Schools Collection, White Lodge Museum with the original films stored in the London Metropolitan Archive.

14 Massine returned to teach on a less intensive basis from 1970 to 1976 and he came to London to meet with those of us who had studied with him in order to complete his book.

Fiercely Alone: Personality and Impersonality in de Valois' Poetry and Work. Patricia Linton

1 This essay is based on a presentation at which recordings of the poems, read by Dame Eileen Atkins, accompanied the talk. Ninette de Valois' poems are published in *Selected Poems* (Manchester: Carcanet Press, 1998), and are quoted here from that edition.

2 *Selected Poems*, p 3.

3 Ninette de Valois, *Come Dance With Me* (London: Hamish Hamilton, 1957), pp 17-18.

4 *Selected Poems*, p 55.

5 See "Song of the Rush Hour (Underground)", *Selected Poems*, p 11.

6 From "'Time Please'", *Selected Poems*, p 34.

7 *Selected Poems*, p 4.

8 Ninette de Valois, *Step by Step* (London: W.H. Allen, 1977), p 5.

9 *Selected Poems*, p 44.

10 Ibid, p 62.

11 Ibid, p 37.

12 Ibid, p 65.

13 Ibid, pp 46-47.

14 Ibid, pp 6-7.

Four Articles for *The Old Vic Magazine* and *The Old Vic and Sadler's Wells Magazine*, Ninette de Valois

1 Edited by Libby Worth and Richard Cave.

2 At the conclusion of the essay in smaller font the following notice appears: "A School of Ballet has been opened at the Abbey Theatre, Dublin, where a permanent teacher is kept. Miss de Valois gives a Ballet Programme in Dublin every three months."

Writing across the Footlights: Ninette de Valois and the Vic-Wells community. Liz Schafer

1 The Old Vic groups and associations acquired the "Vic-Wells" title after the reopening of the Sadler's Wells Theatre in 1931.

2 Although the use of the green leaflets was dying out by the 1930s, one is clearly visible in the portrait of Lilian Baylis painted by Ethel Gabain in 1936.

3 Later the magazine became the *Old Vic and Sadler's Wells Magazine*. It was published 1919-1939. Unfortunately this magazine is not easy to access, being currently only available at the Bristol Theatre Collection, the V&A at Blythe House, and Cambridge University library.

4 For example, "Thoughts on Returning" by Sybil Thorndike (*OVM*, September – October, 1927); "Is Opera a Wash-Out in England" by Ethel Smyth (*OVM*, February, 1934); "*The Snow Maiden* and its Décor" by Elizabeth Polunin (*OVM*, April, 1933); "My First Repertory Season" by Peggy Ashcroft (*OVM*, September – October 1932).

5 See, for example, *OVM*, February, 1925.

6 The essay is reprinted in this volume, pp.149-152.

7 Besides Fairbairn and Anderton, others who worked on dance at the Old Vic include Martha Mayall, the wife of conductor Charles Corri, and a former dancer with the Carl Rosa Opera; Rupert Doone; and, during the First World War, Baylis's sister, Ethel Dunning.

8 The essay is reprinted in this volume, pp.82-83.

9 *Vic-Wells Association Newsletter* July-August 1983.

10 For more on the relationship between Baylis and de Valois, see my *Lilian Baylis: A biography*, (Hatfield: University of Hertfordshire Press, 2006), especially Chapter 9 "Baylis and the Ballet".

11 The essay is reprinted in this volume, pp.83-84.

12 *OVM* May, 1929; the production of *The Shrew* actually played in October, 1925.

13 Edwin Fagg, *The Old "Old Vic": A Glimpse of the Old Theatre from its Origins as "The 'Royal Coburg" First Managed by William Barrymore to its Revival under Lilian Baylis* (London, 1936) p.5.

14 The essay is reprinted in this volume, pp.84-86.

15 The essay is reprinted in this volume, pp.86-87.

16 Others from the dance world lured into writing for the *OVM* included Leslie French on "Movement" (*OVM*, February 1931); Anton Dolin on "The Future of Ballet" (*OVM*, December 1931); Frederick Ashton on 'Ballet and the Choreographer (*OVM*, December 1933); and Robert Helpmann on "Learning to be a Good Dancer" (*OVM*, April 1934) and "Shakespeare and the Ballet" (*OVM*, January 1938).William Chapell also wrote on "Designing for the Ballet" (OVM, April 1937).

The Irish and the Italians: de Valois, the Cecchettis and the "other" ballet mime. Giannandrea Poesio

1 *Tribute to Cav. Enrico Cecchetti 1850-1929* (sic) Sunday, 17 January 1954, Rudolf Steiner Hall, 33 Park Road, N.W.1. Typewritten document consisting of nine pages reproducing addresses by Errol Addison, Cyril Beaumont, Margaret Craske, Ninette de Valois, Tamara Karsavina, Alicia Markova, Marie Rambert, Peggy Van Praagh, Laura Wilson. (Gift of the late Diana Barker, Chair of the Cecchetti Society, to the author.)

2 This was one of de Valois' favourite jokes, and one she loved to repeat on different occasions.

3 Kathrine Sorley Walker, *Ninette de Valois: Idealist Without Illusions* (London: Hamish Hamilton, 1987), p.16.

4 In French, no date. The draft is part of the collections of letters now held in the Biblioteca Comunale Silvio Zavatti in Civitanova Marche, Italy.

5 In French, date not legible, presumably October 1922. (Author's private collection.)

6 Underlined , in the original text.

7 In French, no date, presumably early summer of 1925. See Giannandrea Poesio, *To and by Enrico Cecchetti* (Novi Ligure: Edizioni Joker, 2010), p.78.

8 In French, no date, presumably late October/early November 1927. See Poesio, *op. cit.*, p. 107.

9 See both Beaumont and Addison's addresses in *Tribute to Cav. Enrico Cecchetti 1850-1929*.

10 Laura Wilson in interview with Giannandrea Poesio, taped, May 12, 1992.

11 *Ninette de Valois, idealist without illusions*, p.65.

12 Serafino Torelli, *Trattato dell'arte scenica* (Milano: Albertari, 1866).

13 Antonio Morrocchesi, *Lezioni di Declamazione* (Firenze: All'Insegna di Dante, 1832).

14 According to the nineteenth-century Italian tradition, there was a neat division between principal, "noble" dancers and mime ones.

15 *Ninette de Valois*, p. 14.

16 Mark Perugini, *Mime* (London: *Dancing Times*, 1925).

17 Cecchetti's own notation of *Catarina, la Fille du Bandit* (1888) is held in the historical archives of La Scala Theatre in Milan. His notes on *The Sleeping Beauty* and *Amor* are now part of the author's collection.

18 Held in the Harvard Theatre Collection.

19 See Giannandrea Poesio, "Carabosse revisited: Enrico Cecchetti and the lost language of mime", *Proceedings of the 21st Conference*, The Society of Dance History Scholars (U.S.), University of Oregon, 1998, pp.79-86.

Interviews with Ron Smedley and Simon Rice on the teaching of folk dance and national dance at The Royal Ballet School. Libby Worth

1 Ninette de Valois, "Introduction" in Peter Brinson, (ed.), *The Ballet in Britain: Eight Oxford Lectures*, (London: Oxford University Press, 1962), p.3.

2 At this date Kennedy was Director of the English Folk Dance and Song Society.

3 Douglas Kennedy, "Folk Dance and Ballet" in *The Ballet in Britain*, p. 110.

4 Ibid, p. 110.

5 The original Bampton Morris Team perform a traditional Cotswold Morris dance in the village of Bampton in Oxfordshire at Whitsun every year. With the recent revival in interest, newer groups have been formed as well as the original. For information on this group and its history see http://www.bamptonmorris.co.uk/

6 Ballet teacher at Royal Ballet Lower School since 2005. Trained at The Royal Ballet Lower and Upper School, he joined Sadler's Wells Royal Ballet in 1982, becoming a Principal in 1989.

De Valois' role in the development and dissemination of Benesh Movement Notation. Robert Penman and Victoria Watts

1 See for example Dawn Lille Horwitz, "Philosophical issues related to notation and re-construction", *Choreography and Dance*, 1., 1988, p. 37-53; Brendan McCarthy, "Score-less draw?", *Dance Now*, Summer, 2008, p. 71-80; William C. Reynolds, "Film versus notation for dance: basic perceptual and epistemological differences", *The Second International Congress on Movement Notation*, Hong Kong, 1990; Francis Sparshott, "Recording Dance", *A Measured Pace: toward a philosophical understanding of the arts of dance*. (Toronto: University of Toronto Press, 1995).

2 See previous article in this volume by Ann Hutchinson Guest for details on this.

3 Joan Benesh, "Lines and spaces", *The Choreologist*, 15, Autumn, 1978, p.10.

4 For an overview of the early years of BMN see Institute of Choreology Progress Reports,

in *The Choreologist*, London: Royal Academy of Dance, 1965/1966.

5 A quick glance at the appendix of Ann Hutchinson Guest's book *Choreographics* shows how many systems have been proposed but have come to nothing. My own doctoral research extends her findings. Of 70 new systems proposed in the twentieth century less than a handful gained any traction in the dance community. There is no reason to believe that the Beneshes' system would not have shared the obscure fate of similar systems invented by Sol Babitz (1939), Walter Arndt (1951), Letitia Jay (1955), or Valerie Sutton (1973).

6 Issues of *The Choreologist* from the 1960s and 1970s list small news items reporting on the engagement of notators at companies around the globe.

7 BMN had remained part of the curriculum, taught as part of the A Level Dance course, until it was taken out of the Dance GCE specifications by the AQA Examining Board in 2009. Since then, it has been difficult for The Royal Ballet School to find a time slot in the timetable, but a short introductory course is being re-introduced for Year 10 students this year [Editors' note].

Benesh Movement Notation and Labanotation. Victoria Watts

1 The notation begins just as the Betrayed Girl has put down her sewing and stepped back into 5th position, back of her hands on her waist. She turns to the corner and with a rocking, lunging step makes a pleading/pushing gesture. She makes a half turn to the left with this same gesture to the upstage corner before turning almost a full circle to the right, ending facing upstage. As she turns with a lilting pivot step she leans from side to side, watching as the lower arm curves in and up then down and out as though dropping or gently scattering something. Facing the back, in 5th position *en pointe*, the Betrayed Girl *pliés* and extends her legs three times while stretching her arms out three times in an open 5th with clenched fists. The notation extract ends with the sequence that travels to the dancer's right in a series of *glissade*-like steps *en pointe*. Her head alternates looking from side to side, into and away from her direction of travel. Her arms are held stiffly out to her sides with right angles at her elbows and wrists.

2 Ninette de Valois, Choreographer, *Rake's Progress/Checkmate*, music by Sir Arthur Bliss & Gavin Gordon, Sadler's Wells Royal Ballet, 1982. DVD.

Benevolence in ballet – the philanthropic legacy of Dame Ninette. Clementine Cowl

1 Ninette de Valois, *Come Dance With Me: A Memoir 1898-1956* (London: Hamish Hamilton, 1959), p.39.

2 Ibid. p.98.

3 Ibid. p.100.

4 Ibid. p.97.

5 Minutes from The Royal Ballet Benevolent Fund Archives (1936-2011).

6 *Come Dance With Me*, p.195.

7 Minutes from The Royal Ballet Benevolent Fund Archives (1936-2011).

8 *Come Dance With Me*, p.193.

Ninette de Valois' Turkish adventure. Richard Glasstone

1 Ninette de Valois, *Step by Step* (London: W.H. Allen, 1977), p.165.

2 See Kate Flatt's contribution to this volume, pp.65-70.

3 *Step by Step*, p.171.

Six essays contributed to *Dancing Times* in 1926 and in 1933. Ninette de Valois

1 The essays have been edited here for the first time. Punctuation and spelling have been revised to reflect modern usage. The most significant change in this respect is the substitution of "choreography" and "choreographer" throughout for de Valois' use of "choregraphy" and "choregrapher", which accord with the house-style and preferences of the then editor of *The Dancing Times*, P.J.S. Richardson. Presumably under his influence de Valois had named her school, founded in 1926, as the Academy of Choregraphic Art. Arguably the terms were interchangeable in the 1920s and 1930s. Later in her career de Valois preferred the more conventional usage. Some names have been corrected (Baylis for Bayliss; Braque for Brague); and the quotation from Shakespeare's *As You Like It* has been regularised.

2 De Valois' name is given as the author of the article and then the following description of her is offered in smaller, italic font: *"the young English danseuse who has appeared for two years with the Diaghilev Company, and has also danced in the ballets of the Royal Italian Opera at Covent Garden".* Was this a tactic on the editor's part, to show that de Valois' thinking, as revealed in the ensuing essay, was rooted in substantial experience?

Madam and the betrayed girls: The dancers' perspective. An introduction to the DVD recording, track 6. Nicola Katrak

1 For a fly-on-the-wall view of Madam herself rehearsing each scene in great detail, the Channel 4 1982 documentary made by IFPA and Jaras Entertainment Ltd: *Madam – The Work of Dame Ninette de Valois in Rehearsal and Performance with Members of Sadler's Wells Royal Ballet* cannot be recommended too highly. Further references include archive footage of Maryon Lane as the Betrayed Girl filmed at the Royal Opera House by Edmée Wood in the 1960s, and *Masterpieces of British Ballet: The Rake's Progress and Checkmate* from Video Artists International [4379].

Coaching Roles in *Orpheus and Eurydice* and *Promenade*. An Introductoin to the DVD recordings, tracks 7 and 8. Anna Meadmore

1 Kathrine Sorley Walker, *Ninette de Valois: Idealist Without Illusions* (London: Hamish Hamilton, 1987), p. 236.

Crafting a Collaboration of "Talents". Susie Crow and Jennifer Jackson

1 Ninette de Valois, *Come Dance With Me* (London: Hamish Hamilton, 1957), p.10.
2 Jennifer Homans, *Apollo's Angels: a history of ballet* (London: Granta Books, 2010), p.396.
3 Keith Sawyer, *Group Genius; the creative power of collaboration* (New York: Basic, 2007).
4 "[Vygotsky] formulated his important principle that creative work is profoundly social. Art is the *social* within us, and even if its action is performed by a single individual it does not mean that its essence is individual..." See S. Moran and V. John-Steiner, "Creativity in the Making: Vygotsky's Contemporary Contribution to the Dialectic of Development and Creativity", in Keith Sawyer (ed.), *Creativity and Development* (Oxford: Oxford University Press, 2003, Ebook), p.62. See also C.B. Handy, *Understanding Organisatons*. Harmondsworth: Penguin, 1999), p.9.

5 See Leslie Edwards, *In Good Company* (Alton: Dance Books, 2003), passim; and Kathrine Sorley Walker, *Ninette de Valois: Idealist Without Illusions* (London: Hamish Hamilton, 1987), p.154.

6 Moira Shearer in E. Battersby, "Was British ballet's grande dame a dictator or a genius?",
Observer, 15 November 1987.

7 Ninette de Valois, *Invitation to the Ballet* (London: Bodley Head, 1937), p.171.

8 See John Berger, *Ways of Seeing* (London: British Broadcasting Corporation and Penguin Books, 1972).

9 *Group Genius*, p.46.

10 Frances Harris, "Ninette De V CBE", *Covent Garden Book.* (London: Royal Opera House Publications, 1950), p.14.

11 Leo Kersley in interview with Jennifer Jackson (2008) for research on de Valois and the War Years.

12 The 'somatic' is the *first person* perspective on the body: my body, not as an object perceived from the outside, but as I experience it as a person. Thus Somatic practices challenge classic Western mind/body duality. And see Richard Allen Cave, *Collaborations: Ninette de Valois and William Butler Yeats* (Alton: Dance Books, 2011), especially Chapter Six, pp. 92-119. Also DVD, track 9.

13 David Bintley in interview with Jennifer Jackson (2008) for research on de Valois and the War years.

14 *Invitation to the Ballet*, pp. 175-176.

15 Ibid. p.176.

16 De Valois was unsure of the move to Covent Garden, but Ashton is reputed to have said, "If you don't, I will".

17 Beth Genné, "Creating a canon, creating the classics in twentieth-century British ballet", *Dance* Research, 2000, pp.132-162.

18 *Group Genius*, p. 124.

19 David Bintley in interview with Jennifer Jackson (2008).

20 The music was by Roberto Gerhard with designs chiefly by Edward Burra.

21 See (and compare) the chapter entitled "The Choreographer" in *Invitation to the Ballet*, pp.157-197 and the section headed "Choreography" in de Valois' later autobiography, *Step by Step* (London: W.H. Allen, 1977), pp.112-126.

22 See Richard Buckle, "Ballet: *Don Quixote*", *Observer*, 26 February 1950; and A.V. Coton: "*Don Quixote*: Ballet Lacks Reality", *The Sunday Times*, 26 February 1950.

23 *Ninette de Valois: Idealist Without Illusions*, p.256.

24 Ibid. p.261.

25 *Invitation to the Ballet*, p.178.

26 Richard Sennet's book, *The Craftsman* (Harmondsworth and London: Penguin, 2009), highlights how individual and collective practice is instrumental in developing shared knowledge.

27 *Apollo's Angels*, p.419.

28 Ibid. p.446.

29 Arnold Haskell, *The National Ballet: A History and a Manifesto* (London: A. and C. Black, 1943), pp.16 and 20.

30 Howard Gardner, *Extraordinary Minds: Portraits of Exceptional Individuals and an Examination of Our Extraordinariness* (London: Phoenix Publications, 1998), p.11-12.

31 *In Good Company*, p.44.

32 Peter Wilson in interview with Jennifer Jackson (2011).

33 A discussion of these issues (raised at the *Where are the women?* debate) can be found in our articles for *Dancing Times*, 2010, cited in the Bibliography.

Ninette de Valois, the Bloomsbury Group, and the role of visual culture in the formation of the early Royal Ballet. Helen Hammond

1 The term "early Royal Ballet" is used here to denote also the Vic-Wells and Sadler's Wells Ballet titles under which the Company founded by de Valois danced, prior to its award of a Royal Charter in 1956.

2 Ninette de Valois, *Come Dance with Me: A Memoir 1898-1956* (London: Hamish Hamilton, 1959), p. 112.

3 Rishona Zimring, "'The Dangerous Art Where One Slip Means Death': Dance and the Literary Imagination in Interwar Britain", *Modernism/Modernity*, Vol. 14, No. 4 (November 2007), pp. 707-727. Mary Caws, and Sarah Wright, *Bloomsbury and France: Art and Friends* (Oxford: Oxford University Press, 1999), pp. 169-190. Evelyn Haller, "Her Quill Drawn from the Firebird: Virginia Woolf and the Russian Dancers" in *The Multiple Muses of Virginia Woolf*, ed. Diane Gillespie (Columbia: University of Missouri Press, 1993).

4 Stephanie Jordan, *Moving Music: Dialogues with Music in Twentieth-Century Ballet* (London: Dance Books, 2000). Charles M. Joseph, *Stravinsky and Balanchine: A Journey of Invention* (New Haven and London: Yale University Press, 2002).

5 Arnold Haskell, *Going to the Ballet* (London: Phoenix House Limited, 1950), p. 87.

6 Arnold Haskell, *The National Ballet: A History and a Manifesto* (London: Adam and Charles Black, 1943), p. 23.

7 Ibid, p. 49.

8 Ibid, p. 51.

9 Howe quoted in Kathrine Sorley Walker, *Ninette de Valois: Idealist Without Illusions*, (London: Hamish Hamilton, 1987), p. 114.

10 Beth Genné, "Creating a Canon, Creating the 'Classics' in Twentieth-Century British Ballet", *Dance Research*, Vol. 18, No. 2, (Winter 2000), pp. 132-161, 139.

11 *Come Dance With Me*, p. 113.

12 See Genné cited above.

13 Larraine Nicholas, "The Lion and the Unicorn: Festival of Britain Themes and choreography in the Postwar Decade", (Roehampton Institute, University of Surrey, now Roehampton University, 1999) unpublished Ph.D., Vol. I, p. 21.

14 *Come Dance with Me*, pp.108-109.

15 Christopher Reed, *Bloomsbury Rooms* (London and New Haven: Yale University Press, 2004), p. 101.

16 Brighton, *Radical Bloomsbury: The Art of Duncan Grant and Vanessa Bell 1905-1925* exhibition (Brighton: Brighton Museum and Art Gallery, 2011).

17 Nijinska quoted in *Ninette de Valois*, p. 34.

18 Haller quoted in "'The Dangerous Art Where One Slip Means Death': Dance and the Literary Imagination in Interwar Britain", p. 710.

19 Woolf quoted in *Bloomsbury Rooms*, p. 99. (See footnote 3 above.)

20 Ibid, p. 101.

21 "'The Dangerous Art Where One Slip Means Death': Dance and the Literary Imagination in Interwar Britain", p. 711; Mackrell, Judith, *Bloomsbury Ballerina: Lydia Lopokova Imperial Dancer and Mrs John Maynard Keynes* (London: Phoenix, 2009).

22 *Ninette de Valois*, p. 36.

23 "Creating a Canon, Creating the 'Classics' in Twentieth-Century British Ballet", p. 137.

24 Ibid, p. 137

25 Benois quoted in John Roland Wiley, *A Century of Russian Ballet: Documents and Eyewitness Accounts 1810-1910* (Oxford: Oxford University Press 1990), p. 391. See also Helena Hammond, "Spectacular Histories: The Ballets Russes, the Past, and the Classical

Tradition", *Ballets Russes: The Art of Costume*, exhibition catalogue (Canberra: National Gallery of Art/Thames and Hudson, 2010), pp. 51-68, 54.

26 Ninette de Valois, "Modern Choreography", *The Dancing Times*, March, 1933, pp. 668-670. See this volume, pp.159-162.

27 Unless indicated otherwise, all references and quotations for The Camargo Society are drawn from The Camargo Society Minute Books and related materials housed in the Library of the Royal Academy of Dance, London, and consulted by author in October 2010. For the fullest discussion, to date, of the Society's foundation, see Angela Kane and Jane Pritchard, 'The Camargo Society Part 1, *Dance Research*, vol. 12, no. 2, Autumn, 1994, pp. 21-65.

28 "The 'Camargo' Dinner: A Remarkable Gathering, The Objects of the Society", *The Dancing Times*, March, 1930, p. 717.

29 'Modern Choreography', p. 670. See this volume, p.162.

30 Charles Harrison, *English Art and Modernism: 1900-1939* (London and New Haven: published for the Paul Mellon Centre for Studies in British Art by Yale University Press, second edition, 1994), p. 198.

31 *Ninette de Valois*, p. 141.

32 James Beechey, "Defining Modernism; Roger Fry and Clive Bell in the 1920s", in Richard Shone, *The Art of Bloomsbury: Roger Fry, Vanessa Bell and Duncan Grant, with essays by James Beechey and Richard Morphet* (London: Tate Gallery Publishing, 1999, on the occasion of the exhibition of the same name), p. 49.

33 Frances Spalding, *The Tate: A History* (London: Tate Gallery Publishing, 1998), p. 64.

34 Letter exhibited in "A History of Modern Art at Tate", "History/Memory/Society" strand of the 2005 thematic display of Tate Modern's permanent collection.

35 *The Tate: A History*, p. 48.

36 For a full discussion of the exercise of taste in the construction of the Tate's collections and their articulation of national and cultural identities, see Brandon Taylor, *Art for the Nation: Exhibitions and the London Public 1747-2001* (Manchester: Manchester University Press, 1999), pp. 100-131; Frances Spalding, *The Tate: A History*. (London: Tate Gallery Publishing, 1998); and Jonathan Conlin, *The Nation's Mantelpiece: A History of the National Gallery* (London: Pallas Athene, 2006).

37 *Art for the Nation*, p.129.

38 Anton Dolin, *Markova: Her Life and Art* (London, W.H. Allen, 1953), p. 184.

39 Zoë Anderson, *The Royal Ballet: 75 Years* (London: Faber and Faber, 2006), p. 73.

40 *Come Dance with Me*, p. 152.

41 *Going to the Ballet*, p. 87.

42 "Modern Choreography", p. 670. See this volume, p.162.

43 *Going to the Ballet*, p. 55.

De Valois as Colleague and Collaborator: A Discussion led by Gerald Dowler

1 Transcribed by Elizabeth Marshall and edited by Richard Cave.

Ashton and de Valois. Alastair Macaulay

1 See David Vaughan, *Frederick Ashton and his Ballets*, 2nd Edition (Alton: Dance Books, 1999), pp. 8, 15, 21, 63, 93-5, 106-7, 468-83.

2 Zoe Dominic and John Gilbert, *Frederick Ashton: A Choreographer and his Ballets* (London: Harrap, 1971), p. 76.

3 *Frederick Ashton and his Ballets*, pp. 123, 140-2.

4 *Frederick Ashton and his Ballets*, pp. 76, 168, 202-3, 255-8, 268-9, 314, 419-20, 499.

5 Alexander Bland, *The Royal Ballet – The First Fifty Years* (New York: Doubleday, 1981), p. 140.

6 "Painfully dowdy" were Rambert's words to David Vaughan in the 1970s, as he confirmed to me in March 2011.

7 Belinda Quirey spoke to me often in the 1980s on these and other matters.

8 Agnes de Mille, *Dance to the Piper* (London: Hamish Hamilton, 1951), p. 181.

9 Lydia Lopokova and Frederick Ashton, quoted in *Frederick Ashton: A Choreographer and his Ballets*, p.76.

10 Julie Kavanagh, *Secret Muses: the Life of Frederick Ashton*, Second Edition (New York: Pantheon, 1997), p. 209.

11 De Valois and Ashton in *Secret Muses*, p. 241.

12 *Secret Muses*, p. 290.

13 Frederick Ashton quoted in Keith Money, *The Art of Margot Fonteyn*, 2nd Edition (London: Dance Books, 1975), unpaginated.

14 Alastair Macaulay, "*The Sleeping Beauty* – the British Connection", *Dancing Times*, September 2000; Alastair Macaulay, "Ashton and MacMillan" in E. Dunn and J. Still (eds.), *Revealing MacMillan* (London: Royal Academy of Dance, 2004).

15 Pamela May in conversations with Alastair Macaulay, 1997-2001.

16 Margot Fonteyn, *Autobiography* (London: Allen, 1975), p.52.

17 Lynn Seymour, *Lynn* (London: Granada 1984); Lesley Collier in interview with the Ballet Association (1979).

18 Ninette de Valois in a letter to Joy Newton, dated January 14, 1948 (Royal Ballet School Collections, White Lodge Museum).

19 Ninette de Valois quoted in *Secret Muses*, p. 317

20 Ninette de Valois in conversation with Mary Ann de Vlieg (1980).

21 *Secret Muses*, p. 318.

22 *Secret Muses*, pp. 473-5.

23 Ninette de Valois in a letter to Joy Newton, dated August 14, 1952 (Royal Ballet School Collections, White Lodge Museum).

24 Ninette de Valois, *Come Dance With Me* (London: Hamish Hamilton, 1959), p. 164.

25 Ninette de Valois, *Step by Step* (London: W.H. Allen, 1977), p. 57.

26 *Step by Step*, pp. 60-62.

27 Fonteyn, *Autobiography*, pp. 47-8

28 Arlene Croce, "Split Week", *The New Yorker* (December 29, 1980), reprinted in Croce, *Going to the Dance* (New York: Knopf, 1982), p. 333.

29 Mary Clarke in conversation with Alastair Macaulay in the early 1980s.

30 See Arlene Croce, "Artists and Models" *The New Yorker*, November 1, 1982; also Arlene Croce, *Sight Lines* (New York: Knopf, 1987), p. 72: "British dancers are instinctual actors, but they are at their greatest when the instinct is sublimated."

31 Julia Farron in conversations with Alastair Macaulay, 1997-2010.

32 Zoë Anderson, *The Royal Ballet* (London: Faber and Faber, 2006), p. 23.

33 *Secret Muses*, p. 175.

34 Julia Farron in conversations with Alastair Macaulay, 1997-2010.

35 Frederick Ashton in interview with Alastair Macaulay, 1984.

36 Pamela May and Julia Farron in conversations with Macaulay, between 1996-2001 and 1997-2010 respectively. See also Stephanie Jordan (ed.), *Following Sir Fred's Steps: Ashton's Legacy* (London: Dance Books, 1996).

37 Richard Glasstone in conversation with Alastair Macaulay in the 1990s; *Secret Muses*, pp. 473-5; and *The Royal Ballet*, p. 171.

38 *The Royal Ballet*, p. 200; and Jann Parry, *Different Drummer – The Life of Kenneth MacMillan*, Faber, p. 467.
The author would like to express his gratitude for interviews and conversations to the following: Frederick Ashton (1980, 1984, 1988), Lesley Collier (1979, 1980), Ninette de Valois (1987), Mary Anne de Vlieg (1980), Beryl Grey (1988-1995), Richard Glasstone (1997-1998), Peter Wright (1994, 1998), Julie Kavanagh (1996-2011), Julia Farron (1997-2010), Pamela May (1996-2001), Belinda Quirey (1982-92), Anita Young (2001).

Ninette de Valois and Kenneth MacMillan. Jann Parry

1 Composer and musician whose work for Sadler's Wells Ballet and The Royal Ballet included re-arranging musical scores and operas for ballet.
2 P. W. Manchester, *Vic-Wells: a Ballet Progress* (London: Victor Gollanz, 1946, 1st ed. 1942), p.102.
3 Richard Buckle, "Three Blind Mice", *The Observer*, 15 July 1951.
4 Ninette de Valois, Letter to Kenneth MacMillan, dated 21 February 1957.
5 Ibid.
6 Ninette de Valois, Letter to Kenneth MacMillan, dated 6 March 1957.
7 Ibid.
8 Ibid.
9 Ibid.
10 Ninette de Valois, Letter to Kenneth MacMillan, dated 27 March 1957.
11 Ninette de Valois, Letter to Kenneth MacMillan, dated 30 March 1957.
12 Ibid.
13 Ninette de Valois, Letter to Kenneth MacMillan, dated 12 August 1957.
14 Ninette de Valois, Letter to Kenneth MacMillan, dated 20 October 1957.
15 Ballet Sub-Committee minutes, 22 October 1958.
16 Board minutes,27 October 1959.
17 Board minutes, 23 November 1965.
18 Ballet Sub-Committee minutes, November 1958.
19 Ninette de Valois, Letter to Kenneth MacMillan, undated.
20 Kenneth MacMillan, Letter to Ninette de Valois, undated, August 1960.
21 Ninette de Valois, *Step by Step* (London: W.H. Allen, 1977), p. 100.
22 Ibid, p. 100.
23 Ninette de Valois, Telegram to Kenneth MacMillan, 19 January 1972.
24 Ninette de Valois' poem, *Dancers in Action*, is dedicated to "Kenneth MacMillan and to the dancers of The Royal Ballet in Mahler's Song of the Earth", in *Step by Step*, p. 198.
25 Ninette de Valois, Letter to Kenneth MacMillan, date unclear.
26 *The Stage*, 2 May 1985.
27 Ninette de Valois, Letter to MacMillan, undated [evidently May 1985, author's note].

Re-creating *The King of the Great Clock Tower*. Richard Cave

1 The other three were *Fighting The Waves* (1929), *The Dreaming of the Bones* (1931, revived 1932) and *At The Hawk's Well* (1933). De Valois appeared as Fand, a sea goddess in the first, The Guardian of the Well who transforms into a Hawk in the third, and the Queen in *The King of the Great Clock* Tower. She did not perform the role of the female ghost (Dvorgilla) in *The Dreaming of the Bones* through pressure of work and because of a recent foot injury.
2 The history of the school has been admirably recounted in Victoria O'Brien, *A History*

of Irish Ballet from 1927 to 1963 (Brussels and Oxford: Peter Lang, 2011) and, partly through reminiscences of several of the original students, in Deirdre Mulroolney, *Irish Moves* (Dublin: The Liffey Press, 2006).

3 Yeats thought this production the most fully realised of his plays in this form: "It has proved most effective – it was magnificently acted and danced. [...] It has turned out the most popular of my dance plays" (*The Letters of W.B. Yeats*, edited by Allen Wade (London: Rupert Hart-Davis, 1954) pp.826-827); and de Valois has written memorably of the new creative strengths that came to her from submitting to the particular disciplines that working on one of Yeats's plays demanded of her, of being "absorbed into the whole, never to exist as an isolated part, only as part of the whole" (Ninette de Valois, *Step by Step* (London: W.H.Allen, 1977), pp.179-186, quotation from p.183).

4 It is this lacuna in Irish cultural history that prompted both Victoria O'Brien in *A History of Irish Ballet from 1927 to 1963* and Deirdre Mulrooney in *Irish Moves* to undertake their research. As O'Brien tersely observes: "[...] if there has been no ballet history of Ireland published to date, one could be forgiven for thinking that there is no history of ballet in Ireland" (loc. cit., p.1).

5 The text of the play was published in *The King of the Great Clock Tower, Commentaries and Poems* (Dublin: Cuala Press, 1934). Yeats subsequently revised the play, substituting verse for the prose dialogue of the version that was staged, and it is this second version that has more frequently been printed, chiefly in *Collected Plays* (London and Basingstoke: Macmillan, 1934, revised and extended 1952). Prose and Verse texts are juxtaposed in Russell K. Alspach (ed.), *The Variorum Edition of the Plays of W.B. Yeats* (London and Basingstoke: Macmillan, 1966). The re-creation was staged at The Royal Ballet School, White Lodge on April 3, 2011.

6 For the detailed scenario, see Richard Allen Cave, *Collaborations: Ninette de Valois and William Butler Yeats* (Alton: Dance Books, 2011), pp.92-119.

7 See Richard Allen Cave (ed.), *"The King of the Great Clock Tower" and "A Full Moon in March": Manuscript Materials* (Ithaca and London: Cornell University Press, 2007).

8 The Cuala edition was published on 14 December 1934, some five months after the production went into rehearsal ready to open on 30 July. A first set of proofs survives, dated 24 August, bearing revisions by Yeats notably to the stage directions, especially for the danced elements. The final printing had been completed by 20 October.

9 Though Robinson was nominally the director, Yeats was a constant presence at rehearsal as the ultimate authority to whom details of interpretation were invariably referred. An earlier surviving, heavily revised typescript has the phrase, "6 Copies", written in Yeats's hand alongside the play's title; the two of the six that survive reproduce the revisions exactly. These are to be found in the collection of Lennox Robinson papers in the Special Collections of the Morris Library, Southern Illinois University (SIUC 91/16/10) and the National Library of Ireland (NLI 29,550 – 2). The latter contains the floor plan, discussed below.

10 The programme assigns the name of Dorothy Travers Smith (Robinson's wife) as designer; but what is not clear is whether Robinson made this sketch or whether it was the work of Travers Smith, which Robinson subsequently annotated in relation to how he proposed using the setting in the course of rehearsals and performances.

11 See *Manuscript Materials*, pp.36-37. Edward Gordon Craig, a long-term friend of Yeats and later of his daughter, Anne, had given the Abbey a set of his unpatented screens to use in settings chiefly for Yeats's heroic plays; they were of varying heights and widths and could be hinged together to create varieties of shapes of setting. The manuscript referred to here is in the National Library of Ireland (NLI 8769 – i), while the ensuing typescript is in the Special Collections of the Morris Library, Southern Illinois University ((SIUC 76/1/7).

12 This computerised design work was kindly undertaken by my former colleague from Royal Holloway, Rosie McGuire. It is reproduced in *Collaborations* as plate 41.

13 See W.B.Yeats, "The Reform of the Theatre" in W.B.Yeats (ed.), *Samhain* (Dublin and London: Sealy Bryers & Walker and T. Fisher Unwin, 1903), p.10.

14 SIUC 76/1/7, referred to above. The sketches are reproduced in Manuscript Materials, pp. 343-344.

15 Marius Arnold-Clarke is ICT and Theatre Manager for The Royal Ballet School. He also designed the lighting.

16 See Sam McCready, *The Director's Approach to the Presentation of the Plays of W.B.Yeats* (University of Wales, Bangor: Unpublished MA Thesis, 1975).

17 An undated newspaper cutting showing the photograph of Lennox Robinson is preserved alongside Joseph Holloway's diary-entry about the production, dated May 9, 1926. (His diaries are in the collections of the National Library of Ireland). The photograph of *Fighting the Waves* is reproduced as Plate 46 in *Collaborations*.

18 In Noh performance the masks are representative of a range of stock types, male, female and divine, but are individualised by the narrative context of a given play and by the artistry of the performer playing the central role.

19 See Allan Wade (ed.), *The Letters of W.B. Yeats* (London: Rupert Hart-Davis, 1954), pp.826-827.

20 Macmillan, Yeats's publisher, had gathered material for a collection of his late plays in the late 1930s, including, where plays had been staged, transcripts of the music involved. This material is now to be found in the Macmillan Archive in the British Library. Irwin emigrated to Canada but kept his Abbey scripts in his personal effects (he had sung in several Abbey productions in the 1920s and 1930s).

21 See Kenneth Archer and Millicent Hodson, "Ballets Lost and Found: restoring the twentieth-century repertoire" in Janet Adshead-Lansdale and June Layson (eds.), *Dance History: an Introduction* (London and New York: Routledge, 1983), pp.98-116.

22 I have assembled all this evidence, visual and verbal, while outlining a possible interpretation of the material in both *Manuscript Materials* and *Collaborations* (Chapter Six).

23 Yeats tried to involve her in his future plans on several occasions, particularly when, for a while, it looked as if his work and particularly his dance plays might be performed in conjunction with the Group Theatre; but de Valois always resisted, offering Frederick Ashton as a likely choreographer for a while in her stead, a proposal which came to nothing.

Bibliography

Alspach, Russell K. (ed.), *The Variorum Edition of the Plays of W.B. Yeats* (London and Basingstoke: Macmillan, 1966).

Anderson, Zoë, *The Royal Ballet: 75 Years* (London: Faber and Faber, 2006).

Anon, "Ninette de Valois", *Era*, 23 December 1914, p.11.

Anon, "Robert Roberti [sic] A Clever Dancer", *Era*, 7 July 1915, p.14 .

Anon, "Stravinsky's 'Ragtime'. Russian Dancers at Covent Garden", *The Times*, 4 April 1922, p.12.

Anon, "The 'Camargo' Dinner: A Remarkable Gathering, The Objects of the Society", *Dancing Times*, March 1930, p. 717.

Anon, *Radical Bloomsbury: The Art of Duncan Grant and Vanessa Bell 1905-1925* (Brighton: Brighton Museum and Art Gallery, 2011).

Archer, Kenneth and Millicent Hodson, "Ballets Lost and Found: restoring the twentieth-century repertoire" in Janet Adshead-Lansdale and June Layson (eds.), *Dance History: an Introduction* (London and New York: Routledge, 1983).

Battersby, E., "Was British ballet's *grande dame* a dictator or a genius?", *Observer*, 15 November 1987.

Beechey, James, "Defining Modernism; Roger Fry and Clive Bell in the 1920s", in Richard Shone (ed.), *The Art of Bloomsbury: Roger Fry, Vanessa Bell and Duncan Grant* (London: Tate Gallery Publishing, 1999).

Benesh, Joan, "Lines and spaces", *The Choreologist*, 17 (Autumn, 1978).

Bland, Alexander, *The Royal Ballet – The First Fifty Years* (New York: Doubleday, 1981).

Brinson, Peter (ed.), *The Ballet in Britain: Eight Oxford Lectures* (London: Oxford University Press, 1962).

British Library, *A Timeline of Women's Suffrage*, http://www.bl.uk/learning/histcitizen/21cc/struggle/suffrage/background/suffragettesbackground.html

Browne, Janet E., *Charles Darwin: vol. 1 Voyaging* (London: Jonathan Cape, 1995).

Browne, Janet E., *Charles Darwin: vol. 2 The Power of Place* (London: Jonathan Cape, 2002).

Buckland, Theresa, "Crompton's Campaign: The Professionalisation of Dance Pedagogy in Late Victorian England", *Dance Research*, 25, no. 1, 2007, pp.1-34.

Buckle, Richard, "Ballet: *Don Quixote*", *The Observer*, 26 February 1950.

Buckle, Richard, "Three Blind Mice", *The Observer*, 15 July 1951.

Buckle, Richard, *Diaghilev* (London: Hamish Hamilton, 1984).

Carter, Alexandra, "London 1908: A Synchronic View of Dance History", *Dance Research*, 23, no. 1, 2005, pp.36-51.

Cave, Richard Allen (ed.), *"The King of the Great Clock Tower"* and *"A Full Moon in March": Manuscript Materials* (Ithaca and London: Cornell University Press, 2007).

Cave, Richard Allen, *Collaborations: Ninette de Valois and William Butler Yeats* (Alton: Dance Books, 2011).

Caws, Mary and Sarah Wright, *Bloomsbury and France: Art and Friends* (Oxford: Oxford University Press, 1999).

Clance, P.R. and S. Ament, "The Impostor Phenomenon Among High-Achieving Women: Dynamics and Therapeutic Intervention", *Psychotherapy Theory, Research and Practice*, Volume 15, #3, Fall 1978, pp.241–247.

Conlin, Jonathan, *The Nation's Mantelpiece: A History of the National Gallery* (London: Pallas Athene, 2006).

Coton, A.V., "*Don Quixote* Ballet Lacks Reality", *The Sunday Times*, 26 February 1950.

Croce, Arlene, *Going to the Dance* (New York: Knopf, 1982).

Croce, Arelene, "Artists and Models", *The New Yorker*, 1 November 1982.

Croce, Arlene, *Sight Lines* (New York: Knopf, 1987).

Crow, Susie and Jennifer Jackson, "Talking Point", *Dancing Times*, 100:1194, February 2010, p.12.

Crow, Susie and Jennifer Jackson, "Talking Point", *Dancing Times*, 100:1195, March 2010, p.12.

De Mille, Agnes, *Dance to the Piper* (London: Hamish Hamilton, 1951).

De Valois, Ninette, "The Future of the Ballet", *Dancing Times*, February 1926, pp.589-593.

De Valois, Ninette, "Modern Choregraphy: I - Introductory", *Dancing Times*, January 1933, pp.434-437.

De Valois, Ninette, "Modern Choregraphy: II - [Music]", *Dancing Times*, February 1933, pp.549-552.

De Valois, Ninette, "Modern Choregraphy: III - Production: Theatrical Presentation", *Dancing Times*, March 1933, pp. 668-670.

De Valois, Ninette, "Modern Choregraphy: IV - Décor and Costume", *Dancing Times*, April 1933, pp.9-10.

De Valois, Ninette, "Modern Choregraphy: V - The Classical Dancer of Today", *Dancing Times*, May 1933, pp. 122-125.

De Valois, Ninette, *Invitation to the Ballet* (London: The Bodley Head, 1937).

De Valois, Ninette, *Come Dance With Me* (London: Hamish Hamilton, 1957).

De Valois, Ninette, "Introduction" in Peter Brinson (ed.), *The Ballet in Britain: Eight Oxford Lectures* (London: Oxford University Press, 1962).

De Valois, Ninette, "The Wonder Children", *The Spectator*, 24 January 1964.

De Valois, Ninette, *Step by Step* (London: W. H. Allen, 1977).

De Valois, Ninette, "Lydia Lopokova and English Ballet" in Milo Keynes (ed.), *Lydia Lopokova* (London: Weidenfeld and Nicolson, 1983), pp.106-115.

De Valois, Ninette, *Selected Poems* (Manchester: Carcanet Press, 1998).

Dimbleby, David, "Dame Ninette de Valois: a lifetime in ballet" (From *Person to Person*, BBC1), *The Listener*, 26 July 1979, pp.110-112.

Dolin, Anton, *Markova: Her Life and Art* (London, W.H. Allen, 1953).

Dominic, Zoe and John Gilbert, *Frederick Ashton: A Choreographer and his Ballets* (London: Harrap, 1971).

Edwards, Leslie, *In Good Company: Sixty Years with the Royal Ballet* (Alton: Dance Books, 2003).

Espinosa, Edouard, "An Encyclopaedia of The Ballet", *Dancing Times*, nos. 443- 448, August 1947 to January 1948.

Fonteyn, Margot, *Autobiography* (London: W.H. Allen, 1975).

Friel, Brian, *Making History* (London: Faber & Faber, 1989).

Gardner, Howard, *Extraordinary Minds: Portraits of Exceptional Individuals and an Examination of Our Extraordinariness* (London: Phoenix Publications, 1998).

Genné, Beth, *The Making of a Choreographer: Ninette de Valois and "Bar aux Folies-Bergère"*, Studies in Dance History, No. 12 (Madison, Wisconsin: Society of Dance History Scholars, 1996).

Genné, Beth, "Creating a Canon, Creating the Classics in Twentieth-Century British Ballet", *Dance Research*, Winter 2000, pp.132–162.

Guest, Ivor, *Ballet in Leicester Square: The Alhambra and The Empire 1860-1915* (London: Dance Books, 1992).

Haller, Evelyn, "Her Quill Drawn from the Firebird: Virginia Woolf and the Russian Dancers" in Diane Gillespie (ed.), *The Multiple Muses of Virginia Woolf* (Columbia: University of Missouri Press, 1993).

Hammond, Helena, "Spectacular Histories: The Ballets Russes, the Past, and the Classical Tradition", *Ballets Russes: The Art of Costume*, exhibition catalogue (Canberra: National Gallery of Art/Thames and Hudson, 2010), pp. 51-68.

Handy, C.B., *Understanding Organizatons* (Harmondsworth: Penguin, 1999).

Harris, Frances, "Ninette De V CBE", *Covent Garden Books* (London: Royal Opera House Publications, 1950).

Harrison, Charles, *English Art and Modernism: 1900-1939*, Second Edition (London and New Haven: published for the Paul Mellon Centre for Studies in British Art by Yale University Press, 1994).

Haskell, Arnold, *Ballet* (Harmondsworth: Penguin, 1938).

Haskell, Arnold, *The National Ballet: A History and a Manifesto* (London: A. and C. Black, 1943).

Haskell, Arnold, *Going to the Ballet* (London: Phoenix House Ltd., 1950).

Hindemith, Paul, *Elementary Training for Musicians* (London: Schott and Co., 1974).

Hodson, Millicent, *Nijinsky's Bloomsbury Ballet: Reconstruction of the Dance and Design for "Jeux"* (Hillsdale, NY: Pendragon Press, 2008).

Homans, Jennifer, *Apollo's Angels: a history of ballet* (London: Granta Books, 2010).

Horwitz, Dawn Lille, "A Ballet Class with Michael Fokine", *Dance Chronicle*, 3, no. 1, 1979, pp. 36-45.

Horwitz, Dawn Lille, "Philosophical issues related to notation and reconstruction", *Choreography and Dance*, 1, 1988, pp.37-53.

Hutchinson Guest, Ann, *Dance Notation: the Process of Recording Movement on Paper* (New York: Dance Horizons, 1984).

Hutchinson Guest, Ann, *Choreographics: A Comparison of Dance Notation Systems from the Fifteenth Century to the Present* (Amsterdam: Gordon and Breach, 1989).

Institute of Choreology, "Progress Reports, 1965/1966", *The Choreologist* (London: Royal Academy of Dance, 1966).

John-Steiner, Vera, *Creative Collaboration* (New York: Oxford University Press Paperback, 2006).

Jordan, Stephanie (ed.), *Following Sir Fred's Steps: Ashton's Legacy* (London: Dance Books, 1996).

Jordan, Stephanie, *Moving Music: Dialogues with Music in Twentieth-Century Ballet* (London: Dance Books, 2000).

Joseph, Charles M., *Stravinsky and Balanchine: A Journey of Invention* (New Haven and London: Yale University Press, 2002).

Kane, Angela and Jane Pritchard, 'The Camargo Society Part 1", *Dance Research*, vol. 12, no. 2, Autumn, 1994, pp. 21-65.

Kavanagh, Julie, *Secret Muses: the Life of Frederick Ashton* (London: Faber & Faber, 1996; Second Revised Edition, New York: Pantheon, 1997).

Kennedy, Douglas, "Folk Dance and Ballet" in Peter Brinson (ed.), *The Ballet in Britain* (London: Oxford University Press, 1962).

Keynes, Milo (ed.), *Lydia Lopokova* (London: Weidenfeld and Nicolson, 1983).

Konecny, Mark, "Dance and Movement in the Cabaret", *A Journal of Russian Culture*, 10, 2004, pp.133-146.

Lynes, George Platt, *Ballet* (New York: Twelve Trees Press, 1956).

McCarthy, Brendan, "Scoreless draw?", *Dance Now*, Summer, 2008, pp.71-80.

McCready, Sam, *The Director's Approach to the Presentation of the Plays of W.B.Yeats* (University of Wales, Bangor: Unpublished MA Thesis, 1975).

Macaulay, Alastair, "*The Sleeping Beauty* – the British Connection", *Dancing Times*, September 2000.

Macaulay, Alastair, "Ashton and MacMillan" in E.Dunn and J. Still (eds.), *Revealing MacMillan* (London: Royal Academy of Dance, 2004), pp.71-86.

Mackrell, Judith, *Bloomsbury Ballerina: Lydia Lopokova, Imperial Dancer and Mrs John Maynard Keynes* (London: Phoenix, 2009).

Manchester, P.W., *Vic-Wells: a Ballet Progress* (London: Victor Gollanz, 1946; First Edition, 1942).

Massine, Léonide, *My Life in Ballet* (London: Macmillan, 1968).

Massine, Léonide, *Massine on Choreography: Theory and Exercises in Composition* (London: Faber, 1976).

Masters, Brian, "Why Madam is a winner on points", *The Times*, 6 June 1983.

Miller, Liam, *The Noble Drama of W.B. Yeats* (Dublin: Dolmen Press, 1977).

Money, Keith, *The Art of Margot Fonteyn*, Second Edition (London: Dance Books, 1975).

Moran, S. and V. John-Steiner, "Creativity in the Making: Vygotsky's Contemporary Contribution to the Dialectic of Development and Creativity" in Keith Sawyer (ed.), *Creativity and Development* (Oxford: Oxford University Press Ebook, 2003).

Morrocchesi, Antonio, *Lezioni di Declamazione* (Firenze: All'Insegna di Dante, 1832).

Mulrooney, Deirdre, *Irish Moves: An Illustrated History of Dance and Physical Theatre in Ireland* (Dublin: The Liffey Press, 2006).

Nicholas, Larraine, *The Lion and the Unicorn: Festival of Britain Themes and Choreography in the Postwar Decade*, (Roehampton Institute, University of Surrey, now Roehampton University: Unpublished Ph.D Thesis, 1999).

O'Brien, Victoria, *The Abbey School of Ballet*, Published MA Thesis, *Choreologica Journal* (2005).

O'Brien, Victoria, *A History of Irish Ballet from 1927 to 1963* (Bern: Peter Lang, 2011).

Parry, Jann, *Different Drummer – The Life of Kenneth MacMillan* (London: Faber & Faber, 2009).

Perugini, Mark, *Mime* (London: Dancing Times, 1925).

Poesio, Giannandrea, *To and by Enrico Cecchetti* (Novi Ligure: Edizioni Joker, 2010).

Reed, Christopher, *Bloomsbury Rooms* (London and New Haven: Yale University Press, 2004).

Reynolds, William C., "Film versus notation for dance: basic perceptual and epistemological differences", *The Second International Congress on Movement Notation* (Hong Kong, 1990).

Richardson, Philip, "Dancing in the Christmas Plays", *Dancing Times*, January 1917, pp.139 and 141.

Ripman, Olive, "Wordy", *Dancing Times*, LXIV, no. 766, July 1974.

Robinson, Jane, *Bluestockings: The First Women to Fight for an Education* (London: Penguin, 2010).

Robinson, Lennox, *Ireland's Abbey Theatre 1889-1951* (London: Sidgwick and Jackson, 1951).

Sawyer, K. (ed.), *Creativity and Development* (Oxford: Oxford University Press Ebook, 2003).

Sawyer, Keith, *Group Genius; the creative power of collaboration* (New York: Basic Publications, 2007).

Schafer, Elizabeth, *Lilian Baylis: A biography*, (Hatfield: University of Hertfordshire Press, 2006).

Sennett, Richard, *The Craftsman* (London: Penguin, 2009).

Seymour, Lynn, *Lynn* (London: Granada, 1984).

Singleton, John (ed.), *100 Years of Dancing: A History of the ISTD Examinations Board* (London: ISTD Examinations Board, 2004).

Sorley Walker, Kathrine, *Ninette de Valois: Idealist Without Illusions* (London: Hamish Hamilton, 1987).

Spalding, Frances, *The Tate: A History* (London: Tate Gallery Publishing, 1998).

Sparshott, Francis, "Recording dance" in *A measured pace: toward a philosophical understanding of the arts of dance* (Toronto: University of Toronto Press, 1995).

Stepanov, V.I., *Alphabet of Movements of the Human Body* (Cambridge: Golden Head Press, 1958).

Taylor, Brandon, *Art for the Nation: Exhibitions and the London Public 1747-2001* (Manchester: Manchester University Press, 1999).

Torelli, Serafino, *Trattato dell'arte scenica* (Milano: Albertari, 1866).

Vaughan, David, *Frederick Ashton and his Ballets*, Second Edition (Alton: Dance Books, 1999).

Wade, Allan (ed.), *The Letters of W.B.Yeats* (London: Rupert Hart-Davis, 1954).

Wiley, John Roland, *A Century of Russian Ballet: Documents and Eyewitness Accounts 1810-1910* (Oxford: Oxford University Press, 1990).

Yeats, W.B., "The Reform of the Theatre" in W.B.Yeats (ed.), *Samhain* (Dublin and London: Sealy Bryers & Walker and T. Fisher Unwin, 1903), pp. 9-12.

Yeats, W.B., *The King of the Great Clock Tower, Commentaries and Poems* (Dublin: Cuala Press, 1934).

Yeats, W.B., *Collected Plays* (London and Basingstoke: Macmillan, 1934; revised and extended, 1952).

Zimring, Rishona, "'The Dangerous Art Where One Slip Means Death': Dance and the Literary Imagination in Interwar Britain", *Modernism/Modernity*, Vol. 14, No. 4 (November 2007), pp. 707-727.

List of contributors

VALERIE ADAMS is the former Director of The Royal Ballet Teachers' Training Course.

DAVID BINTLEY is Director of Birmingham Royal Ballet.

RICHARD ALLEN CAVE is Emeritus Professor of Drama and Theatre Arts at Royal Holloway, University of London.

RUPERT CHRISTIANSEN is the dance critic for *The Mail on Sunday*.

CLEMENTINE COWL has been responsible for the management of the Royal Ballet Benevolent Fund since 2004 and, prior to that, for the Dance Teachers Benevolent Fund.

CLEMENT CRISP is the dance critic of the *Financial Times*.

SUSIE CROW works with Ballet Independents' Group and initiated Ballet in Small Spaces in Oxford in 2004.

GERALD DOWLER teaches at the City of London School for Boys and writes for the *Dancing Times*.

DAVID DREW is a Guest Principal Character Artist with The Royal Ballet; he has been a member of the Company for 56 years, and is a former teacher at The Royal Ballet School.

KATE FLATT teaches choreography at The Royal Ballet Upper School and mentors young choreographers.

CRISTINA FRANCHI is Exhibitions and Heritage Publications Manager, Royal Opera House Collections.

FRANCESCA FRANCHI is Head of the Royal Opera House Collections.

RICHARD GLASSTONE formerly taught at The Royal Ballet School and was one-time Director of the Turkish National Ballet.

BETH GENNÉ is Professor of Dance Studies and Professor of Art History at the University of Michigan.

HELENA HAMMOND is Senior Lecturer in Dance at Roehampton University.

PETER HULTON founded Arts Archives at Exeter University in 1993 and remains its Editor.

ANN HUTCHINSON GUEST is co-founder of the International Council of Kinetography Laban.

JENNIFER JACKSON is Senior Lecturer in the Department of Dance, Film and Theatre at the University of Surrey and she teaches at The Royal Ballet School.

NICOLA KATRAK is currently the Year 7 Girls' teacher at White Lodge.

LEVENT KURUMLU is a documentary film-maker and Lecturer in Cultural Studies at Mardin Artuklu University, Turkey.

PATRICIA LINTON teaches at The Central School of Ballet and founded the charity, Voices of British Ballet.

ALASTAIR MACAULAY has been chief dance critic to *The New York Times* since 2007 and has published on Margot Fonteyn and Matthew Bourne.

ANNA MEADMORE is the Curator of White Lodge Museum & Ballet Resource Centre and Head of Academic Dance Studies, The Royal Ballet School.

GERALDINE MORRIS is Senior Lecturer in Dance and Programme Convenor (MA Ballet Studies) at Roehampton University.

VICTORIA O'BRIEN lectures at the Irish World Academy of Music and Dance at the University of Limerick and is Development Officer at the National Dance Archive of Ireland.

JANN PARRY, biographer of Kenneth MacMillan, was Dance Critic of *The Observer* from 1983 to 2004.

ROBERT PENMAN is Head of Contextual Studies and Programme Leader at the London Studio Centre.

GIANNANDREA POESIO is Reader in Dance at the University of Bedfordshire, Chairman of the European Association of Dance Historians, and dance critic for *The Spectator*.

JANE PRITCHARD is Curator of Dance, Theatre and Performance Collections at the Victoria & Albert Museum.

SIMON RICE danced with The Royal Ballet Company 1982–1992 and teaches English Folk Dance at The Royal Ballet School.

ELIZABETH SCHAFER is Professor of Drama and Theatre Studies at Royal Holloway, University of London, and biographer of Lilian Baylis.

EDWARD SMALL is Cataloguer of The Royal Ballet School Collections, White Lodge Museum & Ballet Resource Centre.

RON SMEDLEY was a visiting teacher of English Folk Dance at The Royal Ballet School with colleague Bob Parker from 1969 to 1989.

VICTORIA WATTS is a Lecturer in Dance Studies at the Royal Academy of Dance.

LIBBY WORTH is a Senior Lecturer in Theatre Practice at Royal Holloway, University of London.

INDEX

[While the text has been thoroughly indexed, the Notes have been treated more selectively and are only included in the Index where they incorporate substantially new material. In some instances where the notes to two or more chapters fall on the same page, the note-numbers may not appear to have been numerically ordered (256 n.2 may follow 256 n.7); but they have been recorded in the order in which they appear upon the given page in relation to the sequence of chapters. Scrutiny of the actual notes on the page will clarify the matter.]

Engel, Johan Jacob, 102
English Folk Dance and Song Society, 105
ENSA (Entertainments National Service Association), 51, 242
English National Ballet, 30
Enigma Variations (Ashton), 206
Erasmus Prize, 216
Eshkol-Wachmann Notation, 130
Espinosa, Edouard, 8, 42, 44, 237
Espinosa, Judith, 49, 51
Euclid, 243
Evans, Edith, 83, 92
Evans, Edwin, 23, 171, 237
Evergreen (film), 46
Expressionism (German or Central European), 22, 155, 178, 224

Faber and Faber, 65, 69
Façade (Ashton), 86, 203
Fairbairn, Flora, 90, 258 n.7
Fairy Queen, The (Ashton), 243
Fanatics of Pleasure (Massine), 11
Farron, Julia, 49, 50-51, 52, 54-55, 169, 195, 201, 205, 206
Fawn, The (de Valois), 60, 62
Fedorovitch, Sophie, 171, 243, 250
Festival Ballet (see under London Festival Ballet)
Festival Theatre (Cambridge), 20, 22, 30, 58, 60, 63, 154, 174, 175, 218, 219, 250
Field, John, 245, 246
Field, Lila, 6-8, 9
Fifield, Elaine, 197
Fighting the Waves (Yeats), 223, 256 n.9, 266 n.1, 268 n.17
Firebird, The (Fokine), 237, 243, 253n.10
Flatt, Kate, 70, 256n.4
Fokine, Michel, 6, 21, 22, 23-24, 43, 62, 142, 149, 154, 171, 239, 243
Foley-Martin, Clodagh, 64
Fonteyn, Margot, xii, 46, 85, 93, 171, 173, 178, 201, 202, 204, 205, 206, 240-241, 242, 245, 248
Fortnam, Craig, 224, 225, 227-228
Foster, Dorothy, 10
Four Plays for Dancers (Yeats), 58, 60, 154
Fra Angelico, 68
Franca, Celia, 245
Franchi, Francesca, xi
Frank Sharman Collection, 248

Frederick Ashton Collection, 248
French Players (see La Compagnie des Quinze)
Freud, Sigmund, 187
Friel, Brian, 41
From Morn to Midnight (Kaiser), 59
Fry, Roger, 183
Full Moon in March, A (Yeats), 219
Furse, Roger, 191
"Future of the Ballet, The" (de Valois), 18, 21, 22, 89, 149-152

Gaiety Theatre (Dublin), 236
Gardner, Howard, 179
Gate Theatre (Dublin), 58, 60
Gaunt, Hilda, 201, 241
Gautier, Théophile, 84
Genée, Adeline, 5, 42
Genné, Beth, 176, 185, 187-188
George V, 42
Georgiadis, Nicholas, 37, 209, 244
Gerhard, Roberto, 243
Gielgud, John, 89, 153
Gielgud, Maina, 30, 31-32, 35
Ginner, Ruby, 44
Giselle (Coralli and Perrot), 26, 55, 84-86, 93, 127, 142, 144, 154, 200, 239, 248
"Giselle" (de Valois), 84-86, 93
Glasstone, Richard, 70, 107, 142, 215
Gluck, Christoph Willibald, 171, 203
Gods go a-Begging, The (de Valois), 56, 184
Goldfish, The (Lila Field), 6, 45
Good Companions, The (film of Priestley's novel), 153
Gordon, Gavin, 239, 260 n.2
Gore, Walter, 198
"Gospel of Wealth, The" (Carnegie), 137
Goudin, Alex, 7, 9
Gounod, Charles, 11
Goya, Francisco, 184
Graham, John, 106
Graham, Martha, 24, 178
Grant, Alexander, 198
Grant, Duncan, 11, 183, 185, 186, 189
Grassini, Giuseppina, 85
Gray, Julia, 59
Gray, Terence, 22, 30, 174, 175, 218, 219
Greenaway, Kate, 184
Gregory, Lady Augusta, 61
Gregory, Jill, 62, 256 n.13